ANOTHER
CHINA
CYCLE

Committing to Reform

ANOTHER CHINA CYCLE

Committing to Reform

Wang Gungwu

World Scientific

NEW JERSEY · LONDON · SINGAPORE · BEIJING · SHANGHAI · HONG KONG · TAIPEI · CHENNAI

Published by

World Scientific Publishing Co. Pte. Ltd.

5 Toh Tuck Link, Singapore 596224

USA office: 27 Warren Street, Suite 401-402, Hackensack, NJ 07601

UK office: 57 Shelton Street, Covent Garden, London WC2H 9HE

Library of Congress Cataloging-in-Publication Data
Wang, Gungwu.
   Another China cycle : committing to reform / Wang Gungwu.
     pages cm
   Includes index.
   ISBN 978-9814508919
   1. China--Economic policy--1976–2000. 2. China--Economic policy--2000–   I. Title.
   HC427.92.W34725 2014
   330.951--dc23
                                    2013042754

British Library Cataloguing-in-Publication Data
A catalogue record for this book is available from the British Library.

Im-house Editor: Lum Pui Yee

Typeset by Stallion Press
Email: enquiries@stallionpress.com

Printed in Singapore

CONTENTS

INTRODUCTION

The economic reforms in China launched by Deng Xiaoping after 1978 succeeded beyond anyone's expectations. Today, in every part of the country, younger generations can hardly imagine what China was like 35 years ago. It is, however, important to place on record that Deng Xiaoping and his senior colleague, Premier Zhou Enlai, had tried to introduce reforms several years earlier. The two had offered a blueprint for their country when they were called on to lead the government in 1974. Although very little was achieved because the "Gang of Four" led by Madam Mao opposed their plans, the reform programme that they prepared did have a start. The substance of what they proposed was still on the table when Mao Zedong died in 1976. Thus, when Deng Xiaoping regained power a year and a half later, he could move quickly to get his reforms off the ground.

Thus the will to reform by Zhou Enlai and Deng Xiaoping predates the end of Mao Zedong's Great Proletarian Cultural Revolution. 1976, however, was a watershed. This remarkable year began with Zhou Enlai's death and Deng Xiaoping's ouster less than a month later. I was at the Australian National University (ANU) in Canberra at the time. My colleagues and I had been on an academic tour of China where we learnt something about life under Mao Zedong. When we heard the news, we shared the feelings of loss and foreboding that most Chinese then experienced. For months afterwards, the wish among many young Chinese to mourn the death of Zhou Enlai grew stronger. This came to a head during the Qingming festival when crowds of Beijing people gathered spontaneously in Tiananmen Square. The display of grief was suppressed by force but the desire for reform remained. The earthquake in Tangshan in July then killed up to half a million of its inhabitants

1

and was seen as a sign that the country was about to experience great change. Less than six weeks later, Mao Zedong died.

Mao Zedong's going was accompanied by mixed feelings. There was fear and unease among all who identified him with the People's Republic of China, but great relief among those who realized what economic and psychological damage he had done during the Cultural Revolution. I recall the gloom and uncertainty that followed but was totally unprepared for the dramatic reversals that came soon afterwards to the heart of Beijing politics. Within four weeks of his death, the "Gang of Four" was arrested and the Cultural Revolution decade ended. The outcome was Deng Xiaoping's third return, one that gave him the power to launch his reforms.

The essays in this volume largely concern this desire to reform, and the consequences that have enabled the country to gain a new sense of direction within the country and in world affairs. The beginning of reform through the 1980s was impressive. It raised high expectations that China might become more open and free. As it turned out, that hope came crashing down in the months of May and June in 1989, also at Tiananmen Square. The tragedy was a severe test of Deng Xiaoping's determination to see the reforms through. He and his senior colleagues were soon afterwards confirmed in their determination to proceed by the unexpected collapse of the Soviet Union. Their vision was also steeled by the realization that the Western alliance led by the United States was still pushing for ideological changes that China was not prepared to make.

The essays in this volume take the 1990s following the Tiananmen tragedy as its baseline. They reflect changes in two decades of my thinking about China's developmental path before and after the turn of the 21st century. The emphasis on the will to reform not only brings out the consistency of vision after Deng Xiaoping's Tour to the South in 1992, but also reflects on the confidence that his vision has inspired in his countrymen. The essays trace some of the ways he and his senior colleagues drew strength from their faith in China's ancient civilization and, more directly, from the country's long history.

The book traces the choices that three generations of Chinese leaders from Deng Xiaoping to Jiang Zemin and to Hu Jintao have made to rebuild China and consolidate the reforms first introduced in the late 1970s. It also examines how Chinese leaders are trying to restore China's position in the region; how they are re-connecting with the country's history and re-defining the kind of nation it wants, and also how they hope to establish what they consider to be China's rightful place in the international order.

The outline of the choices that China made the past century and the choices it faces today is based on a lecture given at the Australian National University in Canberra in 2012. It then takes the question of choice back to 1989, on the eve of the Tiananmen tragedy. In May that year, I spoke at Princeton University when the drama was unfolding in the square. I had spent the fortnight before in Hong Kong, Taipei and San Francisco before going to Princeton, and had followed the news every night. I was astonished what the call for reforms did to bring thousands of students on to the streets of so many Chinese cities. Without knowing how the demonstrations would end, I pointed to openness as the factor that had radically improved the lives of Chinese elsewhere and commended the same openness to post-revolutionary China.

The next essay was written three years later under totally different conditions. The Tiananmen tragedy had brought to a close the brief period of euphoria in relations between China and the outside world. The fall of the Soviet Union meant that the West did not need to look to China for help against a common enemy and sought to shut down their links with China as punishment for the military crackdown throughout the country. In Hong Kong at the time, I was deeply troubled by the consequences of that on China's drive to reform. Hong Kong was directly affected by Beijing's concerns, not least by suspicions that Britain's last outpost may be used to inspire democratic forces that China was not ready to tolerate. It was, therefore, with relief that I followed Deng Xiaoping's tour to South China early in 1992 when he reaffirmed his commitment to the reforms he had initiated. My duties at the university did not permit me to attend the conference on "China in Transformation" in Boston that September, but I felt strongly that I should send my views on a "righteous mandate", what I saw as a reaffirmation of faith and a call for reforms to continue apace.

I end the section on revolution and reform with an essay written ten years later when it was clear that Deng Xiaoping's hopes for China were bearing fruit. The world was surprised how well China had overcome the financial crisis that threatened the economies of East and Southeast Asia and how it was taking the lead in a rising Asia. This had led me to take a historical look at the times when China could be described as "rising" and suggest that China could be looking at its fourth rise since the civilization emerged from the small states of the Yellow River plains.

For the second section, I begin by going back to the mid-1990s. By that time, it was clear that the retreat from communist ideology was nearly complete. When asked to address this issue by the International Institute of Asian Studies in Amsterdam in 1996, I pointed to the new efforts to identify Chinese characteristics in socialism and how the emphasis was shifting towards the nationalism that marked the start of modern China. Fast forward to the end of the first decade of the 21st century, I include ten short essays that serve as snapshots of current developments. They trace some aspects of China's growing confidence in dealing with a global economy that is guided by principles of industrial capitalism. Insofar as any large multinational state can be normal, they show that China is normal in getting ready to play its part in the game to shape a future international world order.

This leads to the third section where I explore how the game might evolve by looking at China's challenges in Southeast Asia. That region has gained a strong sense of its potential as an "association of nations"(ASEAN) vital for the peace and stability of the Asia-Pacific system. The opening essay is drawn from a lecture given in 2011 at a conference on imperial China and its southern neighbours. It outlines how China is re-examining its historical relationships with the ten new nations that have been restructured by the last two centuries of globalizing trade. In the second, I go back to the mid-1990s, to a lecture I gave at the Institute of Strategic and International Studies in Jakarta. My Indonesian colleagues wanted to know how China would respond to the new phase of region building, with ASEAN covering all countries of the region. I surveyed efforts by the Chinese to find friends among its southern neighbours with that framework in mind. For China, the conditions were ripe for change. The conflict in Cambodia in which it had been deeply involved had ended. Vietnam had joined ASEAN and everything was ready for the remaining three countries, Myanmar, Laos and Cambodia, to complete the regional family. The third essay takes me to the 21st century when I took part a decade later in a conference at George Washington University to examine the power shift to Asia that was taking place. I include it because the focus on China's sense of its rising wealth and power brings out the lines along which China and Southeast Asia will have to adjust to that shift.

The final section of the book looks beyond the region in response to the idea that China's dealings with the United States are now central, at least to China's future as an economic power. I begin with a re-look at the roots of US-China dealings the past century and what China has most wanted in that relationship. This is based on the lecture I gave to the Lowy Institute in 2011. Finally, I end the volume by going back to my thoughts on China's reaffirmation in the 1990s to stay with economic reform, especially after having seen the disintegration of the Soviet Union. Clearly, Deng Xiaoping's southern tour in 1992 called for courage and renewal. He was adamant about bringing his colleagues of the Chinese Communist Party back "to cross the river feeling for the stones". From that, I realized that he was still unswerving in his belief that reform was the key to China's quest for modernity in a new world order. It was clear that China had to go on doing that in order to ensure that its quest does not end until it can establish its place in a safe and prosperous world. At the same time, it would have to find new ways to re-connect with its distinctive history, one of the most important factors that made its civilization great.

CHAPTER 1

CHINA'S CHOICES*

In 1971, Gough Whitlam, as Leader of the Opposition, challenged the government and went to China to show that Australia was prepared to recognize the People's Republic of China if he was elected. The same year, in the United States, Kissinger reported that he had made a secret trip to Beijing on behalf of President Nixon. Whitlam made the choice even though replacing the ROC with the PRC in the United Nations would have made the choice inevitable.

Earlier, by inviting the American table-tennis team to China, Mao Zedong and his colleagues made their choice public: to reach out to the US and turn away from the Soviet Union. The fact that the Australian and Chinese decisions happened while the Vietnam War was going on was remarkable. The re-alignments happened while China and the Soviet Union were still pledged to support Vietnam against America, Australia and others in that war. The world was not for the timid or the conventionally logical in those game-changing times.

We seem to be at one of those times again. What are the choices ahead? The question is obviously influenced by the ongoing debate on Australia seeking to avoid choosing between the United States and China. My focus will not be that, but some of the deeper concerns about the paths that China might choose to take that would have an impact on Australia and the region.

---

* This is a revised version of a lecture I gave at the Australian National University in September 2012 to commemorate forty years of Australia-China relations. In response to the ongoing debate in Australia about having to choose between China and the United States, I spoke on China's experiences with its choices since the mid-19th century.

China's leaders are known to be capable of making abrupt and unpredictable choices for their country's future. Some of those choices were good for Australia, and others not so good. China's choices are now much more complex. Since the 1980s, it has chosen to open up to the world faster than anyone expected. How much further will it go to bring in more foreign technologies, institutions and ideas that its people still need? China is determined to be modern in distinctive Chinese ways. What can be done to achieve that? If a new Chinese identity becomes powerful, will it alarm the neighbourhood or become part of the soft power that could transform the region? On the other hand, if the United States chose, or is invited, to intervene in the region, what choices would China have?

All countries have a degree of freedom in making choices, but most choices are very limited. As can be seen in China, it had often come down to selecting from a few hard choices, with each likely to affect the choices the next time round. But the Chinese have always relied on learning from the past; to them, the past has never been a foreign country. Thus Chinese leaders and their advisers today are not only looking to the globalizing world outside but also inwards to the Chinese past for ideas to help them think about the future. Many observers were struck by the example of Berkeley-trained social scientist Yan Xuetong turning to the Warring States period of the 4th and 3rd centuries B.C. for fresh thinking about what China should do. Yan Xuetong is not alone. Others have done similar comparisons and we should expect more to follow.

The process of sifting through the past and discarding what failed and adopting what might succeed is something Chinese thinkers have been accustomed to doing for their rulers. Other states do that, except the Chinese have a long past and more experiences from which to look for suitable guidance. From past record, Chinese leaders do not simply react to events, nor are they prone to play by ear. They keep to the principle of acting rationally and using all the knowledge they can gather. This resembles scientific methods of using theory to determine practice, but the Chinese preferred to use their traditions of morally-righteous knowledge to provide help for pragmatic action.

For my purposes, I shall not range too far but only consider choices made in the past 150 years, a period when China had to learn to deal with a world dominated by Western wealth and power. The choices they made are still present in Chinese minds today. The Chinese do not normally think of history as linear progress but consider any lesson from the past useful if it can be shown to be relevant for the present. Here I shall take as starting-point the Deng Xiaoping legacy as China's base position from which the current leaders have to chart the future. From the choices that Deng Xiaoping made, I shall look back at four periods in the past century and a half when Chinese leaders had made other choices. Before that, let me briefly examine the Deng legacy.

It began with Deng's idea of crossing the river, I take that to signify getting away from the nightmares that Mao Zedong had generated, and concentrating on "feeling for the stones" to find the way to other shore. This was a return to pragmatism. Deng Xiaoping's key choices were to keep the socialist heritage as the country's foundation and open the country to a wide range of other choices to bolster that base. He was open not only to the West and China's modernizing neighbours, but also to fresh insights drawn from the Chinese heritage.

The most important part of his choice was to restore credibility to the Chinese Communist Party, one that was not Leninist, nor Maoist. Chastened by the horrors of the Great Leap Forward and the GPCR, Deng Xiaoping wanted a Party that was protected from the whims of a powerful leader, from internal divisions that led to distrust and fear, and from appeals to dogmatic ideology. The core of his idea of political reform required the removal of party seniors from the decision-making centre. The selection process to the Central Committee and its Politburo was restructured and the relationship between Party and the People's Liberation Army redefined. The first generation of new leaders he selected, namely Hu Yaobang and Zhao Ziyang, failed him and the first phase of the reforms ended disastrously in the Tiananmen tragedy in 1969. But the regrouping afterwards did work, and his efforts to establish a stable regime and institutionalize the succession machinery have been successful.

The focused and limited political reform was the capstone of the Deng legacy. China's remarkable economic performance would not have been possible without that. After he died in 1997, few changes were made to the plans that he had presented to his Party colleagues. For example, "capitalists" were admitted to the CCP while several large state-owned enterprises were expanded. Another policy he advocated that may not survive much longer is that China should keep a low international profile. This was carefully followed for a decade after his death but, with China's growing influence as the world's second richest economy, it has become increasingly difficult to avoid being proactive in foreign affairs. Paradoxically, China's increased influence does not give its leaders greater freedom of choice. By becoming more powerful and attracting closer scrutiny around the world, China's every move is now met with new constraints. The Deng injunction to keep its head down is unlikely to survive.

For the long haul, the most powerful impact of the Deng legacy is China's capacity to match anything that the developed nations can do. People selected for their proven talent and performance have provided the country with skilled management. New cadres are expected to be dedicated to advancing the country's growth and these have transformed the quality of CCP membership. Today, most of its 80 million members have had high school education or above. They also include entrepreneurs and younger cadres who have mastered capitalist skills. By opening the door to foreign investment and new ideas and technologies, and by sending the best and brightest abroad to study in the most successful nations of the West, Deng established a new baseline for local initiatives. When the Party reformed its lines of central control and encouraged a large degree of local and regional autonomy, it sought to shape a new kind of state that could avoid rigidity at one end and chaotic division at the other. This capacity to bring stability and predictability to a large and populous country that is diverse and complex should play a large part in determining the future political system best suited to China.

While most Chinese are proud of the economic development that has made China second only to the United States in global influence, not all Chinese agree on all aspects of the growth trajectory. There are perceptions of social inequalities having grown beyond what is endurable, of officials becoming more corrupt than ever in the past, of justice being wayward and not credible, and of moral values having been sacrificed in the race to material success.

There are also concerns that the economy is over-dependent on a capitalist system now in disarray everywhere and that Deng Xiaoping's efforts to protect the CCP at all costs have made further reforms ineffective. The first concern may lead some to want to make China less open and vulnerable and pay more attention to wealth distribution and social justice. The second has seen vested interests grow among party leaders, and there is fear that the incentive to reform the power structure will further diminish. Nevertheless, Deng Xiaoping's legacy still provides the baseline from which to prepare for an unpredictable future. The legacy is rooted in elements of the Leninist state, supported by a party army proud of its revolutionary origins, and built on a bureaucratic tradition hallowed by China's history. That is a formidable structure for future leaders to reform.

Let us say that Deng Xiaoping's river has been crossed. On the other shore, so to speak, are deserts, forests, even jungles, with dangerous fauna and quagmires but no clearly marked roads. The pressure to respond to global changes beyond China's control is increasing each year. China may prefer to have more time to sift and analyze possible future choices but, as global events close in, it has to think and act more quickly. In particular, the current financial troubles of the developed West impinge directly on China's factories and exports, and the uneven economic development within China has distorted its own consumer markets. State interventions have so far been successful but these are hardly sustainable if current global conditions continue to worsen.

Deng Xiaoping's choices have led to success in the eyes of most Chinese, even among those who are dissatisfied with the performance of the present leadership in a one-party state. Although hopes are not high about the next generation of leaders, few Chinese are calling for radical change. They would be content if serious steps are taken to reform the country's governance mechanisms. It seems safe to assume that the Deng legacy shall continue to serve as the foundation on which the next set of choices will be made. In that legacy, we can find examples of what Deng Xiaoping learnt from China's modern history. His success suggests that he learnt the lessons well. Understanding what he learnt from that past can help us know what kinds of choices his successors are likely to consider before they make decisions for China's future. It is not possible in a brief lecture to do justice to the whole range of lessons. I shall merely outline what helped Deng Xiaoping make his choices after 1978.

For that purpose, I propose to identify four sets of choices that are presented chronologically. The four are: Restoration choices; Reform-revolution choices; Nationalism-internationalism choices; and Maoist choices.

RESTORATION CHOICES

These were the choices made by mandarins of the late 19th century, like Zeng Guofan, Li Hongzhang, Wo Ren and Zhang Zhidong, and their advisers like Wei Yuan, Feng Guifen and others. They were impressed by Western military superiority, reviewed what the series of defeats that China experienced could teach them, and used analogies from Chinese history to argue for suitable responses. They also backed their reasoning with Confucian assurance and doses of Legalist realism, and supported that with insights drawn from the strategic wisdom of Sun Zi. They tried to understand what was behind the power of Western science, but thought that most of the non-military aspects of the new knowledge were unnecessary for China to learn. By 1895, the Japanese proved that they were seriously wrong in what they chose to do.

To put that in perspective, Australia was at that time a group of colonies whose choices were guided primarily by Britain's imperial plans. The important work was to lay down the foundations for Australia, a new Britain down under. The colonists knew China as the homeland of thousands of largely Cantonese miners who joined the gold rush, people who were quite different from mandarins of the Manchu Qing who did little to support these miners.

REFORM-REVOLUTION CHOICES

At the turn of the 20th century, Chinese officials and literati chose to adopt aspects of the Japanese model of constitutional government, and introduced the Xinzheng 新政 reforms to save the regime and protect the country's heritage. Others outside the court, however, argued for French and American models, advocating republican nationhood as the engine of progress, and were prepared to take China through revolutionary change. The fall of the Qing in 1912 was unexpected and the decision to establish the republic hastily taken. No steps had been taken to prepare for that outcome. Either of the choices, reform or revolution would have led to discarding key parts of the past. But, given the circumstances, neither the reformists nor the revolutionaries brought the country the unity, order and respect that their leaders sought.

In comparison, Australia had become a federal Dominion in the British Empire, but committed to upholding the imperial values of the Mother Country. It was also determined to stop more Chinese from coming to Australia. At the same time, the Chinese who had lived and worked in Australian cities began to bring innovative ideas back to China, and what they had to offer to their home towns and villages, and also to cities like Shanghai, did appeal to reformers and revolutionaries alike. Australia had begun to be part of the modernity that Chinese leaders are now keen to have.

NATIONALISM-INTERNATIONALISM CHOICES

The desire to pursue openly all features of modernity that new generations of activists admired was overtaken in the 1920s by the narrower choice between nationalism and internationalism:

(a) KMT/GMD nationalism built on pride in 中华文明 (Chinese civilization) that included heritage concerns not unlike the Restoration choices some decades earlier, but they also included militarist lessons from Japanese and German models.

(b) an internationalist agenda began with a progressive programme of 全盘西化 (total westernization) that young founders of the CCP espoused, with a commitment to destroy imperialism and colonialism and improve the world. This period of the 1920s to 1940s was one of division, civil war and Japanese invasion. In the end, the internationalists won, but they actually had a very strong nationalist core.

This period saw the emergence of national consciousness in Australia. It was not a happy one for the Chinese living here while the KMT government in Nanjing encouraged them to be Chinese patriots. At the same time, some radicalized Chinese sailors and workers saw the labour movement in Australian port cities as an inspiring example of internationalism, a phenomenon that also attracted support among workers in China. Eventually, Australians sympathized with a China threatened by Japanese imperialism, and sensed that Australia might one day be similarly threatened. Both countries also had a growing overlapping interest in the Southeast Asian countries in between.

MAOIST CHOICES

This had begun with Mao Zedong determined to industrialize the country as quickly as possible and the progress was rapid. At the same time, he wanted to "sinicize" the internationalist doctrines that had inspired him, become less dependent on the Soviet Union and put China in a leadership position in the revolutionary world. He led struggles within the CCP to push for continuous revolution and, in the end, what he wanted for China baffled even his closest comrades. The mix of Leninist organization and Stalinist practice did prevail, but Mao Zedong's turn to the history of Chinese peasant rebellions as the core of Chinese proletarianism ultimately produced the Great Proletarian Cultural Revolution. His choices came from a combination of what he took from a heresy of European communism and from China's populist heritage. This was not the country's choice, but that of a leader who came to be seen as a failed god-emperor.

By this time, Australia had made a new choice of protector, the United States. It was strongly supportive of the Western position in the Cold War, and highly suspicious of Soviet and Chinese links with its own communists and their Labor Party sympathizers. Mao's choices, the very antithesis of Australia's own commitments, simply confirmed Australia's worst fears. Nevertheless, Gough Whitlam led the Opposition to open doors to China, independently of the US and without expecting the Mao choices to be replaced. The 1970s was a decade of shifting perspectives in Asia, and Australia did its own calculations of its own long-term interests.

The Maoist choices, I believe, offered Deng Xiaoping the most immediate lessons. He certainly did not want to return to the era of the Great Leap Forward or the GPCR. Those had come from Mao Zedong's own ambitions and predispositions. I do not agree that the recent "singing red" manifestations in Chongqing under the aegis of the charismatic Bo Xilai mark a wish to return to that era. Most of Mao Zedong's choices were peculiar to him as a brilliant but obsessive son of peasants, and no one can hope to succeed by choosing to follow that. The Maoist choices belong to a time when political and cultural throwbacks were still possible. The phenomenon should now be considered an aberration. One can say that Deng Xiaoping's first and most painful lesson has been thoroughly learnt by all concerned.

Nevertheless, the Maoist choices had their impact. One dramatic example of that is how Mao Zedong compared himself to several of the great empire-founders. There is little doubt that he wanted his contributions to match those of the first emperor, Qin Shihuang, whose heritage of a unified China rewrote Chinese history. In Mao's eyes, if Qin Shihuang's reign marked the beginnings of China's first rise, his might be the harbinger of the second. Never mind that it was Western imperialism that brought ancient China down, and Western ideas and technology and its revolutionary inspiration that enabled leaders like him to rebuild China. He saw the chance for China to rise again from its 19th century ruins, only the second time in history that a totally different China became possible. Many may be prepared to give Mao Zedong that pride of place.

Another example touches on the Maoist choice to sinicize the Marxist-Leninist model of the future. It comes from another strand in Chinese thinking that draws from Chinese history. The desire to sinicize what China has received from outside reflects the Chinese wish to remain as Chinese as possible even when it wants to become wholly modern. They see no contradiction here. The immediate sources of modernity today are European and developed out of traditions that were largely unique to the Mediterranean region. The different manifestations of modernity around the world have been grafted onto those European roots, even when these products display the use of non-Western criteria in their efforts to be distinctive. China can contribute to the enrichment of what is modern. But if China seeks to establish a sinicized modernity for the Chinese people, it must expect some of it to be unrecognisable to others. The challenge is make the difference something that people elsewhere can respect. From that perspective, Mao Zedong's experiments to sinicize a socialist modernity are not encouraging.

Beyond the Maoist choices, the earlier three are important in different ways. Let me take them chronologically in reverse order and look first at the nationalism-internationalism choices immediately preceding the Maoist choices. During Mao Zedong's last years, internationalism was failing the Chinese, well before the collapse of the Soviet Union and the abandonment of the communist millennium. Most Chinese had experienced the rise of nationalism. Now that China has become more confident of its place in the world, a return to national pride is expected. The people remember the wartime origin of national consciousness and the leaders know how volatile nationalism can become on issues linked to security and sovereignty. As something that people can give free expression to without retaliation by the state, it can arouse passions that are difficult to control. This is a double-edged sword that the Chinese state may encourage only sparingly.

At the same time, there are areas where China needs patriotism to be a constructive force in binding people together to serve national interests. There is much to be done because the task of nation building in China is not complete. Beijing is struggling to win the hearts and minds of many of its peoples, especially among the larger minorities in Tibet and Xinjiang, as it tries to get them to feel proud to be Chinese. There are signs in the social media as well as in published writings that nationalism is becoming a test of political loyalty and cultural cohesion. Chinese leaders are aware how protean this force can be. As a vehicle for enhancing China's global position, it will have to be handled with great care.

With the earlier choices between reform and revolution, however, Deng Xiaoping recognised that the time for revolution was over and reform was the key. Today, even reform has to be re-cast because China will need totally different kinds of reform. The questions are, what to reform, how far and how quickly, in what direction, and also how actually to manage reform under conditions that are so very different form those of the 20th century. The obvious lesson is not to leave necessary reforms until they are too little too late, as the Qing rulers had done, and this is being underlined by many calls to Chinese leaders today.

Another feature of the reform-revolution period of the early 20th century called for choosing foreign models to copy, for example, that of Japan for the Xinzheng 新政 reforms and those of France and America for the republican ideal. Today, Japan is no longer a model and France is too remote. Only the United States is still keen to be a global inspiration and there are Chinese who are interested to learn directly from the American ideal. But it seems clear that the time for any country to be a model for a rising China is over. The choices of the 20th century were cast in somewhat generic even holistic terms, and those are not what China now wants. China will be more selective about they want.

What is interesting is that China is willing to learn from the 19th century Restoration choices about what history and tradition could offer. For the last three decades, the Chinese have looked again at what made China great and have made serious efforts to revisit the highlights of Chinese and world history. They have embraced the extensive work of scholars in Taiwan, Hong Kong as well as the best work by non-Chinese. There is a realization that politics and prejudice have stood in the way of understanding China's past. The cadres who serve the state do not necessarily share this view, but the progress made since the attempts to rewrite history during the Mao Zedong years is encouraging.

In that light, curiosity about what can be helpful in China's past has been reviving during Deng Xiaoping's reforms. Texts are reviewed and forays are made into the ancient classics and all periods of dynastic history. Thus efforts to re-evaluate the Restoration choices of the 19th century should not be surprising. The ups and downs in historical interpretation about this period are revealing. In the early 20th century, there was criticism of everything that was done during the Restoration era. After 1928, the Nanjing government encouraged a reassessment of the patriotic efforts of leaders like Zeng Guofan and the Hunan gentry. But, with CCP victory in 1949, there was a turning away from that as fresh praise was lavished on the Taiping "revolutionaries" and the traditions of peasant rebellion that the gentry had condemned and fought to destroy. Nothing done by the late Qing officials were thought to deserve any attention.

The willingness since the 1980s to look again at what those mandarins sought to do to defend China's interests reminds us of the question whether the literati were blind to weaknesses in China's political culture or were they merely over-cautious? Revisiting that period reflects the mood of Chinese leaders and their advisers today. There is none of the dismissive judgment that once marked their writings. Instead, consideration is being given to what was enduring in the China that the mandarin elites were trying to save.

The Chinese once again find the idea of historical continuity with the ancient past appealing. There is even official approval to write Qing history as dynastic history, suggesting a willingness to consider cyclical features in Chinese history. That way, Chinese civilization can be described as becoming enriched over the centuries despite periods of division, invasions and conquests. It had survived severe tests of its viability, and its enduring qualities have been enhanced after each ordeal. Such an interpretation can be instructive and encouraging for Chinese today.

Mao Zedong's generation compared the 1949 victory of the Communist Party with the revolutionary impact of the Qin-Han unification over 2,000 years ago. The current generation are ready to see that China experienced other rises and that each rise was marked by China bring reunified again. Therefore, the failure of the 19th century Restoration offers lessons about what could go wrong in times of serious threats. Taken together with Deng Xiaoping's views on opening up China and the current affirmation of patriotism, such history lessons can be valuable. The tiyong 体用 representation of retaining Chinese foundations and making use of Western knowledge is no longer mocked. A modern world-view is accepted but the desire to rediscover the value of Chinese foundations has returned. Can Chinese Learning be restored to greatness? If that is not possible, can it be bolstered and given a place of respect by the intelligent application of modern scientific thought?

There are two other areas of continuity with the Restoration period that deserve attention. When China was forced open, two policy changes markedly departed from Chinese tradition. One concerned the Chinese merchants as entrepreneurs adapting capitalism to China's needs. Attitudes towards commerce had been changing since the 16th and 17th centuries, but the new Treaty ports transformed the relationship between the literati and merchant classes. From literati-supervised and merchant-managed 官督商办 enterprises, the role of merchants was better appreciated and, after the end of the Confucian state, this led to a higher status for them in both state and society. In Mao Zedong's China, that was overturned for a few decades but, with the reforms of the past thirty years, entrepreneurial cadres have been rewarded and Jiang Zeming convinced the Party to admit capitalists into its ranks. In a new economic structure in which cadre and entrepreneur could share responsibility, one can see a continuity that came from pragmatic Restoration choices.

The other policy change dealt with the Chinese who were living overseas. Although the ban against people leaving China without permission was still in place, the opening of the Treaty Ports not only allowed large numbers of Chinese to work abroad but also forced the mandarins to rethink their policies towards Chinese who were already living outside China. These officials conceived the idea that these Chinese were only qiaoju 侨居, temporarily living abroad, and adopted a policy of rewarding the successful ones and welcoming them home to invest in China and acquaint their countrymen about the outside world. A great deal has been written about these huaqiao 华侨 as supporters of Sun Yat-sen's nationalist revolution. But it was Qing officials who recognized their importance for China's future and recommended that the court change its policy towards them. It was this policy that prevailed after the imperial ban was lifted in 1893, and is one of few major policy changes of the Restoration decades that are still operative today.

The Republican government after 1912 strengthened it and modified it here and there, but it was never neglected. Similar policies were developed and given new importance every few decades. For example, under the KMT government in Nanjing and during the Sino-Japanese war, the role of the overseas Chinese in raising funds for the cause of national salvation greatly troubled the Japanese. And, in the propaganda wars between the governments in Beijing and Taipei after 1949, competition for the loyalty of the Chinese in countries in Southeast Asia like the Philippines, Vietnam and Myanmar was intense. And that remains a serious factor in the politics among Chinese-Americans today. There was a brief period during Mao Zedong's later years when the returned huaqiao, or guiqiao 归侨, were suspect and mistreated, and their relatives abroad were deeply hurt by that treatment, but that policy was rejected by Deng Xiaoping and a much more open approach towards all Chinese overseas was revived. With China's rise this past decade, and with new cohorts of rich and well educated Chinese from the mainland encouraged to study abroad and seek foreign experience, there will be ramifications for Chinese relations with many more countries globally. There is every possibility that the Chinese modernity that China seeks to shape will have to take into account the potential role of millions of Chinese overseas.

The evidence of historical continuity in the growing numbers of Chinese overseas over the past 200 years is now widely available. At the beginning of the 18th century, they were numbered in few tens of thousands. That figure rose dramatically during the 19th. It stabilized in the early 20th century but the trajectory of growth since the 1970s is steep and is characterised by a remarkable global outreach. The continuity of overseas Chinese policy is symbolic of the ambivalence that most Chinese people feel about the outside world as well as about their past. From the creative response by mandarins in the 19th century, the policy was adapted to the needs of both nationalist and communist regimes. It now serves as a conscious effort to treat the Chinese abroad as a bridging asset between Chinese and modern civilization. It is a many-faceted manifestation of modernity with Chinese characteristics and cannot but become a factor in Chinese thinking about its future.

Let me now try and draw together key features of China's choices that may still be relevant. The over-arching choice has been between pushing for radical change and closing down to consolidate what has been resilient and essential. The sets of choices outlined show that they were not uniformly painful, challenging or exhilarating, but they have all contributed to current thinking about the choices they will have to make for the future. They confirm that, for the Chinese, the past is not a foreign country and their leaders will not allow the past to be too foreign.

In this regard, Australia's choices are comparable. Its historical ties with Europe were re-enforced when it turned to America for inspiration and protection. With that support, Australians could more securely adapt to a changing Asian neighbourhood. But it also called for careful thought about the next set of choices to be made. An analogy may be found in Singapore's choices. The city-state has a strong Anglo-Chinese heritage but is situated in the middle of a Malay-Muslim world. It could have chosen to identify with China or Anglo-America, but it saw that as ultimately precarious and decided to take the Southeast Asian or ASEAN road. Australia, too, has long practiced geographical realism. It is not a question of choosing China but of adapting to a rising Asian mega-region: that is, East, South and Southeast Asia as well as the Western Pacific. To make that choice requires a mindset change as great as what was demanded of the pioneers who came half way round the world 200 years ago. Those founders succeeded, there is no reason why Australians today cannot do as well.

As for China, its people experienced radical change in attitudes many times in their history. They are prepared to re-order their priorities for their future. China's new leaders will start with Deng Xiaoping's legacy focusing on reform backed by economic development. From that, they are likely to stress the value of patriotism as a necessary factor in nation building. But the earlier Restoration choices remain important. They reflect the desire to restore continuity with China's long history, the understanding of which is again seen as essential to China's future. We should not underestimate the value of the lessons learnt from Mao Zedong's excesses and the choices that demonstrated the futility of copying foreign models. And one should not preclude the possibility that totally new paths will be found as China opens its doors wider. What is clear is that openness will not only bring foreign ideas and institutions to stimulate inventiveness but also help define the modernity that China wants. It will also enable the entrepreneurial classes as well as the Chinese overseas to enrich China through their cosmopolitan networks. China has re-affirmed the vitality of reason and historical experience. If there is any way to attain the condition of becoming modern and Chinese, the Chinese people will find it.

CHAPTER 2

EMBRACING REVOLUTION*

When I was asked to give this lecture and look back at the course of the Chinese Revolution, I thought of the 200th anniversary of the French Revolution. My mind turned to the question whether more was achieved by resorting to revolutionary means or whether decisive progress could have been made if China had followed a different road and opened itself to global changes outside its control. I noted that scholars who studied the remarkable growth of Japan in the late 19th century, and again after its defeat in the Pacific War, were led to admire the evolutionary alternatives.

The death of Hu Yaobang on April 15 and the student demonstrations which that aroused — and the way the events that followed dramatised on older anniversary, the 70th anniversary of the May 4th Movements, has led me to change the focus of this lecture. Indeed, the rising tensions suggest that the

---

* For this Walter E. Edge Lecture at Princeton University, I had entitled the lecture, "Outside the Chinese Revolution" and had begun preparing it in April 1989. Not expecting the dramatic developments in May and uncertain how they would end, I made only light changes to my draft before I gave the lecture at Dodds Auditorium in Woodrow Wilson Hall. I did that on May 15, in the middle of the Tiananmen demonstrations, and wondered how the audience would react to the words of an historian. No one in the hall could have anticipated the tragic results of the confrontations but the signs were for some of us ominous.

The lecture was published in Chinese as "中国革命之外" in 《中国何去何从-海外学者的反思》, Teaneck, N.J.: Global Publishing, Co., 1990, pp. 1–19; and the Japanese translation followed in 1991, *Chugoku no zasetsu to meimu*, Tokyo: Gakuseisha, 1991. A slightly revised version was published in *Australian Journal of Chinese Affairs*, Canberra, no. 23, 1990, pp. 33–48; and this was republished as "Openness and Nationalism: Outside the Chinese Revolution", in *Chinese Nationalism*, edited by Jonathan Unger, Armonk, NY: M.E. Sharpe, 1996, pp. 113–125. A Spanish translation of this was published in *El nacionalismo chino*. Barcelona: Bellaterra Publishers, 1999.

70th anniversary of May 4th might well over-shadow the 40th anniversary of the PRC. How could this happen? What does it mean? Educated Chinese everywhere, not least the CCP leaders themselves, have been very conscious of the May 4th Movement, especially of its two major slogans of Science and Democracy. I had been invited to two major conferences, both held in May in Beijing, to discuss "the spirit of May 4th" and China's Modernisation. While I was unable to go to those two, I did accept an invitation to speak on the "Uncompleted Mission" of May 4th at a forum in Hong Kong — and this took place on April 29th, the first of a series in Hong Kong of talks, conferences, exhibitions scheduled for the week before May 4th this year. In short, like many others, I had May 4th and the 70th Anniversary of the Movement on my mind during the past few months. But I do not believe anyone of us antici-pated that the students in Beijing would confront the government as they have been doing these past weeks and make the May 4th historically significant again. Now that this has happened, I have been unable to go back to the 40th anniversary of the PRC without looking at the 70th anniversary of May 4th. In fact, I was reminded of what I had written ten years ago on the 60th anni-versary of May 4th. (*Pacific Affairs*, 52:4) Let me quote some of my conclud-ing remarks in my 1979 essay on the *60th* anniversary of May 4th and the *30th* anniversary of the PRC: I had first quoted from a lecture on "Conflict of Cultures" in 1931 by Hu Shi which went as follows . . .,

> "My own attitude is that we must unreservedly accept this modern civilisation of the West because we need it to solve our most pressing problems, the problems of poverty, ignorance, disease and corruption".

I then went on to say,

> "Some ten years after May Fourth, these brave words were very much in the spirit of cultural revolution. Thirty years after, when the People's Republic was proclaimed, the problems seemed about to be solved. Cultural Revolution in the hands of the Communist Party had won. Yet this year, in 1979, on the 30th anni-versary of the People's Republic, the Chinese sound as if they have hardly begun, especially when the May Fourth slogans in 1919 of Science and Democracy once again appear appropriate and reflective of China's most urgent needs".

I was not content to leave it at that. Here are some sentences from my concluding paragraphs:

> "… A whole new generation has grown up in the PRC . . . a new kind of Chinese, sceptical of cant and humbug, but also rootless and disillusioned. They may not be satisfied by words like revolution any more. They may want the opportunity to think every question afresh, and coolly examine the old slogan".
>
> "… A close unemotional look is now needed, at what the West is really like, at Marxism-Leninism around the world today, at the strengths and weaknesses of tradition in China, and not least at the historic role of tradition in the modernisation process. Time as usual is short and panaceas, of course, are irresistible. But the greater danger, from the Chinese experience of the cultural revolution remedy, may be the myths and historic slogans that discourage free and scientific thought. It might not be a bad idea when the Chinese are being asked to be fiercely critical of the GPCR to ask also that they be critical of the May Fourth Movement as well".

Forgive me for quoting at such length. During the past four weeks, I have had many good reasons for reflecting on the inadequacy of treating the May Fourth Movement as an earlier failed "cultural revolution". Reading the many articles commenting on the 70th anniversary and reading the many slogans that have emerged since 16 April 1989, it is all too clear that many articulate Chinese do not now want to see the 1949 Revolution as the culmination of the Chinese Revolution, that is, as the *true* revolution that followed 38 years after the abortive one in 1911. The Chinese Communist Party had off and on played down the 1911 Revolution as nothing more than a bourgeois nationalist movement that failed to lead to a genuine revolution. Instead, it had preferred to associate itself with the May Fourth Movement of 1919 and linked the Party's origins (it was founded soon afterwards, in 1921) with the Movement's initial successes. In contrast, the Nationalist or KMT historians have ignored the 1919 movement and affirmed the 1911 Revolution as the actual beginning of revolution in China. They have always maintained that their party carried the flag for the 1911 Revolution and this led to the foundation of the Nanjing regime in 1928. There have been other views, but the two main interpretations are about whether there had been only *one* revolution, that is, with part one in 1911 and part two either in 1928 or in 1949; *or* whether the 1911 Revolution was never a revolution and, therefore, the only real revolution was the one in 1949.

I have not subscribed to the view that the 1949 Revolution was the only real revolution; I have long supported the view that 1911 was part one and 1949 was part two, and that the 1949 Revolution was a most dramatic culmination of the process that had begun in the late 1890s with Sun Yat-sen and his supporters, as a process of restoring China to greatness through radical change, even revolution. The events re-affirming the May Fourth Movement this past month have reminded me of a deeper underlying continuity, if only because its slogans have proved to be remarkably appropriate and because so much that had been hoped for at the beginning of the 20th century remains still unaccomplished.

Thus the question I had begun to ask, about whether more was achieved outside the Marxist-Leninist-Maoist framework of the 1949 Revolution than inside may be clearer and more interesting if I placed it in the context of a two-part revolution. That is to say, I should ask what was achieved under the revolution that started in 1911 and is still going on today; and compare that with what has been achieved on the mainland since 1949. You can see I am still exploring the question. Even if I get that right, answering it may still be beyond me.

The Communist leaders of the 1949 Revolution had set high standards of revolution for themselves — standards on par with the Soviet Union, in their view the most revolutionary society at the time; they even thought themselves capable of by-passing that to create the first communist society. In comparison, what happened in the name of the 1911 Revolution always looked modest, although, in the long run, perhaps no less revolutionary. The question that I asked might be worded in another way. Now that we can see that the impossibly high (even romantic) aims of the 1949 Revolution under Mao Tse-tung have not been attained, could we ask if a smaller revolution, cumulatively a series of little modernisations outside the 1949 Revolution, had not occurred? In particular, we might note that the changes outside the PRC have been modernising and progressive, and that they have steadily transformed the Chinese communities living in the Asian region and beyond.

Let me briefly outline the main points that enable us to say that there has only been *one* Chinese revolution. In broad terms, the 1911 Revolution was inspired by the American and French revolutions, but from the start lacked the universal elements of both. Sun Yat-sen wanted to overthrow the *ancien regime* and the monarchy, and argued for a republican democracy. To do this by violent means certainly made it a revolution. But there was one major element that made it a Chinese, and not part of world, revolution. Sun Yat-sen had to overthrow the Manchus, a non-Han minority who had conquered the Han majority more than 260 years earlier. Indeed, almost all his supporters were initially more concerned with this factor than with any other. His Triad or Secret Society colleagues thought no further. His literati or intellectual followers helped him raise this goal to a more sophisticated appeal for a modern Chinese nationalism. Only very few understood Sun Yat-sen's wish to establish a republic, an ultimately democratic republic. And although he did have his way, and the Republic miraculously survived the machinations of President Yuan Shikai and the warlords after him who thought of restoring the monarchy, the 1911 Revolution was essentially a nationalist revolution to restore the rule of the Han majority and make China strong and prosperous again. And because the warlord era was chaotic, a pre-condition of such revolutionary success was for China to be reunified.

By the standards of world revolution (whether American or French), much of this would not be rated as revolutionary goals. Only the goal of a democratic republic would qualify, and a modern nationalism that transformed imperial subjects "scattered like loose sand" (一盘散沙, in Sun Yat-sen's words) into a politically conscious citizenry was certainly a necessary step towards the success of such a republic. In short, at the start, it was a *Chinese* revolution and not one that claimed to have lessons for the betterment of the human condition.

Nevertheless, modest though it was, it marked the beginnings of a revolution for China. It did achieve a republic and there was no turning back; after 1918, no further attempt was made at monarchical restoration. But, up to 1919, this was a most imperfect republic, far from democratic, not even nationalist, did not unite China, least of all make China strong and prosperous. Hence the importance of the May Fourth Movement. The Beijing students behind this Movement in 1919 began by highlighting new standards of modern nationalism, focusing on anti-imperialism even more strongly than Sun Yat-sen. What was more, they were inspired by a new generation of intellectuals who elaborated on Sun Yat-sen's ideals and articulated them better than he ever did. Sun Yat-sen had trained in science and believed that China's future depended on advances in science and technology; he also believed in government by the people, but stopped short of the universal ideals of "liberty, equality and fraternity". Indeed, he had a fatal misunderstanding about China that could be traced to his superficial knowledge of Chinese history. He believed that Chinese society was already free and indeed had too much freedom. What China needed instead, he thought, was discipline and strong government that would curb the dangers of fragmentation and disunity.

During the May Fourth Movement, two men, both professors, were outstanding in trying to give new direction to the Chinese revolution, in trying to make it more revolutionary and less bogged down in mere national revival. The first was Chen Duxiu who was educated in Japan and whose most famous statement was a manifesto for Science and Democracy. The second was Hu Shi [Hu Shih], educated in the U.S., who launched a *baihua* (spoken language) movement essential for modern nationalism and for both scientific thinking and the democratic spirit. His most outstanding message, however, was liberalism, freedom of thought and speech, of faith, of association etc., all supported by laws that protected private property and human rights. In the context of China in 1919, both Chen and Hu were advocating ideals that would have made the 1911 Revolution more revolutionary and less Chinese.

Both Beijing professors were influential among the students, but the messages did not get very far. It is significant that, even today, the liberalism of Hu Shi that was associated with total Westernisation, as outlined in the famous statement in 1931 that I quoted earlier, is suspect. As for Chen Duxiu's most famous defence of Science and Democracy, it is remarkable that in 1979, and now again in 1989, scholars both in Taiwan and the mainland have repeatedly quoted it with approval — clearly emphasising its relevance for today; because neither the spirit of science nor that of democracy is healthy in *both* parts of China. This is such an influential statement that I would like to quote it here. Please bear in mind that Chen Duxiu said this about the time he was to become the first secretary-general of the newly-founded Chinese Communist Party. He said it in January 1919, a few months before the May Fourth demonstrations at his university, but they have become symbolic of the Movement thereafter (i.e. for the next 70 years). Let me quote his defence of his magazine, 新青年 (New Youth):

> "Our magazine has done no wrong. Only because we defended the two gentlemen, Mr. Democracy and Mr. Science, did we commit some great crimes. In order to support Mr. D, we could not but oppose Confucianism, the practice of rites, chastity, old morality, old politics. In order to support Mr. S, we could not but oppose old art, old religion. In order to support both Mr. D and Mr. S, we could not but oppose "national essence" and old literature . . ."
>
> "Westerners who supported Mr. D and Mr. S had to create much disturbance and spill much blood to rescue them both from darkness and bring them forth into the bright world. We now know that these two gentlemen can save China from the darkness of its politics, its morality, its learning. In support of these two, we will not decline to accept every oppressive action by the government, every attack and denunciation by society, even to bleed from our lopped off heads."

The fact this statement was made in 1919 is important. It was just after a disastrous World War I for the West and a little over a year after the October Revolution in Russia. Suddenly, the ideals of the 1911 Revolution and Sun Yat-sen's methods of seeking assistance from Western Powers and Japan seemed suspect and even backward. For the next few decades, Western values associated with capitalism and imperialism were portrayed as flawed. An exciting *world* revolution was seen as being in the making. Liberal democracy of the Anglo-American variety was being rejected by the new Soviet Union, by Mussolini's Italy and then by Hitler's Germany. Why then should China waste time with gradualism and evolution? Why not leap forward to the advanced forms of collective revolutionary action? It was therefore understandable, if tragic, that most Chinese intellectuals were tempted by what they saw as short cuts to achieve both the *Chinese* revolution and a revolutionary China. Chen

Duxiu was quickly converted and turned to the Communist Party. Sun Yat-sen was half-converted and allied with the Soviet Union. Hu Shi alone remained with the small minority that continued to argue for liberal democracy and the scientific spirit — these few, largely intellectuals, were lonely voices trying to sustain the momentum of the May Fourth Movement.

Yet, ironically, the May Fourth Movement marked a watershed of a kind. Up to that time, everyone who claimed he was a revolutionary was inside the Chinese revolution, fighting for national salvation as patriots but prepared to be as radical as necessary. After 1919, Sun Yat-sen and his followers, who stood for the 1911 Revolution, saw themselves alone as truly inside the *Chinese* Revolution. To them, the leaders of the Chinese Communist Party who looked to Marx and Lenin, and whose senior cadres were trained abroad by Stalin, were clearly outside. These communists might claim to be more revolutionary, but their revolution was certainly not Chinese! As for Hu Shi and his liberal friends who favoured modernisation through learning directly from the West, both sides rejected them as being both un-Chinese and un-revolutionary. In short, the May Fourth Movement ended by creating a deep division among its supporters into two major revolutionary groups.

This potted history and what I am about to say may be over-simple, but I believe it reflects the course of events during most of the 20th century. The Chinese revolution led by Sun Yat-sen's successors turned away from his revolutionary ideals and became more intensely Chinese in its quest for national legitimacy; in its efforts to survive against treacherous warlords, an expansionist imperialist Japan and on alien Soviet-led Communist Party. Under the circumstances leading to the Sino-Japanese War of 1937–1945, these efforts became increasingly popular, appealing to a pervasive anti-Japanese nationalism all over China and among Chinese overseas. Saving China was China's revolution — almost nothing else mattered as long as China was in danger.

The pressure on the Chinese Communists to be nationalist was no less acute. For their own survival, they too had to play down their revolutionary ideals. They also needed to be inside the *Chinese* revolution, emphasising both their patriotism and their genuine concerns for the peasantry who formed some 80 per cent of the population. Mao Tse-tung's success over the

Stalinist cadres, who returned from USSR in the 1930s, marked the resurgence of the *Chinese* over the internationalist elements in their revolution. In fact, by the end of the Sino-Japanese War, they had turned the tables on the KMT government by showing that the peasant nationalism which they had aroused, and which they now led, was far more Chinese than the nationalism of the landlord and bourgeoisie classes who supported the KMT. The communists were ready to demonstrate that the KMT were not only reactionary (i.e. against revolution) but also not really Chinese!

Let me not go into the reasons why the CCP won and the KMT lost in 1949, nor argue here who was inside and who was outside the Chinese Revolution. Both parties obviously believed that theirs was the true Chinese Revolution. Mao Tse-tung and his party had good reasons for believing that they had won because they were both revolutionary and Chinese, and that the KMT lost because they were neither Chinese nor revolutionary. By their victory, it would appear to the CCP that the Chinese people had spoken; the Mandate of Heaven was theirs; at the same time, they also thought theirs was a victory for world revolution and human progress with China thus contributing for the first time to global history.

Mao Tse-tung and the CCP lost no time in resolving an inherent contradiction. Throughout the Civil War in China prior to the CCP victory in 1949, only the loyal party members of each of the main contenders for power really counted as insiders. After their victory, however, the Communist Party quickly rectified this by a constitutional device. They introduced the inclusive formula of people (as in People's Republic) by defining whole classes of all peasants and workers as people and therefore, by constitutional right, inside the Revolution. This was also broadened to include sympathetic bourgeoisie and intellectuals who had supported the CCP at critical stages. Only the enemies of the people, that is, counter-revolutionaries, Kuomintang reactionaries who followed Chiang Kai-shek to Taiwan and abroad, certain classes of unrepentant landlords, compradores, and common criminals, were outside the Revolution. By using this device to define who should, and who should not be, legally recognised as citizens of the People's Republic, they claimed that theirs was truly a revolution of the people.

In theory, China was in revolution under a visionary leadership guided by scientific Marxist ideology and functioning through what was called democratic centralism. Therefore, every citizen was about to experience revolutionary change. In reality, however, the Revolution was determined and controlled by the Party. It soon became clear that most people were controlled by members of the Party at every level and therefore were more the objects of education and indoctrination than active participants. Again, on paper, this meant that everyone so indoctrinated was accepted inside the Revolution and, therefore, in time, everyone would become a revolutionary and share in the fruits of the Revolution. Everyone ultimately would be inside and no one would be left outside. But this was not to be so, for several reasons. Firstly, there were class enemies within, false revolutionaries and potential traitors, dissidents and recalcitrants who resisted education and indoctrination. Secondly, there was a dangerous world outside, of capitalists and imperialists, of socialist backsliders (even in the USSR) who wish to restore capitalism (even the USSR came to be seen as "social imperialist" and "hegemonist"), all of whom threatened the Chinese Revolution. And not least, thirdly, there were millions of Chinese outside China who were potential sympathisers or enemies; or who simply wanted nothing to do with the Chinese Revolution.

The net result of all these factors was that the Revolution that had begun by being inclusive became, over the next 30 years until the end of the so-called Great Proletarian Cultural Revolution, more and more exclusive. Let me briefly explain. Mao Tse-tung discovered by 1956–1957 that education and indoctrination by conventional means was not reliable. Intellectuals outside the Communist Party could never be trusted, and were always potential enemies of the Revolution. They were therefore placed outside the Revolution, many of them jailed and sent to labour camps, others simply not allowed to use the skills that they had. And then, it was discovered that hundreds of millions of peasants could be converted to revolutionary enthusiasm very easily — thus swelling the ranks of those inside the Revolution. But in so doing, Mao Tse-tung also found that many of his colleagues within the Party did not agree with him, or thought he was going in the wrong direction. He was moving away from world revolution and "sinicising" it instead; that is, turning the revolution inward into a peasant-based and backward, feudal Chinese uprising. Mao, however, concluded that it was his comrades who were not true revolutionaries; many were too timid, and conservative, merely greedy for privileges and power, and that some were sympathetic with "capitalist roaders" led by Soviet leaders under Khrushchev. It must have been disconcerting, if not disheartening, for him to find that so many of his comrades were not inside *his* Revolution, but actually distancing themselves from him. The Cultural Revolution of 1966–1976, therefore, was the result of his effort to cleanse the Party from within. During that decade of unprecedented confusion, thousands were deemed to have been *outside* the Revolution whilst millions of others were quickly brought inside the Party. No one was clear what the criteria were for being good communists. A mixture of enthusiasm, boldness and native cunning taken with the memorisation of some key Maoist texts was probably enough for most of the new members. Good education, advanced technical skills and even years of loyal work experience for the Party were denigrated if they were not accompanied by constant affirmations of Maoist loyalty.

In total, more members joined the Party during the Cultural Revolution decade and it might well be argued that more people were now inside the Revolution than ever before. In fact, there was so much confusion that no one knew who was a revolutionary any more — and this was perhaps the one clear result of the Cultural Revolution. For those older members who managed to survive, the Old Guard, it must have been a great relief when Mao Tse-tung died in 1976 and they were able to restore everything to the conditions before 1957. To many, they had lost 20 years. But, at least for the Old Guard, the Party was not totally destroyed and there was the opportunity to rebuild a Party that had so nearly lost its way. But what was left of the 1949 Revolution for them to rebuild?

Deng Xiaoping and the remnants of the Old Guard led a dramatic new start after 1978. Everything pertaining to Mao Tse-tung's mistakes since 1957 was quickly swept away. Verdicts were reversed, those wrongfully jailed or dismissed were restored; old standards for education and party membership were brought back; a socialist legal order, still largely modelled on that of the Soviet Union, was re-established. A new Open Door policy was introduced that built bridges to the capitalist world. The initial results were stunning, at least at the economic level. Reforms in the countryside, the resurgence of rural, and then low-level urban, entrepreneurship, the rise of new medium-sized industry at all urban centres, and the increase in foreign trade — some of the developments were unbelievable, and most Chinese people were delighted with the changes. Slowly, somewhat uncertainly at first, and then more and more confidently, a new and more open kind of Chinese Revolution emerged.

But something else also became clear. On the one hand, Mao Tse-tung's efforts to place his Revolution in the vanguard of world revolution had failed. He had, intentionally or not, taken the road back to something more Chinese, more traditionally peasant-based and unmistakably feudal and pre-capitalist, and in effect anti-revolutionary. On the other hand, by changing gears and opening up China, Deng Xiaoping could not return to the ideals of world revolution of the 1940s and 1950s. The world itself had radically changed during the years when Mao had kept the PRC in isolation. By 1979, there was no world revolution to join or return to. Instead, it was a world of relative capitalist success, of remarkable advances in science, industry, communications and international trade, and a world increasingly aware of human rights as it grows smaller and smaller. And not least, the face of East and Southeast Asia had changed and great things were now expected to happen in a vigorous and increasingly prosperous Asia-Pacific region.

In this new political and economic environment, Deng Xiaoping and his team, notably Hu Yaobang and Zhao Zhiyang, were shaping a new start, not for a revolutionary society for the new socialist man, but for a more familiar *Chinese* Revolution. Just about everyone, inside and outside China, wanted China to be opened up, wanted Deng Xiaoping to let in more light, and open more minds to new ideas coming from the outside in order to give the Chinese revolution a new lease of life. In this context, recalling the 1911 Revolution and the May Fourth Movement seemed perfectly natural — that was how the Chinese Revolution had begun, and the 1949 Revolution was meant to be that Revolution's culmination. But partly because the 1911

Revolution was still very much the KMT and Taiwan's own special ancestor, and still regarded as too narrowly conceived in nationalist terms, i.e. merely for China's unity, strength, and prosperity, it was the May Fourth Movement that caught more attention among Chinese intellectuals from the start.

It was not an auspicious start. In 1979, within months of Deng Xiaoping's return to power, when the PRC was preparing to celebrate its 30th anniversary, the intellectuals debated the meaning of the May Fourth Movement on its 60th anniversary. It was immediately pointed out that the "Four Modernisations" espoused by Deng Xiaoping did not include a fifth modernisation, *political* modernisation. There was no mention of the urgent need for democratic reform. I have already mentioned my impressions of what people expected in 1979 of the May Fourth Spirit, that they must learn from the outside world, and turn to experiences outside Mao Tse-tung's revolution.

It is now clear that many in China since 1979, especially young Chinese students, have taken a hard look outside their country and have digested some of what they have found. Not least, among many other things, they have found that the two major slogans of the May Fourth Movement, of Science and Democracy, are once again what China urgently needs. But during the past ten years, their experiences have not been encouraging. Scientific thinking is being limited to technology and industrial productivity. Cries for democratic reforms have been brushed aside. The Democracy Wall came to an end and the leaders of the small democracy movement were incarcerated. Others were sacked from the Chinese Party and otherwise punished. But, so much else was being achieved during these years in the economic sphere that what protests there were remained minimal and could, in fact, be safely ignored by the CCP leadership for another ten years.

All that has changed during the past month. The Chinese economy is not well; corruption is rampant; the 30 per cent inflation has frightened even the optimists and the stout hearted. The students in Beijing had been preparing for yet another decade's anniversary of the May Fourth Movement to express their concerns, when Hu Yaobang's unexpected death last month hastened the emotional outpourings that followed. This time, much public sympathy was shown and this has strengthened and emboldened the students. Suddenly the calls for Mr. Science and Mr. Democracy seem very appropriate again. And, if they are indeed that appropriate, they would show that the 1949 Revolution is no longer part of the world revolution the CCP had wanted to join, but is now very much an extension of the Chinese Revolution of 1911. And May 4th, 1919 is the key link that confirms that there has only been one Chinese Revolution and that the 1949 Revolution was really only a part of it. What had distracted us for three decades was Mao Tse-tung's bold but misguided effort to rise above that. When his revolution became a disaster during the Great Proletarian Cultural Revolution, it sealed the fate for revolutionary China and returned China to the earlier model.

Let me now return to the question I had asked at the beginning of the lecture about how one might evaluate whether more revolutionary change was achieved outside the Marxist-Leninist-Maoist framework of 1949 than within it. Put in another way, I asked if a smaller revolution, consisting of little modernisations accumulated outside the 1949 Revolution, has in fact occurred among Chinese peoples elsewhere. I would like now to suggest that we might try to answer the question by looking at the reasons why the two slogans of the May Fourth Movement, Mr. Science and Mr. Democracy are still relevant today.

I do not wish to open a debate about nature of the May Fourth Movement. But it is significant that the Movement is now such a powerful symbol, especially as one that highlights the goals of Science and Democracy. First, the call for more Science. This is on the surface puzzling insofar as much praise has been heaped on scientific advances in the PRC, how China has kept pace in many areas of technology and produced a number of fine scientists. There is, of course, much still to be done and Chinese scientists are quick to admit that they are far behind in several fields of high technology and lack solid foundations in the basic sciences. The real problem, however, does not lie in advances in technology. Many Chinese now recognise that the much more complex issue is the reluctance to use the scientific method in critical thinking about society, culture, politics and economics.

This is a problem that is very difficult to unravel in China because it questions the foundations of CCP ideology. The problem arises because the PRC had started with the proposition that Marxism-Leninism is scientific and encompasses all the scientific thinking the Chinese Revolution would ever need. It also argues quite unconvincingly that all other forms of scientific thought are class-based (usually bourgeois class) and therefore biased and ultimately unscientific. Only Marxism-Leninism is Science. The continued acceptance of this premise in Mainland China would make it very difficult to introduce new ideas about society, politics, economics and culture that do not start with Marxist premises and assumptions.

When the new Open Door Policy began ten years ago, there was a reluctant acknowledgement that capitalism has not only survived but has also brought great economic and technological progress to the countries that espouse it. But it was recognised that these advanced sciences and technologies would be invaluable for China. Catching up with the West in many areas was only a matter of time. Given the Chinese abilities in mathematics and basic sciences, few doubted that China would get there before long. But in fact, many Chinese realise that the country needs more science than that. Scientific thinking and methods are equally important in economics and management, in social and political policy-making. And the hardest of all is the willingness to think about the humanities and the social sciences (however imprecise their results may be) beyond the Marxist-Leninist framework.

There is yet another aspect about Science that has now been highlighted. This concerns national investment in education at every level. This is not only to ensure that the best talents are found for advanced studies and scientific work, but also popular education and the broad base that was invaluable for modernisation. Science training and the early introduction of the scientific method in schools require an enlightened policy towards teachers and school curricula. This the authorities in China now admit has been pathetic except for a small number of key schools, colleges and universities. Note what Chen Duxiu had said in 1919. He was not worried about technological advances but about "old religion", that is, about superstitions, ignorance and the power of unscientific ideas on ordinary lives. Hence he talked about saving China "from the darkness of its politics, its morality, its learning". On none of these three has there been progress comparable to, say, China's defence sciences and military technology, to take but one obvious example.

Here is why Mr. Science has been seen in China as inseparable from Mr. Democracy. If Chinese intellectuals are given freedom only to advance technology and the natural and physical sciences, but not to apply scientific non-Marxist thinking to social, political, cultural and economic phenomena, then there can be little progress in the kind of knowledge that supports and enlightens a democratic society and environment. Mr. Science needs freedom, to be free to think, to innovate, to challenge and criticise, free from obscurantist bureaucrats and rigid authoritarian systems, no less than Mr. Democracy does. Of course, not all these freedoms are found outside China. But when they are found, they have provided great assistance to the scientists that have advanced the wealth, as well as the quality of life, of so many democratic societies.

The Chinese have always had far greater difficulty agreeing on what kind of animal is Democracy. The reasons are obvious. After experiencing for 2000 years a powerful system that centralises all power in the hands of the emperor and his mandarinate, how are they to think in democratic terms? Sun Yat-sen had begun to talk about this at the beginning of the century. Twenty years later, Chen Duxiu in 1919 identified the issue as one that was vital for China, and 70 years after that, the Chinese are still wondering how they can introduce more democratic institutions into China.

They have not been helped by the fact that the PRC since 1949 believed that it already was a democracy and that somehow, the "democratic centralism" that had been erected by the CCP is more scientific (because it is Marxist-Leninist) than any other form of democracy. Any other form suggested is therefore likely to be seen as anti-Marxist and unscientific. And if that form should come from outside China, it is also unpatriotic and possibly treasonable.

Both these obstacles to democracy, the imperial tradition and Marxist-Leninist dogma are well known. Together, they are so deep-rooted and strong that it may well be that Mr. Democracy, (as Chen Duxiu, Hu Shi and others knew it) may be impossible for China in the foreseeable future. It is understandable why Chinese intellectuals now argue that it may not be essential to borrow democratic forms from outside China. What may be more important in the long run is the emergence of the democratic spirit, protected by a respect for human rights and freedoms that is embodied in a fair and efficient legal system. What to them is crucial now is an environment where there is free speech, where there are checks and balances to counter corruption and maladministration, where it is lawful to criticise those in power.

And here another difficulty may face the democrats in China. As Chen Duxiu put it, "In order to support Mr. D, we could not but oppose Confucianism, the practice of rites, chastity, old morality, old politics". Within China, but often rejected by Chinese revolutionaries, are forces of tradition still alive today. These forces are not all inimical to the democratic spirit. Some are still greatly respected because they help progress; for example, there is the tradition of support for education; and there is the this-worldly attitude towards hard work, thrift, material success and entrepreneurship. What does stand in the way of democracy, however, is the traditional authoritarianism of emperor and father sanctioned by state Confucianism, which has been translated to the bureaucratic machinery of the modern state and political party. Those in power regularly reject any criticism of this aspect of the tradition by appealing for respect for all the traditions that made China a great civilisation. It is therefore very easy to attack democrats who appear too eager for change by accusing them of unpatriotic, un-Chinese, acts against tradition. One of the great ironies of the Chinese Revolution is that cultural values that were at times severely condemned could, at different times, be defended because they are Chinese and therefore should only be judged by Chinese and not outside standards.

I think I have said enough about Mr. S and Mr. D and the problems they face in China today. What about the revolution outside that of 1949 on the Mainland? The revolution of 1911 started as a nationalist one to be achieved in a republic that would establish a prosperous, strong and united China. It would in time also to be democratic and scientifically advanced and even re-distribute wealth to the poor. By 1928, some twenty years later, that revolution had achieved no more than a nationalist republic. And another 20 years after that, after 1949, it was struggling to re-build its base in Taiwan, and depended on the support of old KMT members and anti-Communists all over the world. By that time, uniting China from Taiwan was widely seen as a myth, and all its other revolutionary ideals seem to have been couched negatively in anti-Communist rhetoric. If the 1949 Revolution in the PRC had lost its way through Mao Tse-tung's romantic zeal, then the 1911 Revolution in Taiwan from 1949 was kept in a frozen state for more than 25 years. Only in the 1970s was it possible to think afresh about the consequences of comparative prosperity. Science and technology had developed to match manufacturing needs and stimulate new industries. And following that, with prosperity and confidence, more scientific thinking has been permitted to extend into examining China's great cultural traditions and this in turn has opened more minds to the possibility of democracy.

Beyond Taiwan, there is Hong Kong, and there are the large communities in several cities in Southeast Asia and, more recently, growing communities in a few cities in North America and Australia. For most of them, there had been divisions between those Chinese who had identified with the 1911 Revolution and the KMT and those who had sympathised with the 1949 Revolution. They had other things in common. Among the most important was the fact they were free from traditional political and social norms. Many, of course, are still deeply concerned for the goals that the Chinese Revolution has yet to achieve: namely unity, prosperity and strength for China; while many of the younger Chinese would call for the spirit of both science and democracy. Despite the fact that no Chinese outside can really do anything significant now for the Chinese Revolution, their lives outside that Revolution have given them rich insights into what their present adopted countries have done, with or without revolution. The one striking fact that all Chinese can now see is that Chinese outside China who had lived in, or still remain in, communist or so-called socialist countries (now very much fewer in number) have done very poorly. In contrast, those who live in liberal capitalist countries have done immeasurably better. This is not merely because these countries have either had their revolutions a long time ago or had never needed one, but also because these open and liberal societies have educated them to bring the scientific method of thinking into their daily family lives, into every aspect of their education and have, in most cases, introduced them to the value of living in a democratic environment. They already have what the May Fourth Movement wanted in 1919 and what the Chinese in China still want 70 years later.

Ladies and Gentlemen, I have taken you quickly through a vast subject. I feel, like the Chinese in China, there is no time to take breath. I have not avoided saying some disheartening things about the Chinese Revolution. Nor did I fail to point to the advances the Chinese people have made both inside and outside China. There is still much that needs closer study from the historical record, also much to speculate about and hope for. But several points are now clearer than they have been for some time. The Chinese Revolution had been much influenced by revolutionary ideas from the outside but (and this should not really surprise us) it has been far more Chinese than revolutionary. In the most painful and tragic ways, it has brought changes and some progress to the Chinese in China — but has yet to contribute to world revolution, least of all to world civilisation. But there are signs that, outside the Chinese revolution and I mean both outside China and outside the idea of revolution as the Chinese have conceived it, progress among Chinese people elsewhere is having an impact on those within China. For this to have any lasting effect and ultimately transform China, there needs to be sustained openness to the world. I believe we all deeply hope that China has passed the stage of depending on a violent big-R revolution to achieve its goals. Its two-part revolution of 1911 and 1949 has brought to the surface what is possible and what is not, what can be fruitful and what is not. The experiences have been so rich and varied, and so many millions both inside and outside have learnt so much, that we can now hope that China remains open to the world. I believe that most Chinese everywhere now realise that only through this openness, and the trials and changes that would bring, can China fulfil the expectations its peoples have for so long had for the Chinese Revolution. Is there a message here? If there is, the message today would be something like this: Be open to the world and then you can be as Chinese as you like!

CHAPTER 3

RIGHTEOUS MANDATE: TO REFORM A REVOLUTION*

When the Republic of China was proclaimed on January 1st, 1912, Sun Yat-sen called its government that 'of a revolutionary era'. Two months earlier, when he was in the United States and heard that the uprising in Wuchang was succeeding, he thought that only the governments of the United States and France, which had had their own republican revolutions, would support the Chinese revolution, while the German, Russian and Japanese governments would not. British support was crucial. Although the government was undecided, the people were sympathetic. Thus when he reached London a month later, he spoke of the unstoppable tide of enlightenment and progress that would soon enable revolutionary China 'to join the civilized and freedom-loving nations of the world'.[1] Thus, China acquired parts of a modern face.

---

*This paper was sent to the American Academy of Arts and Sciences Conference on China, held in Boston in September 1992. I was unable to present it because of urgent commitments at the University of Hong Kong. Stephen R Graubard and Tu Wei-ming edited it for publication in the Academy's journal as "To Reform a Revolution: Under the Righteous Mandate", *Daedalus*, Spring 1993, vol. 122, no. 2, pp. 71–94; reprinted in Tu Wei-ming (ed.), *China in Transformation*. Harvard University Press, Cambridge, MA, 1994.

[1] Interview with a journalist of *The Strand Magazine* in London, published in the March issue, 1912, vol. 43, no. 255, as 'My Reminiscences', pp. 301–307, translated and collected in *Sun Zhongshan quanji*, Zhonghua Press, Beijing, vol. 1 (1890–1911), pp. 547–558. The Proclamation in Nanjing by Sun Yat-sen as Provisional President of the Republic of China on January 1st, 1912 is collected in *Sun Zhongshan quanji*, vol. 2, pp. 1–3.

I am reminded that, thirty years afterwards, in 1942, *geming* or the so-called Right of Revolution was noted as 'a sort of ideological preparation for democratic institutions which, there is good reason to hope, will enable [China] in future to assume her rightful place among the world's great democracies', in Derk Bodde,

Sun Yat-sen saw the Republic as having broken from the past and from all the futile efforts to reform and save the imperial Confucian system. It had become part of modern world history.

There was to be no looking back. A new generation of educated Chinese, including Mao Zedong, picked up the call during the May Fourth Movement after 1919 and many wanted China to go much further. This second genera-tion produced the leaders who established the People's Republic of China in 1949 as an advanced country in 'the vanguard of world revolution'. Mao Zedong himself was impatient to realise this ideal and finally launched a vio-lent 'cultural' revolution to achieve that goal. Consciously or not, he did so by putting on parts of a Chinese face, invoking those features of authority and power that had the effect of reversing recent trends and restoring older politi-cal values and structures.[2]

After his death, the word reform regained efficacy and replaced the word revolution in China's policies and goals. Since the disintegration of Soviet power after 1989, the word revolution has lost its universal appeal even more rapidly. The Chinese word for reform, *gaige*, is now used for everything. *Geming*, the Chinese word for revolution, however, is widely greeted with indifference and a tinge of fear. But some of the third generation of educated Chinese has shown, especially during the decade leading to the tragedy at Tiananmen on June 4th, 1989, that they are prepared to contemplate radical changes amounting to yet another revolution in political and cultural values. What do these words, reform and revolution, *gaige* and *geming,* tell us about modern Chinese, the country's struggle to free itself from the past, and the brave new world it has so much wanted for its people?

Essays on Chinese Civilization (edited by Charles Le Blanc and Dorothy Borei), Princeton University Press, Princeton, 1981, p. 138 (reprinting an essay, 'Dominant Ideas in the Formation of Chinese Culture', first published in *Journal of the American Oriental Society*, vol. 62, December, 1942, pp. 293–299.
[2] Wang Gungwu, 'Juxtaposing Past and Present in China Today', *The China Quarterly*, (London), 61, March, 1975, pp. 1–24; also in a collected volume of my essays, *The Chineseness of China: Selected essays*, Oxford University Press, Hong Kong, 1991, pp. 209–229.

The question reminds us that it has always been difficult to approach any subject about one civilisation using terms derived from another. Should we use indigenous terms in original contexts to try and portray reality as the local people see it themselves? Should we translate the terms as best we can, but interpret them in language familiar to the foreign audience we write for? Or, should we assume the oneness of history and accept the language of discourse dominant at any one time and define everything accordingly? These are old questions for which answers become even more difficult when we deal with what appears to be global events in modern history. And the more complex the phenomena and the more entangled the current developments are in a civilisation's traditions, the harder it is to understand and explain what is happening, least of all predict future changes.

Not surprisingly, this is especially difficult with events in China. The densely knit cultures within its borders hide a great deal, even from its own people. Its long history of dynastic empires thrusting out beyond existing borders or pulling into itself, and its image as a country that had experienced cycles of cultural and institutional sameness have been specially misleading. Certainly, the size of territory and population had led its rulers, whether imperial, nationalist or communist, to give priority to, and use all available resources to ensure, unity and conformity and to encourage bureaucratic simplification of the institutions of social and political control. If necessary, reality could always be made to fit the current ideology.

Students of modern Chinese history cannot but be struck by the distance between hopes, intentions and goals of every generation and the compromises, betrayals and what may be described as the burdens of China's history. Another kind of distance is that between the modern ideal of seeking to meet the needs and demands of the ordinary people (however defined) and the reality of their helplessness in the face of the traditions of centralized power. There are also other kinds of cultural distance derived from the dissonances between imported ideas and technologies on the one hand and native pride and inspiration on the other.[3] Whichever kind of distance it is, our efforts at explaining contemporary

---

[3] Such distances can be measured differently, in terms of industrial entrepreneurship, political action, philosophy, scientific education, literature and the arts; for general

China remains a continuous struggle, because each manifestation of distance is not created by mere ignorance or naivete, nor even by dishonesty. It is implicit in the idea of China, whether as a country, a civilisation, an empire, a nation-state, a cultural sub-continent, or an integral part of an interdependent world.

It is in this context that the words reform and revolution, as taken from Western and world history and applied to China, are explored here. In their Chinese manifestations, revolution is compared with *geming*, the tradition of a violent but righteous (Heavenly) mandate to rule which is deeply rooted in Chinese history, and reform with *gaige* which is often taken for granted and rarely explicit as each dynasty renews and strengthens itself.[4] These comparisons immediately bring out the fact that there are many paradoxes prevailing in China today.

Among them are those that suggest that the old men of today who had launched the communist revolution now want nothing but reform and the younger ones who have tired of revolution are willing to contemplate a new kind of revolution to replace the one that had failed. This may not really be so, nor is it unique to the Chinese. Much depends on what meanings are attached to words like reform and revolution and what qualities are emphasized. For example, if the speed and dimensions of change are stressed in the

---

surveys, Jonathan D. Spence, *The Gate of Heavenly Peace: the Chinese and their revolution, 1895–1980*, Viking Press, New York, 1981; and W.J.F. Jenner, *The Tyranny of History: The Roots of China's Crisis*, Allen Lane, The Penguin Press, London, 1992.

A heightened view is best presented by the writers and artists. For an earlier period, Leo Ou-fan Lee, *The Romantic Generation of Modern Chinese Writers*, Harvard University Press, Cambridge, Mass., 1973, provides a valuable framework for understanding the present. For developments during the past decade, two collections of Chinese writings are outstanding: Geremie Barme and John Minford (eds.), *Seeds of Fire: Chinese Voices of Conscience*, Far Eastern Economic Review, Hong Kong, 1986, and Geremie Barme and Linda Jaivin (eds.), *New Ghosts, Old Dreams: Chinese Rebel Voices*, Times Books, New York, 1992.

[4] Benjamin I. Schwartz, *The World of Thought in Ancient China*, The Belknap Press of Harvard University Press, Cambridge, Mass., 1985, pp. 102–117. The concept of reform was expressed indirectly, often through Heavenly warnings that suggested that something was seriously wrong and therefore needed reform; for the theory behind this, see Michael Loewe, 'The Religious and Intellectual Background', *The Cambridge History of China*, vol. 1: *The Ch'in and Han Empires, 221 B.C.–A.D. 220*, Cambridge University Press, Cambridge, 1986, pp. 708–713.

definition of each word, reform suggests the gradual improvement of a work-able system and revolution connotes total comprehensive change that has been swiftly, and often violently, achieved. On the other hand, if it is the protagonists who deserve attention, then it may matter whether they have organised for changes from above to meet elite interests or from below to establish new and more responsive power structures.

In the language of modern scholarship, reform and revolution, reformists and revolutionaries, are opposed in order to assist analysis. In reality, the contrasts apply best only during a specific period when the differences seem clear cut. Once past the time when sharp distinctions can be made, however, successful reforms could lead to radical change and even amount to a revolu-tion, and revolutions that faltered or failed might need to be saved by reforms.

In that context, China today may be no different. It could be demon-strated that the revolutions of 1911 and 1949 have successively lost their way. When the first failed to deliver on its promises, a new set of leaders tried to save China by the second, a more thorough and genuine revolution. But when the second also faltered, ironically despite desperate attempts to galvanize the peo-ple to greater efforts at revolution, the old leaders fell back on reform in order to save what they have. Suddenly, the rhetoric was significantly changed and all the good words connected with reform were brought in to replace the strident expressions associated for decades with revolution. This change of direction may not be peculiar to China. Much of it may be compared with developments elsewhere and conform to modern political and economic imperatives. Never-theless, there are unique features in the Chinese condition that reflect subtle continuities and recall a powerful and not yet forgotten past.

These features mark the ambivalent face of China. There is for China a distinctive intertwining of past and present, of a past that had once seemed so unchangeable with a present which now defies predictability. The search for modernisation in China has given this relationship a new manifestation. In addition, we have been led to an image of apparent elusiveness by the prism of our modern analytical concepts like reform and revolution. These words as applied so richly to Western history should be adequately lucid.

But, in Chinese, they both have ancient roots that are evocative and layered with meanings which have persisted to this day.

The term *gaige* may be set beside other modern terms for reform like *weixin*, or *ziqiang*, or *bianfa*, but the strong echoes of historic efforts to save the country or a dynasty are unmistakable whichever term is used.[5] Revolution as in modern England, France and the United States is more complicated, but the word *geming* is not a bad translation, even though it was first used in China more than 2,500 years ago to describe the victories of Tang and Wu, both founders of dynasties, those of Shang and Zhou respectively. Given the dynastic connotations of the term, they remind us of the concept of mandate, whether in its traditional sense of *tianming* or Mandate of Heaven, or the modern idea of 'given power' as mandate. The latter would be translated as *shouquan*; that could mean, for example, the mandate of the people, which is an openly demonstrable form that could be compared with Mencius' idealized *tianming*.[6] In this essay, I shall combine the two senses of heavenly and secular by using the phrase 'righteous mandate'. It helps to remind us that there are always echoes of the past in the Chinese present. This paper will attempt to use such resonances to explore what lies behind the ambivalent face of China.

Let me begin with the revolution. Every Chinese alive today has lived with the idea of *geming* as revolution since his or her youth. How many meanings has that word had? When Sun Yat-sen, the first internationally acknowledged leader of revolution in China, was asked a question in London, and in English, in 1896 about his '*revolutionary* business', he avoided answering the question but, later the same day, he claimed, again in English, to have been arrested 'for sending a memorial for *reform*'.[7] He had read enough of

---

[5] Both *gai* and *ge* in the term *gaige* appear under the same hexagram *Ge* in *I Ching* (The Book of Changes) and both explain and extend the idea of change in the context of 'great progress and success' and 'coming from what is correct', implying improvement and reform, *I Ching* (based on the translation by James Legge), edited by Raymond Van Over, The New American Library, New York, 1971, pp. 249–252.

[6] The term *geming* also first appears under the hexagram *Ge* in *I Ching*. In its direct association with *tianming* or Mandate of Heaven, it is most fully developed in *Mencius* Book IV, Part A of D.C. Lau's translation, Penguin Books, 1970, pp. 117–127.

[7] *Daily Chronicle*, 24 October, 1896, and then *Evening Standard*, 24 October, 1896, both quoted in J.Y. Wong, *The Origins of an Heroic Image: Sun Yatsen in London*,

Western history to know the difference between the two words and was being evasive. In fact, he had been plotting the overthrow of a failed dynasty ruled by the Manchus, a hated foreign people in the eyes of the many southern Han Chinese who supported him. The Qing rulers and their literati functionaries saw him primarily as a rebel and so did many of his admiring followers who wanted nothing more than to rebel successfully with him.

It is doubtful that Sun Yat-sen thought that what he was saying to his followers when he founded his Xingzhong Hui, or Revive China Association, in 1895 was in the language of modern revolution. He was at that stage influenced by the traditions of the secret societies of South China and Xingzhong was more likely to have echoed the idea of Zhongxing, or dynastic restoration, used during the reign of Tongzhi emperor 30 years earlier, after the Taiping rebellion was finally crushed in 1864.[8] The inversion of Xingzhong and Zhongxing brings out a difference between the 1860s and the 1890s, between restoration of imperial power and national (Han Chinese) revival, but implicit in both is an evolving patriotism about the dignity and power of an ancient state, sustained by a great civilisation. This civilization-state had experienced a considerable battering by the Western powers, and the humiliating defeat by the Japanese in 1894–1895 was, especially for the Han Chinese elites, the last straw.

Soon after the failure of his first attempt at open rebellion in Guangzhou in 1895, Sun Yat-sen saw the word *gemingzhe*, or revolutionary, applied to him in the Japanese press and he quickly recognized what he stood for. The ambiguity in the term *geming*, however, remained between the traditional sense of overthrowing a dynasty that had lost its Heavenly Mandate and the

---

1896–1897, East Asian Historical Monographs, Oxford University Press, Hong Kong, 1986, pp. 169 and 172.

[8] The language of the constitutions of the Xingzhong Hui of Honolulu (1894) and Hong Kong (1895) may be compared with that in the proposal for reform which Sun Yat-sen sent in 1894 to Li Hongzhang, *Sun Zhongshan quanji*, vol 1, pp. 8–24. For his early association with secret societies and other traditional groups, Harold Z. Schiffrin, *Sun Yat-sen and the Origins of the Chinese Revolution*, University of California Press, Berkeley, 1968, pp. 56–97; and Lilia Borokh, 'Notes on the early role of secret societies in Sun Yat-sen's republican movement', in Jean Chesneaux (ed.), *Popular Movements and Secret Societies in China, 1840–1950*, Stanford University Press, Stanford, 1972, pp. 135–144.

modern meaning of replacing a political system that was no longer viable, by force of arms if necessary. For Sun Yat-sen and his young lieutenants, this ambiguity was probably useful. They were aware that the vast majority even of their own followers were not ready to accept that their modern ideals were derived principally from studying Western political institutions. What most Chinese really understood was the idea that the Qing dynasty's mandate was near its end and therefore the time had come to replace it. Already, for practical reasons, there had begun the fudging of foreign ideas that needed to be explicated in Chinese terms.

Sun Yat-sen had himself, in 1894, sent a memorial advocating reform to the Qing senior minister Li Hongzhang. At that time, the *yangwu* or 'Western affairs' experts who offered modernizing reforms for the self-strengthening (*ziqiang*) of the dynastic system had suffered a loss of power because of the disastrous defeats by the Japanese. They were soon challenged by a new group of younger literati who wanted radical changes to the system comparable to Japan's Meiji Restoration or *weixin* (another way of expressing renewal through transformation).[9] They failed and were accused of trying to stage a coup, that is, *zhengbian*, through the Guangxu emperor in 1898. In traditional language, this was treason punishable by death and indeed six of the leaders were executed. Historians have now settled for the equally traditional term *bianfa*, or changing the laws, to describe what this younger group led by Kang Youwei was prepared to do. The term traces back to the reforms of Shang Yang (4th century, B.C.) which transformed the Qin state before it unified the whole of China; after that, the most famous example of *bianfa* was the lifelong effort by Wang Anshi to reform the Northern Song dynasty (11th century). Nevertheless, conservatives in China have always frowned on the

---

[9] Ting-yee Kuo and Kwang-Ching Liu, 'Self-strengthening: The pursuit of Western Technology', in John K. Fairb®ank (ed.), *The Cambridge History of China, vol. 10: Late Ch'ing, 1800–1911, Part I*, Cambridge University Press, Cambridge, 1978, pp. 491–542; and Hao Chang, 'Intellectual change and the reform movement, 1890–1898', in John K. Fairbank and Kwang-Ching Liu (eds.), *The Cambridge History of China, vol. 11: Late Ch'ing, 1800–1911, Part 2*, Cambridge University Press, Cambridge, 1980, pp. 274–338.

idea of *bianfa* and the Self-strengtheners, the conservative *yangwu* experts, were no less hostile to what Kang Youwei and his supporters advocated.[10]

In this way, the reform camp was split between the conservatives and the radicals, those still in high office within the system and those now outside court circles, including those who were outlaws exiled in Japan and elsewhere. Facing these reformers, who made half-hearted attempts to unite with Sun Yat-sen's more or less revolutionary groups, were those who sought to change the mandate altogether, *geming* instead of *bianfa*. As Mary Wright and her colleagues have demonstrated, neither camp was talking about reform and revolution as understood through the history of the English, the French or the Americans.[11] It would be another two decades or more into the 20th century, after the reformists had failed and the revolutionaries of 1911 had won, before a new generation of intellectuals began to see the need to redefine *geming* and equate it with modern Western examples of revolution.

By that time, revolution had acquired another dimension and many turned to it in the shadow of the October Bolshevik Revolution in the Soviet Union. Thus, these young activists sought to divert the Chinese people from their traditional historical operas and novels and the connotations of dynastic change so deeply rooted in their consciousness. They sought cultural or *mentalite* revolution: it was anti-superstition, anti-Confucian, anti-religion as well as anti-imperialist and ultimately anti-Western and even xenophobic. It was a real baptism in several fierce currents of hostility in search of what the new kind of *geming*, as revolution, should stand for.[12]

---

[10] Hsiao Kung-chuan, *A Modern China and a New World: K'ang Yu-wei, Reformer and Utopian, 1858–1927*, University of Washington Press, Seattle, 1975; Hao Chang, Chinese *Intellectuals in Crisis: Search for Order and Meaning (1890–1911)*, University of California Press, Berkeley, 1987. For the most famous effort at *bianfa*, James T.C. Liu, *Reform in Sung China: Wang Anshih (1021–1086) and his New Policies* (Harvard East Asian Studies, no. 3), Harvard University Press, Cambridge, Mass., 1959.

[11] Mary C. Wright (ed.), *China in Revolution: The First Phase, 1900–1913*, Yale University Press, New Haven, 1968; a more recent account is Michael Gasster, 'The republican revolutionary movement', in Fairbank and Liu (eds.), *Late Ch'ing, Part 2*, pp. 463–534.

[12] Chow Tse-tsung, *The May Fourth Movement: Intellectual Revolution in Modern China, 1915–1924*, Harvard University Press, Cambridge, Mass. 1960; and Lin Yu-sheng, *The Crisis of Chinese Consciousness: Radical Anti-traditionalism in the May Fourth Era,*

After eliminating several alternative ideologies inspired by more or less Western political parties, there remained only nationalism and socialism, both protean words that could be applied to many situations. For example, nationalism could encompass *liberte, egalite, fraternite* as well as capitalism, socialism and representative democracy while socialism could be accommodated by liberal democrats, communists as well as fascist dictators. Not very helpful for clear thinking idealists, one must say, but being very modern and equated with world trends and universalist movements persuaded them to conform to the laws of modern history. It was certainly enough differentiation for two major political parties to emerge in China to fight a bitter civil war.

Although the two parties did combine briefly for a national salvation anti-Japanese war, there was no hope of any reconciliation and eventually the socialist definition of revolution won a decisive victory over the nationalist one. After 1949, what was considered the more genuinely revolutionary force thrust the lesser one out of the mainland of China. Historians after that were extolled to adopt a holistic interpretation of what appeared to be the apotheosis of a modern revolution on par with that of the French and the Soviets and on a larger scale than all the great revolutions that had gone before. Clearly, there could be discerned a common thread of an elitist departure from the past, spurning the Great Tradition in favour of a new modern/Western (including Marxist and Soviet) and populist/peasant Chinese culture, an ideology and polity that would, together and thoroughly, redefine *geming* as revolution for every Chinese, whatever their class origins.[13]

Thus did the grand view of revolution appear *both* sinicized and global, the object of new pride because it laid the foundations of a new Chinese

---

University of Wisconsin Press, Madison, 1978. An excellent study of the developments that followed is Vera Schwarcz, *The Chinese Enlightenment: Intellectuals and the Legacy of the May Fourth Movement of 1919*, University of California Press, Berkeley, 1986.

Also the succinct account by Benjamin I. Schwartz, 'Themes in intellectual history: May Fourth and after', in John K. Fairbank (ed.) *The Cambridge History of China, vol. 12: Republican China, 1912–1949, Part 1*, 1983, pp. 406–450.

[13] Wang Gungwu, *China and the World since 1949: The Impact of Independence, Modernity and Revolution*, Macmillan Press, London, 1977, and 'Outside the Chinese Revolution', *The Australian Journal of Chinese Affairs*, (Canberra), no. 23, January 1990, pp. 33–48.

civilization that could face down the world. It is now doubtful how much substance lay behind the rhetoric, the violent action and frenetic political campaigns that followed for the next three decades. Even if there were, there was hardly enough time for the new worker-peasant military-industrial complex to replace the literati-peasant military-agrarian one that had dominated China for 2,000 years. What was certain, however, was that Sun Yat-sen and his nationalist and communist heirs had broken the dynastic mold by violent revolution. There would be no more Sons of Heaven. Theirs was the Republic or People's Republic and the modern Chinese nation had been given a fresh start.

But it is also true, among ordinary Chinese steeped in myths and local lore, that the new leaders could yet be thought to have founded a new kind of dynastic structure, ruling till death without office or title of any kind, becoming ancestors entombed in mausoleums, possibly even new deities in revived temples or protagonists doomed to become tragic wandering spirits. In addition, had they not, like many of their predecessors in history, turned on one another in succession as revolutionary leaders, first in civil wars and then during the Great Leap Forward and the Cultural Revolution? It has not helped that their brands of nationalism and socialism had led to comparative poverty on the mainland and that similar socialisms that had celebrated their revolutions and been so dominant elsewhere in a once hopeful world have collapsed altogether. The recent experiences after a decade of extensive economic reforms in China and after the end of the Soviet Union have begun to undermine the *geming* that a whole generation of Chinese had redefined. At the very least, they threaten to cancel out the many efforts by the present Chinese leaders to distinguish their market socialism from the capitalist democracies on the one hand, and from the residual continuities of the Great Tradition on the other.

There has, in short, been a return to historical ambiguity here. This is a feature of modern Chinese culture that has persisted through the century more strongly than the idealists and revolutionaries expected. The ambiguity has acquired fresh intensity now that erstwhile revolutionaries speak so passionately of reform. The idea of reforming a revolution grates against the more familiar one of *consolidating* a revolution and has to be seen as a contradiction.

But, in the Chinese context, it not only brings back echoes of reform at the beginning of modern Chinese history in the late 19th and early 20th century, but also calls for a reappraisal of the deep-rooted idea of *geming* itself.

The reform that is now so strongly espoused cannot avoid being compared with what is normally associated with the *yangwu* experts and the *bianfa* radicals of the 19th century. There were, of course, other near contemporaries who also claimed to have been reformers. They were minor and peripheral players outside these two distinctive camps and shall not concern us here. The distinction that needs to be made would be clear from the two main groups. The reformers in China today have chosen yet another term, *gaige,* to distinguish their reforms from the earlier ones. This term, too, has an honorable ancestry. Although it is not identified with any dynasty or period in history, it too has, by common usage, connotations of removing old ways and replacing them with new ones, but usually by peaceful means. The questions that have brought about continual debates and divisions, however, have always been — which of the old had to change, how quickly that was to be done, and how new the new had to be.

On the surface, there is so much today that reminds us of the bitter struggle at the centre between the *yangwu* self-strengtheners and the radical supporters of the Hundred Days Reform in 1898 while, on the periphery, a few bold activists, with some outside support, try to harass both groups. Indeed, it is tempting to produce a collage which mounts a number of modern names, faces and slogans beside or on top of the comparable ones from the period of Li Hongzhang, Kang Youwei and Sun Yat-sen. Of course, nothing would quite fit, nor should we expect that. If they did fit and China looks like having returned to square one after a hundred years and countless million lives sacrificed, that would certainly give reason for despair. But there are times, as if through a distorting mirror, when the audience feels that it is looking at the same picture. What they actually see, of course, is the ambivalent face of China. A few examples of what this means for various reform measures would suffice. They range from the insistence on minimal change to attempts at grudging reform, from clearly radical ideas to policies revealing much indecision and confusion.

The example of minimal change in an area widely perceived as needing urgent reform is in the power structure. Although the network of cadres within Zhongnanhai today are obviously different from the Qing court mixture of Manchu-Mongol-Han aristocrats and officials, the determination to change the political and ideological framework as little as possible is remarkably similar. All the reformist vocabulary skirts around what the Qing court and the Chinese Communist Party both regard as the moral core of their respective belief systems.[14] This includes the image of Deng Xiaoping as the 'head of household', the retired elder, without office or title, with something like an untestable mandate; also the myth of non-existent factionalism; and, most of all, the sacred rituals of political succession. The last is particularly striking, down to the long-lived untitled ruler governing from behind the curtains awaiting some yet unforeseeable opportunity to pick the right heir. For all Chinese who love and speak through the idiom of historical analogies, there is a real feast here for future operas, literature and the visual arts.

The reality is much more complicated. The power structure today, borrowed at the same time as the revolutionary ideology, may be alien in origin, but through the efforts of Mao Zedong had been much adapted to Chinese usage.[15] It had successfully crushed the old world of landlords and literati, and their family-dependent commerce, but it had built its power base on a neo-traditional alliance of peasant armies and state-controlled workers.[16] These latter are comparable to court and state-appointed artisans, only they

---

[14] The essays in S.R. Schram (ed.) *Foundations and Limits of State Power in China*, School of Oriental and African Studies, University of London and The Chinese University of Hong Kong Press, London, 1987, provide an excellent background to this question, notably, Marianne Bastid, 'Official Conceptions of Imperial Authority at the End of the Qing dynasty', pp. 147–185; and David S.G. Goodman, 'Democracy, Interest and Virtue: The search for legitimacy in the People's Republic of China' pp. 291–312.

[15] Two studies by Frederick C. Teiwes explore this topic most successfully: *Leadership, Legitimacy and Conflict in China*, Macmillan, London, 1984; and *Politics at Mao's Court: Gao Gang and Party Factionalism in the Early 1950s*, M.E. Sharpe, New York, 1990. Also Lucian W. Pye, *The Mandarin and the Cadre: China's Political Cultures*, Center for Chinese Studies, University of Michigan, Ann Arbor, 1988, especially chapter 5, 'The Mystique of Leadership'. pp. 135–173.

[16] Wang Gungwu, 'China: 1989 in Perspective', *Southeast Asian Affairs 1990*, Institute of Southeast Asian Studies, Singapore, 1990, pp. 71–85.

are now much larger in number and potentially very powerful in their own right if state controls over their freedom of political action were lifted. Thus, although the rhetoric is new, the structure is built on historically familiar groups of majority interests.

But, thanks to decades of abuse and mismanagement under several over-enthusiastic revolutionary leaders, the power structure has rapidly lost credibility as one that was supposed to have fully replaced the Confucian state. The revolution has done enough to ensure that there is no return to the decrepit imperial system, but it has not yet been accepted as its permanent replacement.[17] The disasters that have befallen all the Communist states around the world during the past few years make it unlikely that the Chinese people would ever accept that Communist system in its original form.

Perhaps that is recognized by those still in power. Is this why they have concentrated on reforms in other spheres, partly because they need to keep control of the structure in order to stay in power longer? And partly because they hope that successful non-political reforms might save them ever having to change the structure and the ideology that supports it? Or is it really because, under the circumstances, any call for political reform would raise the specter of *geming* or a total change in the regime? This would be gambling for very high stakes, not only for the future of the Party's elites and their revolution, but also that of the country and the people. But most immediately for the Chinese people is the series of selective reforms to prevent the need for another revolution, or at least avoid reminding the people about *geming* as a total change of regime.

Among the areas selected for reform, that of economic reform has been agreed to by almost everyone in China. Most people seem to have been enthusiastic about, and grateful for, the little freedoms that enabled them to trade, to profit from productive labour, to learn new technologies from

---

[17] Tang Tsou, *The Cultural Revolution and Post-Mao Reforms: A Historical Perspective*, University of Chicago Press, Chicago, 1986. Three of the essays are particularly insightful: 'Back from the Brink of Revolutionary-"Feudal" Totalitarianism', pp. 144–188, 'Political Change and Reform: The Middle Course', pp. 219–258, and 'Reflections on the Formation and Foundations of the Communist Party-State in China', pp. 259–334.

abroad, even to enjoy themselves. This is nothing new, simply a return to some of the little pleasures and privileges that the Chinese people had had earlier in the century under the previous regime or during the centuries before that under the last two dynasties. All the same, the package of reforms aimed at stimulating the economy is more systematic than anything that the earlier regimes had attempted and there is a decisiveness about ends and means in the efforts to achieve dramatic results that is quite new. Clearly, these include modern responses to the new international trading system, to the mature capitalism that produced that system and to the growing pace of technological progress. Not least, the Asian Pacific neighborhood has undergone a sea-change and China now has a chance to become an economic power, if not to restore its traditional position of superiority, at least to take its rightful place as one of the region's modern and leading nation-states.

Nevertheless, what one sees is grudging economic reform. For example, it is constrained by the need to avoid any change that might weaken the existing power arrangements and ideological shibboleths. It seems to be pushed in directions which would favour those cadres and networks trusted by the power centre and close to officialdom. This power centre is clearly determined to prevent the emergence of an indigenous merchant class. The first two are by-products of the minimal reform approach mentioned earlier which reflects traditional concerns about protecting the political structure and existing groups of elites and their families in every possible way. The third is not unrelated to power concerns, but is harder to understand given the willingness to encourage foreign capitalists, including those of Chinese descent, and businessmen from capitalistic Hong Kong and Taiwan as well as more recent overseas Chinese emigrants to be active and invest in increasingly large sectors of the Chinese economy.

If the reforms were meant to be modern, why is there no place for those of merchant background still living in China to resume their professions and maximize the commercial and industrial benefits they could bring to the country? Instead, the reforms have encouraged independent business activity at the lower levels but are applied only minimally to the enterprises managed by the state. Again, one cannot resist some comparisons with the *yangwu* self-strengtheners who believed that one of the economic reforms China badly needed was to have high-minded officials supervise the entrepreneurial merchants.[18] In fact, the reforms today have gone further than that: China now has policies to train a commercially sensitive bureaucratic cohort to buy and sell for China, to market China's manufactures at home and abroad and to supervise foreign and overseas Chinese capitalists operating in China. But these measures are carried out with ambivalence, using recognisably Marxist-Leninist language that has been softened by traditional merchant values and by capitalistic managerial standards.[19]

Reform does not preclude radical ideas. On the contrary, some reforms require drastic action before anything could begin to change. This is particularly true of an enormous country with such a large population. The *yangwu* experts were never radical and the *bianfa* reformers were not allowed to be radical. In contrast, the present regime in China, going against the exhortations of their revolutionary hero Mao Zedong, adopted one of the most radical reform policies the Chinese people have ever experienced.[20] I refer to the

[18] Albert Feuerwerker, *China's Early Industrialization: Sheng Hsuan-huai (1844–1916) and mandarin enterprise*, Harvard University Press, Cambridge, Mass., 1958; Wellington K.K. Chan, *Merchants, mandarins and modern enterprise in Late Ch'ing China*, Harvard University Press, Cambridge, Mass., 1977.

[19] Dorothy J. Solinger, *Chinese Business Under Socialism: The Politics of Domestic Commerce, 1949–1980*, University of California Press, Berkeley, 1984, especially on policy conflict, pp. 60–123; also two more recent essays: 'Capitalist Measures with Capitalist characteristics', *Problems of Communism*, 38, January–February, 1989, pp. 19–33; and 'Urban Entrepreneurs and the State: The merger of state and society', in Arthur Lewis Rosenbaum (ed.), *State and Society in China: The Consequences of Reform*, Westview Press, Boulder, 1992, pp. 121–141. Three studies in Brantly Womack (ed.), *Contemporary Chinese Politics in Historical Perspective*, Cambridge University Press, Cambridge, 1991, are useful updates of the central issues raised by Solinger in 1984: Edmond Lee, 'A bourgeois alternative? The Shanghai arguments for a Chinese capitalism: The 1920s and the 1980s', pp. 90–126; Peter Nan-shong Lee, 'The Chinese industrial state in historical perspective: From totalitarianism to corporatism', pp. 153–179; Hong Yung Lee, 'From revolutionary cadres to bureaucratic technocrats', pp. 180–206.

[20] Song Jian, 'Population development — Goals and Plans', in Liu Zheng, Song Jian, *et al.*, *China's Population: Problems and Prospects*, New World Press, Beijing, 1981, pp. 25–31; Judith Banister, *China's Changing Population*, Stanford University Press, Stanford, 1987; John S. Aird, 'Coercion in Family Planning: Causes, Methods and Consequences', in *China's Economy looks Towards the Year 2000: Vol. 1, The Four Modernizations*, U.S. Congress, Washington D.C., 1986, pp. 184–221.

one-child policy as a measure for population control, which is really an essential part of radical economic reform. If it succeeds in the face of persistent resistance, even partially, it would not only help raise the standard of living of the people but also do more to transform the whole fabric of traditional society than any other single reform in Chinese history. This, of course, is merely a policy of reform. It would not have been anything that would have interested professional revolutionaries like Sun Yat-sen and Mao Zedong, yet it could be potentially more revolutionary in effect than most measures those two leaders have advocated.

Radical reforms of this nature may be compared with the industrial revolution which took several decades to take effect in every country, and with the urban, both bourgeois and proletariat, revolution that changed everyone's lifestyle and produced the most effective population control results in history. Is the one-child policy reform then an example of a modernizing *revolutionary* breakthrough, fundamentally departing from tradition? This is only a superficial ambiguity of language. A deeper ambiguity stems from the fact that the policy cannot succeed voluntarily. It would have to be accompanied by crude indoctrination methods at all levels of education and training. It would have to be supported by strong authoritarian measures, together with draconian ways of intervening in the private lives of every child-bearing individual in the country.

With these decisions coming from above, it recalls the traditional policies of *yimin shibian* (moving people to support border areas as military colonies) and *yimin tongcai* (moving people to ease economic conditions, usually for the survival of whole districts because of famine or other natural disasters), when the traditional state transported millions of people over long distances, often against their will.[21] These were population redistribution measures for reasons of security and livelihood and not, of course, for purposes of population control. Certainly they were carried out when China had fewer people and more undeveloped land. But the application of interventionist state

---

[21] This ancient tradition was perfected during the period of the Warring States 4th–3rd centuries, B.C.; Hsu Cho-yun, *Ancient China in Transition: An Analysis of Social Mobility, 722–222 B.C.*, Stanford University Press, Stanford, 1965.

power in social engineering is well within the tradition. The difference is that of degree: modern systems and technology can penetrate deeper and the effects can be much more drastic and even irreversible and, if sustained for long periods, nothing less than revolutionary.

The reform of any structure can produce much indecision and confusion, but nowhere is the uncertainty more manifest than in the present regime's policy on intellectuals.[22] The idea of *zhishi fenzi* or intellectuals is ambiguous. It distinguishes them from the scholar gentry who traditionally shared power at the top and wielded great power in the countryside. At the same time, these intellectuals could also be recognised as new types of experts and professionals who could be treated as 'knowledge workers' in the socialist workers' state. Had it been possible to remain clear and consistent about such definitions, this would have given intellectuals both respectability among other workers and allowed them to partake of the power the working class was supposed to have. It would also have freed them from the stigma of association with the traditional *shi* or mandarin-literati and placed them among the benign category of *gong*, or artisan. In this way, they could have been accepted as a sort of literate artisan sub-class instead of being seen as ambitious and discontented remnants of the overthrown scholar gentry. If this had been a firm step towards modernisation and not primarily an act of power seizure by revolutionaries, the ambiguities about the terminology during the transitional period would probably not have been too great.

But this was not to be for three reasons. Firstly, the *shi* tradition was so strong in Chinese history that the modern intellectuals could not easily escape the sense of moral and spiritual responsibility for the future of the state and for Chinese civilisation. They would not be content to become better-educated artisans. At the least, in modern terms, they would claim the status of professionals, with all the connotations of independence, autonomy and self-regulation. Secondly, access to higher learning and intellectual output

---

[22] Merle Goldman, *China's Intellectuals: Advise and Dissent*, Harvard University Press, Cambridge, Mass., 1981, provides the most lucid account of the shifts in policy since 1949. This has been updated in Merle Goodman, 'The Intellectuals in the Deng Xiaoping Era', in Rosenbaum (ed.) *State and Society in China*, pp. 193–218.

outside China has confirmed them in the belief that there is an important role for free-thinking intellectuals in any modernisation process. It is not enough that they be loyal and well-trained technocrats. The privilege of having knowledge required that they actively participate in the checks on, if not the exercise of, power on behalf of the people and the nation. This self-chosen role of independent critic has caused great difficulty for the policy on intellectuals, whether under Mao Zedong or Deng Xiaoping.[23]

The reason for this confusion and ambiguity is the fact that most people in China look upon the Party cadres as having seized the reins of power from the traditional mandarins. Their monopoly of power both at the centre and in the provinces has impressed everyone. As long as they also manifested a similar aura of moral integrity and respect for learning, they would indeed be seen as having successfully replaced the old discredited literati. The new revolutionary elites were expected to be superior, more modern, efficient and caring than the corrupt representatives of a bankrupt tradition. If they could sustain such an image of themselves, even righteous modern intellectuals might be prepared to shed their links with the past, and their admiration for liberal ideals, to support them.

But the four decades after 1949 clearly showed that this was not so, partly because these cadres were no more immune to abuses of power than mandarins, and partly because they would not tolerate the independently critical role that the modern intellectuals want. What added to the indecision in the Party's policy on intellectuals was that forty years of indoctrination could not

---

[23] The Communist Party's recent policies towards intellectuals are examined in Part Four of *China's Intellectuals and the State: In Search of a New Relationship*, edited by Merle Goldman, with Timothy Creek and Carol Lee Hamrin (Harvard Contemporary China Series), The Council on East Asian Studies, Harvard University, Cambridge, Mass., 1987: essays by Lynn T. White III (pp. 253–274) and Carol Lee Hamrin (pp. 275–304). The contradictions in the idea of 'knowledge workers' contributed to the breakdown of order during the Cultural Revolution, see Lynn T. White III, *Policies of Chaos: The Organizational Causes of Violence in China's Cultural Revolution*, Princeton University Press, Princeton, 1989. The political distance between the regime and young intellectuals seems to have grown during the 1980s, Han Minzhu (ed.), *Cries for Democracy: Writings and Speeches from the 1989 Chinese Democracy Movement*, Princeton University Press, Princeton, 1990.

eliminate the intangible heritage of the literati nor prevent the assimilation of the professional and intellectual ideal from the world outside. There is no greater ambiguity in China today than in the efforts to reform and redefine the relationship between what the Party wants from the new generations of intellectuals who had grown up since 1949 and what these intellectuals want for themselves.

So much for reforming the 1949 Revolution. There remains the ambiguity underlying the meaning of revolution, expressed as *geming*, eighty years after the fall of the last dynasty. It stems from a view that has been over-simplified and then over-drawn. That is, that this new kind of *geming* as revolution is quite different from changing dynasties in an unchanging China, and that it really represents a major break with the past, comparable to the massive change that followed the unification of China under the Qin-Han empire. Indeed innumerable comparisons have been made both within and outside China with what the First Emperor Qin Shihuang in the 3rd century B.C. achieved, including crude analogies that smacked of wishful thinking about this regime not lasting any longer than the Qin dynasty, that is, only a few decades followed suddenly by *geming* and a new dynasty.[24]

It must be clear that the 1949 Revolution did produce a social upheaval. That is not in question. What is doubtful is the picture of unchanging China since the fall of the Qin dynasty. As long as this remains the perception outside China, and as long as such images permeate discourse within intellectual circles in China, then the term *geming* would be, despite its origins in Chinese history, considered inappropriate for application to the dynastic changes during the intervening 2,000 years. Instead, the modern *geming* should only be equated with revolution as understood in Western Europe, the United States and the Soviet Union. If this should become the only legitimate meaning of the word, I suggest that it will diminish our understanding of the role of the

---

[24] Many historians and polemicists in Taiwan and on the Mainland have drawn attention to these analogies. The practice reached something of a climax during the Cultural Revolution, especially in the early 1970s. For some examples, see Wang Gungwu, 'Burning Books and Burying Scholars Alive: Some Recent Interpretations Concerning Ch'in Shih-huang', *Papers of Far Eastern History* (Canberra), no. 9, 1974, pp. 137–186.

past in China's current development. Indeed if this and other similar terms taken from classical texts should assume only the meanings of the western words they have been used to translate, it would reduce our ability to provide the many-layered explanations needed for many of the more interesting faces of modern China.

With the term *geming*, this should become clear from a brief look at its use in dynastic history. Let me return to a common view about imperial China. This says that there have been dozens of dynasties after the fall of Qin in 206 B.C. Most of them had been overthrown by violence, but continuity was greater than change under each new ruling house. Therefore, *geming*, or changing the mandate, consisted largely of a change of dramatis personae and a similar cyclical plot accompanied by some moving of furniture on the stage of history. The Confucian rhetoric of the Mandate of Heaven remained more or less the same and served no more than as a device to say that one group was no longer worthy to hang on to power and had to be replaced by another. Thus the picture of stagnation and little progress for China. This view is not totally unjustified, simply over-stated to the point when the nature of *geming* can be easily misunderstood.

To begin with, we need to distinguish the minor changes of dynastic houses from the major political upheavals that launched powerful new dynasties. The former would come under the phrase *gaichao huandai*, or change of ruling houses; they had no effect on the political system they inherited and they fit the stereotype of being mainly a change of personnel. Most of these occurred during long periods of disunion between the fall of the Han dynasty and the rise of the Tang dynasty and a few occurred when the Tang fell in the 10th century. Of the 55 or so dynasties recognized in official histories, more than 40 belong to this category and they occupy about five of the 21 centuries of imperial history. The remaining 16 centuries saw six major dynastic houses. The founding of each of these, especially the founding of the Tang, the Song, the Yuan, the Ming and the Qing, would clearly count as having experienced a real change of mandate, or *geming*. Four of these six happened during the past thousand years. It would be helpful to be reminded briefly of what changing the mandate means for the four closest to our century.

The founder of the Song dynasty had a deceptively easy time ascending the throne. But his accession came after two centuries of painful changes underlying several violent but indecisive upheavals. The periods of continual disorder came to head with the Song. Thus, the changes which the Song founder and his successors brought to the dynasty were deeper than what appears on the surface. Underneath the Confucian language they used, which was drawn from the state documents of the Tang dynasty, was a major transformation of elite society. This society had been one in which a few aristocratic families had dominated for centuries. In its place was developed one in which a new kind of literati representing different economic and regional interests helped the imperial court to control the empire.

The civil service was transformed, the military centralized and the indirect business activities of both civil and military officials more widely accepted. A new merchant culture linked closely to mandarin family values, without the aristocratic constraints of earlier periods, was evolving. By the end of the dynasty, a robust and totally new formation of Confucian philosophy had emerged out of three centuries of vigorous debate. The dynasty had also seen the strongest and most systematic attempt to launch radical reforms that any ruling house had ever known, the sustained reforms of Wang Anshi and his zealous and politically active supporters. Although the Song emperors were low-key actors who did not win great wars or boast of dramatic successes, their social and economic reforms led to long-term and enduring changes.[25] Their achievements fit the traditional picture of a dynasty that had truly gained the Mandate of Heaven, in short, it fully justified the act of *geming* that had put its founder on the throne.

The Mongol conquerors of the Song were clearly not a simple change of dynastic house when they united all of China under their rule. They had succeeded the Jurchen conquerors from Manchuria who had overcome their

---

[25] Robert M. Hartwell, 'Demographic, Political, and Social Transformations of China, 750–1550', *Harvard Journal of Asiatic Studies*, 42, No. 2, 1982, pp. 365–442. Also Liu, *Reform in Sung China* (note 9 above); and more recently, Patricia Buckley Ebrey, *The Aristocratic Families of Early Imperial China*, Cambridge University Press, Cambridge, 1978; and Robert P. Hymes, *Statesmen and Gentlemen: The Elite of Fu-chou, Chiang-hsi, in Northern and Southern Sung*, Cambridge University Press, Cambridge, 1986.

predecessors, the Khitan invaders who, like the Mongols, had come out of the Mongolian steppes. Both the earlier conquest dynasties had been shrewd enough to employ Chinese and use aspects of Chinese rhetoric for their states, but they never had a credible mandate because their control in China was only partial and the Song to their south was the only legitimate dynasty in the eyes of the majority of the Chinese people. The founder of the Yuan, Kubilai Khan, however, did conquer the whole of China in 1278. He employed even more Chinese to help man the vast administrative structure the empire needed, but it is anachronistic and really stretching Confucian rhetoric to identify Yuan as a Chinese dynasty. Bureaucratic historiography demanded neatness, so Yuan had to be fitted in. Otherwise, the whole system of historical explanation would have had an unacceptable gap in which an overthrown dynasty had not passed on the mandate to its successor. The Mongols did great violence to the concept of mandate; no amount of rationalization could disguise the fact that there had not been a righteous mandate of any kind, merely brutal conquest and systematic exploitation of the Chinese people.[26]

This became clear when the Han Chinese who drove out the Mongols and founded the Ming dynasty in 1368 emphasized the return to the roots of Chinese civilisation, the restoration of Han and Tang glories, the Confucian rhetoric of administration, the elements of nationalistic and even xenophobic fervor and, not least, the righteous mandate. In this case, there was not simply a change of ruling house. On the contrary, it was a liberation of the Han Chinese and a restructuring of the political system which brought great strain to the Ming rulers and the new set of mandarins of plebeian background.

It was also a much more ruthless and authoritarian rule than the Han, Tang and Song. Totally new privileged elites were given more direct power to

---

[26] Herbert Franke, *From Tribal Chieftain to Universal Emperor and God: The Legitimation of the Yuan Dynasty,* Verlag der Bayerischen Akademie der Wissenschaft, Munich, 1978; Chan Hok-lam, 'Chinese official historiography at the Yuan court: The composition of the Liao, Chin, and Sung Histories', in John D. Langlois, Jr. (ed.) *China under the Mongols,* Princeton University Press, Princeton, 1981, pp. 56–106. Also Jennifer W. Jay, *A Change in Dynasties: Loyalism in Thirteenth-century China,* Center for East Asian Studies, Western Washington University, Bellingham, Wash., 1991.

intervene in matters like education, policing, punishments, land distribution, people movements, regulation of trade, than earlier dynasties. The agrarian base of the imperial economy, of course, did not change. Hence, understandably, a picture could be presented of yet unchanging life on the 'good earth'. But the remodeled power structure, despite the Confucian flavor, fully justified the view that the Ming founder had a successful *geming* and fulfilled the new mandate given to him by Heaven.[27] Six centuries later, after succeeding a similar conquest dynasty like the Manchu Qing, both the 1911 and 1949 revolutionary leaders allowed comparisons to be made between their modern *geming* and the traditional one of the Ming founder. This should not surprise us. It reflects the sense of continuity that helped to imbue the new leaders with respectability and reinforce their legitimacy to ordinary Chinese.

Finally, the Qing Manchu elites seized the Ming throne in 1644. Their cultural distance from their Han Chinese subjects was not as great that of the Yuan Mongol tribesmen 300 years earlier. They also took greater pains to convince their subjects that they could claim the right to rule and carefully demonstrated that they could rule China as their predecessors had done, if anything, better and in a more orthodox way. The agrarian economy remained the mainstay of the state and the Chinese literati who were asked to share in the empire's governance were encouraged to return to classical scholarship. On the surface, most scholar gentry families were eventually reconciled by the Manchu show of respect to Chinese civilisation to accept that the conquest had finally given these alien people a righteous mandate.[28]

---

[27] Frederick W. Mote, 'Introduction', and John D.Langlois, Jr. 'The Hung-wu reign, 1368–1398', in Frederick W. Mote and Denis Twitchett (eds.), *The Cambridge History of China, vol. 7: The Ming Dynasty, 1368–1644, Part I*, Cambridge University Press, Cambridge, 1988, pp. 1–10, and 107–181. Also Wang Gungwu, 'Early Ming relations with Southeast Asia: A background essay', in John K. Fairbank (ed.) *The Chinese World Order*, Harvard University Press, Cambridge, Mass., 1968, pp. 34–62.

[28] By the end of the K'ang-hsi Emperor's reign (1662–1722), the majority of the people of North and Central China had accepted that a conquest dynasty was in full control and, therefore, legitimate; see Frederic Wakeman, Jr., *The Great Enterprise: The Manchu Reconstruction of Imperial Order in Seventeenth-century China*, University of California Press, Berkeley, 1985.

In fact, the new dynasty was not a mere change of ruling house. There were considerable innovations to the political and military power structure. Much greater efficiency in administration and financial management was achieved by reforms to the Ming system of government. After several fierce and brutal campaigns of suppression, especially in South China, and much tightening of intellectual controls over the literati, a great peace descended on the land of the Han Chinese and a longer period of prosperity was enjoyed by more people in the 18th century than at any time over the past thousand years. Insofar as the Manchu rulers delivered on their mandate, their claim to *geming* was credible and could even be described as righteous. It is no accident that they survived through the 19th century despite the terrible humiliations at the hands of the Taiping and other rebels within the empire and the red-haired 'imperialists' from without, whether coming from overseas or overland. The Qing court by that time had won the bulk of the literati to their common cause, having made them feel that they too shared in carrying the responsibilities of the mandate.[29]

For the past thousand years, each change of the four major dynasties had been accompanied by great violence and disorder, accompanied by transformations of the political structures, more gradual in the Song though no less far-reaching, but brutal and oppressive in the other three. The empire's economy remained primarily agrarian throughout and its wealth came mainly off the backs of the peasants. Imperial rhetoric governing all four dynasties was carefully made consistent with the orthodox ideology and endorsed by court historians. These facts, however, should not be allowed to diminish the extent of *geming*, or political change, under each of the dynastic mandates which the Chinese people experienced before the 1911 Revolution. Given the record of such experiences over the centuries, most people at the end of the Qing dynasty were prepared to take the political restructuring offered by the Republican Nationalists in their stride. Similarly, when that was followed

---

[29] This is succinctly outlined in Kwang-Ching Liu, 'The Ch'ing Restoration', in Fairbank (ed.) *Late Ch'ing, Part I*, pp. 409–490; and Marianne Bastid. 'Official Conceptions of Imperial Authority', in Schram, *Foundations and Limits of State Power*, pp. 147–185.

by further transformations introduced by the Chinese Communist Party, there was also willing acceptance of them all as the results of the new mandate still recognizable in the modern use of the term *geming*.

Only those who lost out in the competition for power were aggrieved and only those Confucian loyalists who saw the damage done to the fabric of their most ancient and glorious civilisation were outraged. For the rest, whether inside or outside the country, they looked to the social and economic betterment to come with expectation and hope. If the new righteous mandate brought about a successful uplifting in standards of living and a more secure livelihood for everyone, and therefore wealth for the country as a whole, so much the better. But their experiences and the tradition of *geming* as the righteous mandate promised them that the social and economic benefits would come over time with effective reform after the revolution of violent political change was over.

It is with this background in mind that one understands why, for the present regime, *geming* is now a word of the past and *gaige*, especially economic reform, the key to salvation and progress. *Geming* is historically associated with violence and upheavals and the people have had enough of those during the two decades from 1956 to 1976, if not the years from 1911 to 1949 as well. *Gaige*, on the other hand, assumes that the *political* structure is here to stay. The structure may need improvement in order to survive, but this can come about when the necessary economic reforms are achieved: for example, the raising of the standard of living from subsistence levels, the enrichment of the country in order to enable it to play its proper role in world affairs and, if safe and necessary, a greater opening of the country to foreign and modern ideas about technology, culture and lifestyle. Thus political reform at this stage is seen as a dangerous ambiguity, easily confused with *geming*, or a new mandate to overthrow the regime and replace it by another.

What of the future? I referred earlier to China's present which now 'defies predictability'. What follows, therefore, is highly speculative but not groundless. Reports of what the Chinese elites are preparing for, taken together with the country's immediate and deep-rooted history, suggest that some speculations are more probable than others. From this China-focused point of view, there remain fears among the Party elites that even the *gaige* that they have sponsored may endanger their power structure. In the longer run, their economic reforms could lead to some form of 'peaceful evolution' that ultimately amounts to a revolutionary, or as they see it, a retrograde or reactionary, change from socialism to capitalism.[30] Such fears could be a reflection of their insecurity verging on paranoia, but these fears are not unjustified if retaining their present power structure is the final objective of the current economic reforms.

These reforms, however carefully and grudgingly implemented, will engender changes which in turn will produce further need for change. Indeed, many moderate critics of the present regime look forward to precisely the chain reactions that would ultimately bring about a fundamental shift in the political system. But this does not mean *geming*, that is, another change of mandate or a violent revolution. On the contrary, if skillfully managed by the successors of the present generation of leaders, they could themselves be the beneficiaries of such a shift when it comes. This may not be the same as the liberal democratic revolution which others may hope for. But, when it becomes clear that *geming* is undesirable and any revolutionary action unnecessary, a new generation of political leaders allied to loyal and experienced technocrats may be ready to produce an improved, more representative, responsible and accountable, system of government that might win over liberal and democratic lobbies.[31]

Outside China and drawing upon historical examples in other parts of the world, the 'peaceful evolution' argument seems less likely. But those who reject this scenario do not necessarily agree as to why they disbelieve in it. The two main kinds of speculation are also influenced by different sets

---

[30] There have been several terms in use in the Chinese media on the Mainland: 'Bourgeois liberalization' and 'peaceful transformation' in addition to 'peaceful evolution'. All have played a part in internal and external political debates and struggles; see Hsi-sheng Ch'i, *Politics of Disillusionment: The Chinese Communist Party Under Deng Xiaoping, 1978–1989,* M.E. Sharpe, New York, 1991, pp. 257–276.

[31] This issue has been passionately argued by many commentators. One of the clearest statements to date is Edward Friedman, 'Permanent Technological Revolution and China's Tortuous Path to Democratizing Leninism', in Richard Baum (ed.), *Reform and Reaction in Post-Mao China: The Road to Tiananmen,* Routledge, New York, 1991, pp. 162–182.

of modern events. Those knowledgeable about the nature of market economies and the kinds of infrastructures they need, including an open and fair
political and legal environment, would be sceptical of China's present authoritarian and inefficient framework of government. They see China as just
another modernizing nation-state, but one which had adopted a communist
system of government. Therefore, what happened to communist governments elsewhere will soon happen in China.[32] They believe that modernizing
economic reforms without concurrent political reforms will not succeed, and
that the consequent economic failures will soon bring the whole structure
down. They expect dramatic changes to happen quickly; when they do, they
would produce something like a modern revolution that follows when
reformists fail. This view may be underestimating the capacity of the Chinese
people to produce enough economic successes to offset the political inadequacies of the system and the corruption and incompetence of its officials,
but there is clear evidence that all communist systems find it very difficult to
adapt to market conditions.[33] The Chinese face an uphill struggle.

There are other commentators who are more fearful of the nature of
authoritarian governments supported by a politicized military and are also
aware of recent Chinese history. They expect that the political and military
factions at the centre who represent nobody but their narrow selfish interests
will fight openly for power when key members of the Old Guard die. If that
happens, the administration will break down, massive discontent will surface
and forces demanding political rights and freedom will be unleashed. Those
more optimistic in their speculations believe that, after perhaps years of

---

[32] Victor Nee and David Stark (eds.), *Remaking the Economic Institutions of Socialism:
China and Eastern Europe,* Stanford University Press, Stanford, 1989, examines this
view critically. Developments since the Tiananmen tragedy of 1989 have not affected
the main points made in the volume; see Cyril Zhiren Lin, 'Open-ended Economic
Reform in China', pp. 95–136; Martin King Whyte, 'Who Hates Bureaucracy? A
Chinese Puzzle', pp. 233–254; and the opening essay by the editors, 'Toward an
Institutional Analysis of State Socialism', pp. 1–31.
[33] Two other thoughtful essays in Baum (ed.) Reform and Reaction, are Connie
Squires Meaney, 'Market Reform and Disintegrative Corruption in Urban China',
pp. 124–142; and Jean C. Oi, 'Partial Market Reform and Corruption in Rural
China', pp. 143–161.

disorder and division, political progress will be made and something like a liberal democratic revolution would be given a chance to win the final victory. Those less sanguine would despair at the damage that prolonged civil war could bring to China as a unified state and to the fabric of Chinese society and culture. They would have little hope for a strong and prosperous China after such a period of division and no reason to expect that liberal and democratic ideals could succeed in the impoverished country that resulted.

Such speculations depend on whether the Chinese people would react as other peoples might do under similar circumstances or whether their patterns of behaviour would be more deeply influenced by the cultural determinants they have inherited. If most Chinese have become modern by following the ways of the peoples of Western Europe and North America and do, in fact, think and act wholly in terms of the modern concepts of reform and revolution, then analogies can easily be drawn with their modern counterparts elsewhere. What this essay suggests is that, despite the experience of revolution in 1911 and then in 1949, it may be too early to assume that this is appropriate.[34] Throughout Chinese history, it has always taken great force to move the people to make major changes to their way of life, even more to provoke them to political action. For most of them, the difference between modern revolution and the more familiar *geming* could hardly be significant. Everyone appears to know that *geming* as revolution has already taken place: the Republic had become part of modern world history and the People's Republic tasted the bitter fruits of 'world revolution'. As long as this transforming struggle to join the civilized and freedom-loving nations of the world is still garlanded with a righteous mandate, no further *geming* as revolution would seem to be called for. If the mandate has not been exhausted, another drastic *geming* would not be necessary. Until then, most Chinese would be content with *gaige*, especially if the reforms generated are to strengthen or save not only the existing system or regime, but also the country and possibly also the civilisation as well.

---

[34] Tsou Tang, 'The Tiananmen tragedy: The state-society relationship, choices, and mechanisms in historical perspective', in Womack (ed.), *Contemporary Chinese Politics*, pp. 265–327.

CHAPTER 4

THE FOURTH RISE OF CHINA*

This chapter focuses on the cultural changes occurring in China today, in the context of the challenge and threat that a strong and prosperous China might pose to the region. I shall therefore not only deal with culture as conventionally understood, that is, as a culture of values seen through the people's religion, social cohesion, education, and the creative arts, but also offer some thoughts on political culture and the culture of trade, industry and economic development.

Clearly the phrase, "the rise of China", governs the significance or otherwise of China's culture on its neighbours and beyond. If China were not rising, China's cultural problems would only have been of interest to the Chinese themselves. When you consider historical examples where the cultural developments of a country actually become significant, there was always an assumption that the countries' wealth and power had determined whether that culture had notable impact on the cultures of others. If that culture was not accompanied by wealth and power, it is likely to have remained a set of local phenomena that might be intellectually or aesthetically interesting and, therefore, worthy of belonging to museums when it is appreciated beyond the country's borders.

It is on record that Chinese culture had made universalist claims as a civilisation in the past. I shall not discuss whether those claims were justified or not and whether much of the culture was essentially a local expression of one

*The article was first published as "The Cultural Implications of the Rise of China for the Region", in *The Rise of China and a Changing East Asian Order*, edited by Kokubun Ryosei and Wang Jisi, Tokyo and New York: Japan Center for International Exchange, 2004, pp. 77–87.

people's genius that had influenced other peoples in China's neighbourhood. One could also ask if the culture of modernity that is predominant today (that is, the modernity that has been globalized by the West, in fact, largely originating from Western culture) is justified to make the universalist claims that it does. This culture of modernity has been successfully proactive in the region for more than a hundred years, and it is now one that most countries, including China, have accepted as the major guiding culture of the future. Is this modern culture universal? If so, then once that culture is widely accepted, all the countries that embrace it could eventually be expected to share in the same cultural values. If given that scenario, what would be the significance of China espousing that culture? We should allow for the possibility that a China that has truly risen would so transform that culture of modernity in its own way that a new manifestation might emerge. If that were to happen, what would the implications be, not only for the region, but also for what we now describe as modern culture?

These are some of the questions in my mind when writing this paper. What then does "the rise of China" this time round really mean as compared with the many times in the past that China may be said to have risen. For example, I can refer to three main eras when China rose to become the most powerful and prosperous country in the region. These were, first, the Qin-Han unification of the first bureaucratic empire that lasted from 3rd century B.C. to A.D. 3rd century; second, the Sui-Tang reunification that followed a series of tribal invasions and the ascendancy of Buddhism within China; and third, the last and most powerful rise before modern times of the Ming and Qing dynasties when the Confucian tradition was reconstructed and reinforced as a new orthodoxy. From that longer perspective, the present rise of China after 100 years of decline since the late 19th century, and 40 years of division between 1911 and 1949, may be quite different from the previous three. It may be argued that China's reunification will not be complete until Taiwan returns to the fold, and that the current division is an active component of the rise of China today. It is certainly necessary to consider whether the past has left indelible marks on the leaders today and what this might mean for China's future position in the region.

The title of this paper suggests that, for there to be cultural implications beyond its own territories, the rise of China this time round needs to be seen in a longer perspective. We need also to note what the experiences of China's neighbours were during the previous times when China was wealthy and prosperous.

We know that the Qin-Han centuries left a strong impression on the cultures of the various Yue peoples of what is now southern China. It has also been argued that the influence of that culture was so extensive that the commonly adopted name of China had come from the name of Qin because of its success in unifying such a large empire. Also, the people who created the core of that culture have borne the name of the Han dynasty for two thousand years. These are examples of the impact of the Qin-Han empires' political culture. Of course, the cultural implications of Chinese power could be distinguished between the direct and the diffuse. The direct impact was felt in the agricultural lands among its immediate neighbours, notably Korea and Vietnam, countries that absorbed major elements of Chinese culture for a long period of time. While the impact was long lasting, it was confined mainly to the elites of those two countries. The diffuse implications, however, were more extensive. They include the impact of China's export goods and technology, the best-known of which being silks, paper and printing, ceramic ware, and features of military and maritime technology. In both these examples, it was China's economic culture that impressed itself upon all China's neighbours.

Where the culture of values was concerned, Qin-Han China seemed to have been far less successful. Indigenous religions and their rituals and practices did not spread much beyond its borders. The educational ideals offered were elitist if not esoteric even for the Chinese populace itself. The written language was unique and complex and, from the start, hard for anyone to master. The ubiquitous family system was so intensely linked with an almost sacred place for male ancestors that many neighbouring societies that did not share that particular emphasis on lineage simply rejected the culture that stressed its importance. As for the creative arts during this first period of prominence, except for the techniques and designs associated with the trade in manufactured goods and thus associated with economic culture, not much seem to have been appreciated outside China's borders.

By the time of the second rise of China, there can be observed the powerful culture of the Tang empire that was consolidated all over southern China and then spread overland towards the "Western Region" and to what was later known as Manchuria and Mongolia. In addition, key elements of that culture crossed the sea to Japan, and the memory of that culture contact still resonates in Japan today. But, with the exception of Japan and the parts of Manchuria closest to the Tang border, much of that culture did not take root and most of the western and northern areas of penetration shook off that culture when the Tang dynasty fell. Nevertheless, Tang political culture was quite different from that of Qin-Han. It was the product of a mixture of Buddhist spiritual and tribal military conquest, some popular and localised religious responses, and an elitist Confucian restoration. Within China, this political culture was indeed a powerful amalgam and together shaped the cosmopolitan culture that is often identified with the Tang capital Changan. But its appeal as political culture outside China was limited. More important was the culture of trade, industry and development based on that openness for which the Tang empire has always been associated. As a result of that, foreign merchants and travellers came from afar and did much to enrich the lives and tastes of all Chinese. The new cultural ingredients that were brought to China during the period of division between the 4th and 6th centuries had strengthened Chinese culture and led to one of the truly efflorescent periods of Chinese history.

The question of how much the culture of values that emerged had impacted on the region is harder to determine. The advance of Buddhism to Korea and Japan may be included because certain key features of Mahayana Buddhism had undergone Sinicization before transmission. In Vietnam, as in parts of Southwest China like the Nan Zhao kingdom in Yunnan, the Buddhism that took root was influenced by other sources as well. In any case, apart from religion, the impact from Tang Chinese classical and literary education and the creative arts (including music and dance, painting and calligraphy, architecture and the plastic arts) was greatest among the aristocracy and the official classes. This was even truer of the Confucianism that had been diminished for over 200 years and restored to importance in the 7th century. Whatever influence this had was packaged with the more popular features of Buddhism and Taoism before being exported. Indeed, despite its overwhelming wealth and power, Tang China probably imported as many cultural artefacts from great distances as it exported to its immediate region. It would seem at the time that, what might have been seen as universal was China's Buddhist manifestations which had already begun to permeate many parts of Chinese philosophy and the creative arts. The rise of China did have cultural implications in what it exported. What was equally important, however, was what it imported that enhanced its own cultural richness.

In comparison with the Qin-Han and the Sui-Tang images of power and wealth, the third rise of Ming and Qing dynasties, with the peak of development occurring between the 15th and the 18th centuries, was less spectacular but no less powerful. China's cultural impact during this period was of a different quality. By this time, after having its brilliant culture of the Song dynasty virtually demolished by the Mongol invasion and subjugation (the Mongol Yuan dynasty lasted over 90 years), Chinese political culture had become far more conservative and inward-looking. The Ming founders concentrated on the physical defence of its borders and on restoring the great institutions of the Han and the Tang. Indeed, apart from the networks of officially approved trade and the aberrant maritime expeditions of Zheng He to the Indian Ocean, the Chinese were not much interested in projecting their culture. Chinese scholars themselves recognize that the closed-door policy of the Ming itself had become a source of weakness. When this policy towards its maritime frontiers was largely retained by the Manchu conquerors after 1644, and Chinese culture became increasingly protective, it is no wonder that there was little capacity to resist the incoming new cultures brought to the region by enterprising and aggressive Europeans. The Manchus and their northern frontier allies, the Mongols, did expand overland into Central Asia when they thought it necessary for their own security. But what was significant was that they retained much of the political culture of the Ming Chinese. This had by then become highly integrated and very complex, and somewhat daunting to people not familiar with its main features. In short, it was not a culture that the Manchu Qing could or wanted to export much beyond the neighbourhood, notably the yet to be sinicized parts of southwestern China (Yunnan and Guizhou, in particular) and the neighbouring states of Korea and Vietnam, and even there and in Japan, it was largely a question of what the rulers and elites of these countries were prepared to accept.

Underlying this was the relatively closed and tightly controlled trading relations with foreign states. This was reinforced by an official ban on private Chinese trade abroad that inhibited the growth of a more extensive entrepreneurial culture. It may nevertheless be argued that, despite such discouragement, Chinese economic or trading culture did greatly affect the development of the port cities and kingdoms of Southeast Asia. But, since this coincided with the advent of far bolder merchants from Europe who were backed by their ruling classes, the cultural implications were relatively subdued and indirect.

Between a defensive political culture and a constrained economic culture, it would have been surprising if the culture of values could have been more prominent. But there were exceptions, mostly to do with the Chinese sojourners who did manage to leave China and make their homes in the region. At one level, the members of the literati who escaped to Japan, Korea and Vietnam at the fall of the Ming dynasty in the 17th century, and at another level, the anti-Manchu Chinese and their supporters who did the same after several failed rebellions during the 19th and 20th centuries. There were, therefore, pockets of exported Chinese values that survived throughout the region wherever small communities were able to form. Some of these migrants replicated cultural institutions as manifested in art and architecture; temples, shrines and cemeteries; drama and classic stories; even some educational centres where families had settled down. But, apart from Japan, Korea and Vietnam, there are few signs to show that their culture of values reached out among the peoples among whom these Chinese settled.

This fact, and other indications that China's culture during this period of the rise of China did not travel far, alert us to two complementary interpretations that may appear contradictory. The first says that this third time that

China rose under the Ming and Qing cannot be compared with the first two so far as their regional impact was concerned. This was because the world, and also the region, had not remained unchanged. There had been considerable developments, including those arising from imported ideas and institutions from outside the region, and not least because of earlier Chinese influences. Also, simultaneously, there was the presence of peoples from the West who were more technologically advanced and who had their own dynamic cultural values to offer against the relatively stagnant if not decadent Chinese values that severely limited Chinese influence. The second would question the link between cultural implications and China's rise. The fact that China has risen may not necessarily have cultural implications. Much depends on the total environment in which China may be said to have risen. For example, rise of China relative to what, and what kinds of rise would be meaningful? We need to look closely at the guiding ideas and institutions that lie behind the rise.

This brings me to the rise of China today. Bearing the two interpretations in mind, we may legitimately wonder if the current rise of China is not a lesser phenomenon than many people suppose. We may also question if China's rise would necessarily have cultural implications of great significance.

We could assume that China's rise to regional power for the fourth time will have cultural implications for the region. How significant these implications could be determined either by comparing with the three earlier times, or by using new sets of criteria to meet the dramatic changes in the world that have occurred since the 19th century. We could compare the present with the first flush of power of the Qin-Han, or the second burst of revivalist strength during the Tang, or the third complacent and defensive phase. Which is the most relevant?

It would be quite easy to argue that the revolutionary force of modern China may be compared with the explosive power of the Qin-Han unification. To a similar degree, that force totally transformed the polities that existed before and established new kinds of relationships with China's neighbours. It is also possible to show that China today is more like the Sui-Tang recovery. It is an example of a country whose power has been renewed after fighting off invaders, absorbing new foreign ideas and opening the country to external trade and new technology. And there is the view that focuses on the borders of the Qing empire as the foundations of a new modern nation-state. These borders are new and encompass dozens of recognized minority nationalities, and the impact of such an idea of nation is still to be fully felt. Here is a credible appeal to continuity with the Ming-Qing heritage that is central to the new force of Chinese nationalism.

But what is most striking is that all three of the earlier eras may have contributed to the shape and direction of China's rise today. Mao Zedong as Qin Shihuang the great unifier, and the PRC as a redefined Han empire, recalls the first rise. A China opened to an outside world of new ideas and technology and new markets remind us of the second, a cosmopolitan Tang China. And the challenge of ethnicity and nation moulding after been introduced to new concepts of sovereign borders tie the present to the third, the immediate past of the Manchu Qing. These analogous features of the past three eras do not make the task of examining of future cultural implications any easier, but they are important in helping us recognize the many unpredictable elements in China's long history. We would need to place all these elements in a global 21st century perspective.

The world has clearly changed beyond recognition after European colonialism and imperialism. The dominance of the region by the West for 200 years and the present superiority of American wealth and power provide a totally different backdrop for this fourth time that China is rising. It is tempting to say that China's past is not relevant as long as the new power equations remain. But there are some given factors that will not go away. For example, the size of China in the region and the political weight that this carries cannot be wished away. Also, the memory of its historical power both within China and among its neighbours, albeit dormant for the time being, is not far from the surface of regional consciousness. If proof is needed, this Project itself reflects the theme's potential to engender concern and uncertainty. Not least, there are the implications of the cultural vestiges transmitted to some neighbours via language and value systems to be taken into account. In addition, how do the Chinese feel about the cultural challenges ahead?

What resources do they have to deal with the culture of modernity and what do they expect to contribute to that culture? Trying to answer both these questions may be the most useful way to tackle the cultural implications of the rise of China this time round.

I shall be brief about political and economic culture and deal more with the culture of values in the rest of this paper. On political culture, it is so obviously important that I shall simply assert the following. China's decision in the early 20th century to jettison the Confucian state in favour of a revolutionary creed was a major shift in political culture. This new creed derives from the historical experiences of Western Europe that vainly projected a Utopian ideal, a liberation from the cycles of endless tension, from the Darwinian culture of war that nation-states needed in order to survive. It has left a legacy of aggressive nationhood that China as a new nation-state has to learn to cope with. The failure of revolutionary socialism has now opened China to the rival secular and materialist faith in capitalism. Under the conditions China faces today, any attempt to return to a traditional political culture is likely to fail. The continuing struggle to forge a new cultural amalgam without accepting the full force of liberal ideology that accompanies capitalism will engage China's leaders for a long time to come. The implications for the region are that China needs to be left alone to digest and internalise these changes, but it would be keenly sensitive to any kind of threat to itself during a difficult period of re-adjusting to the new stage of global politics. Given its size, China only needs to be internally stable and united for it not to fear its immediate neighbours. But it knows enough history to fear that a power further away, like the United States, could invoke a "China threat" scenario to instigate a hostile alliance in the region against China. It seems to me that, under the circumstances, it would be sheer stupidity for China to provide any power with that excuse to disrupt China's own developmental and survival agenda.

A new economic culture is needed to help China survive the challenge of a globalized market economy. Here the commitment to development is absolute and the cultural implications of an increasingly competitive environment for the Chinese people are grim. But China has passed the point of no return on two vital points: it has to meet the expectations of its 1.3 billion people and it has to generate adequate resources to prevent the country from ever being successfully invaded again. Thus the task of keeping up the rapid economic growth it has so far achieved, and organising an equitable distribution of the new wealth created (a sharp test of social justice?) into some kind of balance, will be so demanding that it is likely that China will have to stay on this treadmill at all costs. It seems to me, therefore, misleading to talk of China catching up and threatening other great powers. What is at stake are the following: the survival of the Communist Party in the face of massive discontent, the stability of existing social institutions, and ultimately the fate of a China trying to stay united within its present borders. The implications of this economic culture are that it needs peace and goodwill, particularly within the region. This need is not just for now, but for the long haul, for the unenviable task of attaining a relatively fair and equitable *xiaokang* (little prosperity) society for its enormous workforce.

What about China's culture of values? Does it provide a counterweight to the apparent leaning towards modern political and economic culture, or does it inevitably follow where politics and economic lead? Like Japan, India and the Islamic world, China has a deep-rooted ancient culture of values and, in its own way, it has tried to resist having this culture replaced altogether by the values from the West. It recognizes that there is much in the new values that are appealing because they are modern and progressive. The Chinese people, inheriting a humanist and rational tradition, are prone to opt for the secular alternatives to their outworn ideas and institutions. In the act of rejecting Confucianism and all manifestations of religion, the generation of revolutionary leaders have made it easier for all Chinese to embrace the scientific and philosophical premises of the Enlightenment Project. The result of this acceptance of totally new assumptions for the building of the new state and society has been profound. It has rendered it far more difficult for the next generation of Chinese to contemplate any return to an earlier set of cultural values. This is not to deny that traditional values have survived well in the countryside among the millions of rural families and lineages. But the rate at which urban and industrial society is growing and the necessity for rural workers to seek their livelihood in that society is posing a great challenge to the values these workers are either happy to abandon or are forced to leave behind.

The last 100 years have been a most trying time for the majority of Chinese to keep faith with their culture of values. The transition has been long and bitter. The battle for a convergence of the old values that people are comfortable with and the new values that promise to free them from drudgery and poverty is likely to go on indefinitely. For the moment, if we observe what is going on among the young in the major towns and cities of China, it might appear that the result is a foregone one. The culture of modern values, whether coming directly from the West or indirectly from Japan, Korea, or Chinese communities in Taiwan, Hong Kong and Singapore, are winning hands down. Only a handful of the older urban elites and their counterparts in the countryside care enough to try to recover respect for older values. It seems clear to me that they are in no position to reverse the tide, certainly not by the old methods of moral exhortation and upbraiding.

Does this mean the end of the inherited culture of values for China? I am not sure, but I do not believe that developments in history follow logic and straight lines. The roots of that heritage are deep and manifest themselves in many different ways. The gains and losses registered so far have been in political and economic culture but the impact of that transformation can be both a threat to, and an inspiration for, the culture of values. And precisely because cultural values are diffusely found at all levels of society and can permeate people's consciousness deeply, because they are notoriously slow to change in every society, what happens to them are unpredictable. In aesthetics and philosophy, through literature, drama, film, music and dance and the fine arts, in every classroom and lecture hall, and through every kind of design and fashion, creative convergences occur readily that can give fresh life to older values. Even the challenge of new religions, whether indigenous or foreign in origin, can produce unexpected consequences. As more and more Chinese seek spiritual expression in their lives, they have the collective power to transmute inherited values into new manifestations that could serve new and yet unforeseen needs.

As China's recent rise exposes its people to such radical changes in the culture of values, what are the implications for the region? The mental and emotional turmoil the Chinese people have experienced during the 20th century is still little known today among China's neighbours. And, as long as the Chinese themselves are engaged in the travails of reinventing themselves, their culture of values are unlikely to be exemplary for others. Most of China's recent experiences seem to have been particular rather than common to the region, and the task of identifying some of its universal features to warn others who are striving for similar changes has yet begun. There are, of course, lessons in China for others to learn from if they choose to. But, as far as I can tell, the more immediate lessons are those pertaining to its political and economic culture rather than its culture of values. Until such time when the Chinese can demonstrate how they have retrieved and revived key parts of that culture of values through their innovative use of the modern culture that they have full-heartedly accepted, the cultural implications of China's rise is likely to be peripheral and unconvincing. But the region will do well to study the history of China's multiple struggles. However painful and devastating these have been, they have jolted most Chinese to a fresh energy and dynamism that China has not seen since the first unification of China over 2,000 years ago.

CHAPTER 5

NATIONALISM RESTORED*

For the past decade, words like patriotism and nationalism have resurfaced in the People's Republic of China. This has been attributed, among other things, to the decline in Marxist or Maoist faith, or to the resurgence of Chinese power in the nation-state system, or to the potent combination of the two. It is symptomatic of the concept of nationalism that nationalism could be regarded as much the product of weakness and insecurity as of renewed strength. Also, it is never clear which is cause and which is effect. Is it because a government has become strong that nationalism is aroused, or is it weakness that leads a country's leaders to resort to nationalist appeals? Whether cause or effect, the very word has acquired such historical baggage that it is likely to arouse fears of aggression and irrationality whenever anyone mentions it.

Commentaries on the rise of nationalism reached a climax in Beijing's display of military might over the Taiwan Straits and in the use of threatening language over what Beijing sees as a domestic affair, a residue of an earlier civil war. Comparisons have been made around the world with the rise of German nationalism under the National Socialists and that of expansionist Japan under the military nationalists. Both had arisen earlier this century, about the time that the Chinese turned to Soviet Communism for inspiration against Fascism and Japanese imperialism. It would be a great irony for the Chinese if that inspiration were now to turn full circle and become itself the cause of the revival of what is seen as an aggressive creed.

---

*This article was first published as *The Revival of Chinese Nationalism* (IISS Lecture), Leiden: International Institute for Asian Studies, 1996.

Nationalism in the West has had largely a negative image in international politics and academic discourse since the end of the Second World War. Only in the post-colonial states of the developing world has it been given a more constructive face, that of self-respect, unity and the kind of purposefulness that colonialised people had never had. This form of nationalism was used to rally disparate peoples to create new nations. It was often highly defensive, but over time, it has matured considerably in most of these new nation-states. The word can still arouse some enthusiasm but now rarely produces the violent emotions that had originally been such an essential part of it. Why does it still remind us of fearsome power when it applies to China?

Obviously, there is China's size, its population, its past as a great empire, and its mammoth needs. Lately, following the reforms of Deng Xiaoping, there is the remarkable performance of its economy. The coastal provinces experienced almost unbelievable successes, having responded swiftly to the stimulus provided by the entrepreneurs of Hong Kong and Taiwan as well as those Chinese who have settled overseas in foreign countries. There has even been the growing perception of a Greater China, sometimes projected as a Chinese commonwealth that is regional if not global. Although formulated in economic terms, it represents nationalist impulses stemming from the ambitions of southern and coastal Chinese who have always looked across the seas and oceans for their livelihood and prosperity.

But there is another China, that of the rural interior. Its heritage and state of mind is found in the values of the traditional mandarins and literati, but would commonly be expressed through peasant suspicions of cultural change. For that silent majority, the economic miracle of the past decade is still distant, if not beyond reach. The developments are seen to have been generated by external forces overseas, and the benefits found only in the coastal areas and a few large cities. They have been accompanied by sharp contrasts in living standards between those regions and the interior and by lurid anecdotes of moral decline. If the nationalist aspirations of that mental hinterland is aroused, they would appeal to quite different memories and instincts.

What the outside world sees as an outbreak of nationalism is multifaceted. Within China itself, there is no single inspiration for it, and there are many expressions of doubt and misgiving. In contrast to the swell of patriotic calls to action, there are serious questions about the dangers of nationalism, at least of certain kinds of nationalism. A couple of recent examples are representative of the sceptics; one of them says,

> "Nationalism may not succeed against the West without but may arouse national divisions within, and thus become a double-edged sword that could wound ourselves but not hurt the enemy" (Ge Jianxiong 1996, 14).

Another, from an advocate of "rational nationalism", says,

> "Narrow nationalism demands that China abandon its opening to the outside world and its reforms and, by strengthening its distinctly Chinese ideology and political institutions, that it challenge the West. As I see it, such a China would console itself politically and ideologically, but would sacrifice the real interests of the nation on a large scale" (Wu Guoguang 1996, 30).

It is perhaps no accident that both voices come from young intellectuals writing out of Shanghai and Hong Kong. This wider context of deep differences among the Chinese themselves brings me to my subject today, "the appeal of restoration nationalism."

Nationalism is usually qualified by a name or an adjective. Most commonly, it is preceded by the name of the country or territory, or the people who see themselves as a nation of one kind or another. For other purposes, generic adjectives are used. Political, economic and linguistic nationalism are some common examples, but also religious nationalism, developmental, multinational, ideological, cultural, historical, revolutionary, and so on. Some of these usages have been applied to China at one time or another during this century. None however can be said to have sustained strong emotions for long. Only one form of cultural and historical nationalism seems to have been persistent and widespread. It is not unique to the Chinese, but there are particular features to it which make it distinctive. For reasons which I shall explain, I call it restoration nationalism. Anthony Smith uses two terms for a range of post-independence nationalisms. One was "Preservation" and the other was "Renewal". He applies the latter term to the nationalism of

Sun Yat-sen, among others (Smith 1971, 224). What I call restoration nationalism combines elements of both preservation and renewal, but ties in the faith in a glorious past more directly with a vision of a great future.

Restoration nationalism has several faces. The most common face concerns questions of polity and stresses the recovery of sovereignty, the unification of divided territory, and national self-respect. Another is the civilisational face. This emphasises moral order and the preservation, or a rediscovery, of traditional values. For most Chinese, this leads back to Confucianism and also various popular religious practices, notably those of the Buddhists and the Taoists. Among Chinese elites, what they want restored is the relevance and universality of what has recently been called "Cultural China" (Tu Wei-ming 1991). But there is also a reactionary face, which yearns to assert superiority and dominate other peoples, and hankers for the glorious past of a great empire. And finally, there is a peripheral and symbolic face that is found among Chinese sojourners who live outside China, whose well-being, and even survival, is perceived as being dependent on the restoration of China's wealth and power.

These restorationist urges link the future to a much admired past and give a sharper focus to a people's sense of identity and continuity. Chinese nationalism has appealed to the image of restoration many times this past century, and its recurrence during the past decade is not surprising, nor is it alarming in itself. As suggested earlier, this restoration nationalism has several faces. The most prominent would be best summed up in the following, which I shall use as my text for this talk. It comes from Sun Yat-sen's letter to Herbert A. Giles in 1896, written one hundred years ago:

> "To drive out the bandit remnants and reconstruct China (*zaizao* Zhonghua) in order to restore the order of the Ancients and follow the ways of the West, and thus cause myriads of people to be revived and all things to flourish, this is a task that fulfils Heaven's way and meets the wishes of Man."

This was soon after Sun's release from the Chinese Legation in London. Sun wrote this in response to a request to supply information for Giles' *Chinese Biographical Dictionary*, published in 1898 (Sun Yat-sen 1981, 46–48. The letter is undated, but the editor thinks it was written in November 1896).

The literature on the elusiveness of the concept of nationalism is now enormous (Kohn 1944; Deutsch 1953/1966; Kedourie 1960; Emerson 1960; Kamenka 1976; Anderson 1983; Gellner 1983). The recent volume of essays on Chinese Nationalism edited by Jonathan Unger (1996) explores the very wide range of forces that have acted on Chinese leaders, and on ordinary people as well. That wide range underlines some of the ambiguities which are peculiar to China as a civilisation, as a former empire, as a potential and abnormal nation, or as revolutionary state with universal appeal, and so on. My own work, *The Chinese Way* (1995), explores these constructs as seen from outside. Other studies have emphasised the contradictory limits to the label of Chinese nationalism that have been seriously challenged. The most dramatic examples of the challenges, each very different in nature, are the demand for foreign citizenship by most Chinese emigrants now settled over-seas (Wang Ling-chi 1994), the evolution of a Taiwanese national identity (Wachman 1994; Hughes 1995) and the persistent challenge of Tibetan nationalism (Shakabpa 1967).

The historical approach is used here to highlight the multi-layered nature of Chinese nationalism. One can analyse and even successfully de-construct this body of complex ideas and images, but the best way to bring out the total impact that the multiple layers can have on the Chinese people is to examine the condition of the country at that particular time, the issues that divided and united its leaders and its people, and the external pressures that were exercised on them. Of the many layers (the anti-Manchu layer, the xenopho-bic, the self-strengthening, the anti-imperialist, the restorationist, and the fascist, socialist, or communist), whatever was summoned to perform a par-ticular task may be said to represent the content of nationalism for that period. Each layer may then be studied with at least the following questions in mind:

> Where did it come from and what is its appeal?
> What gives it the most force?
> What will make it dangerous, and what will dampen it?
> And, not least, how valid is it for its time?

For the past five years, the increasing manifestations of nationalism in the PRC and in Taiwan have produced different responses. Many countries have shown varying degrees of sympathy and scepticism towards the nationalism in Taiwan. But where the PRC is concerned, there have been almost hysterical reactions. The nationalism has been described with adjectives like visceral, assertive, aggressive, arrogant, bullying, dogmatic, xenophobic, irredentist, expansionist, territorially ambitious, reactionary, and so on. What has made this nationalism so tendentious and even alarming?

The form that is prevalent is historically familiar. It stems from the break-up of the Soviet Empire since 1989 (Rezun 1992; Smith 1995; Guibernau 1996) and the challenge that that event posed to the system of government of the People's Republic of China (Nolan 1995). The Soviet collapse had not been predicted. It gave the Chinese leaders little satisfaction to know that the Russians had got their reform programme wrong while the Chinese had found the better formula. By being unexpected and catastrophic, that event has reminded many Chinese of their own history, of the dramatic last years of the Qing Empire and the threats to its sovereignty and to Chinese civilisation itself. After its fall, the failures of the Republic of China from 1911 to 1949 to bring any kind of moral or political order to the successor state are obvious to, and even within living memory of, many of the present leaders. In that context, two factors are obviously prominent. Firstly, there is the idea that there has been an incomplete reunification of China after several civil wars. Secondly, there is the pervasive sense of cultural loss, with the Chinese people stranded between tradition and modernity. I suggest that these two also brought to surface a third, that is, the continental reaction against the open and progressive materialism that coastal China stands for. This is why the return to restoration nationalism is not a straightforward one.

We can understand this phenomenon by starting with the words of Sun Yat-sen which I used as my text for today. The line of thinking was found in the first externally-inspired political party in Chinese history, the Xingzhong hui (The Society to Restore China's Prosperity) founded by Sun Yat-sen and his Xiangshan (now Zhongshan) county followers in Honolulu in November

1894. The text came two years after the Xingzhong hui was founded, but echoed the key idea in the party's constitution,

> "To advance China's prosperity and preserve national prestige (*zhenxing Zhonghua, weici guoti*)",

and epitomised in the oath the members swore:

> "To drive out the Tartar barbarians, restore China (*huifu Zhongguo*) and establish a united government (*hezhong zhengfu*)" [the indeterminate terminology inspired by the example of United States republican democracy].

We all know how small and forgettable the Xingzhong hui was. Its members were, as Martin Wilbur describes them, "businessmen, traders, cooks, clerks, tailors, labourers, farmers, and local government employees" (Wilbur 1976, 13). The tradition they represented was closer to that of the anti-Manchu, Restore Ming, secret societies (Triads) than to any modern political party we know. In itself, the society and all its branches would not have gone very far. But what Sun and his very ordinary supporters said did capture a strong and growing feeling among all Chinese outside China and among most of those who lived along the China coasts and who had direct experience of Westerners and understood the power and achievements of the West. That feeling may have begun from the periphery, but it was unmistakably nationalistic.

What they lacked was the concept of nation as understood in Europe. They did not have the word for it until Liang Qichao introduced it into Chinese a few years later from the Japanese *minzoku*, and thus the Chinese *minzu* had a strongly racial flavour from the start (Dikotter 1992). But it fitted well with the "drive away the Tartars" aspect of the Xingzhong hui manifesto. Once that concept was verbalised, it slipped easily into the political and righteous nationalism of *minzu zhuyi* which threw out the Manchus. This was the first of Sun Yat-sen's Three Principles of the People, the basis of all nationalist education under the Guomindang after 1928 (Peake 1932). They remained the pillar of the Nationalist government in Nanjing and followed the government to Taiwan in 1949.

Although Mao Zedong was polite when speaking of Sun Yat-sen, the term *minzu zhuyi* barely survived in the PRC during Mao's lifetime. Only since the beginning of Deng Xiaoping's economic reforms, when statements about nationalism became acceptable, and Sun Yat-sen was respectable again, did the idea of nationalism reappear in public debate. But there are serious sensitivities about the term *minzu* in the PRC, and official usage has so far confined itself to *aiguo zhuyi*, or patriotism as applied to the country or the state, rather than to the concept of nation in nationalism. It is this patriotism which is arousing concern because it is considered as a mere euphemism for nationalism. It is also this layer of patriotic arousal and excitement that I identify as restoration nationalism. This is the meaning that provides the content of nationalism in the PRC today, and has been summoned to perform a certain task at a particular time. It may be accepted, even shared, by many Chinese in Taiwan and among Chinese nationals overseas, but it is quite distinct from the content of the nationalism in Taiwan. It has also to be distinguished from the nationalism experienced by Chinese outside China who have acquired foreign nationality and live in quite different national environments.

WHERE DID THIS RESTORATION NATIONALISM COME FROM AND WHAT IS ITS APPEAL?

Within China, it came from the radical changes to the socialist economy following from the recognition that the Leninist-Maoist model had failed. Deng Xiaoping's initial little 'restoration' of the values of the Chinese Communist Party of the 1950s before the Great Leap Forward was meant to be reassuring to his Party colleagues, especially those of his own generation who suffered most from the ravages of the Cultural Revolution. But his reforms were more wide-ranging than many of his contemporaries expected.

The ramifications of those changes have reached out to areas which the Party had held sacred, in particular the idea of political reform and the relaxation of bureaucratic control (Shirk 1993). But the influx of foreign learning and its impact on Marxist ideology, and even on Deng Xiaoping Thought, has become worrying. As for public morality, it became obvious that party discipline no longer could keep at bay the power of money and greed (See the reports to the National People's Congress in March this year, *Fazhi Ribbao* 1996). Advances in education in the natural and applied sciences at the expense of 'redness' also now seemed unavoidable. Only in the humanities and the social sciences could defensive barriers still be held, and even here they were only selectively effective. As for literature and the arts, the thirst for the new was so great that foreign ideas poured in as flood waters onto a dusty plain, and draconian measures had to be introduced to contain the highly stimulated imagination of the younger generation (Barme and Jaivin 1992; Barme 1996).

Much uncertainty has followed, especially among the people for whom economic reforms have not brought security, dignity and self-respect. Thus the atmosphere has been created in which greater visions of restoration have now appeared. They are still largely inchoate and directionless, and range widely from a return to some sort of Maoist framework to a restoration of traditional values, whether they be Confucian, Taoist, or Buddhist, especially in their populist manifestations (Liang Xiaosheng 1995; Lin Min 1995). Among the restorations that have considerable appeal is the idea that the separation of Taiwan from the motherland is now a serious problem and that the task of reunification of China is still incomplete.

All of these have an external dimension, some more obvious than others. They certainly can be highlighted as aspects of external interventions in China's affairs. For example, the theme of restoring essential parts of Maoism can find many echoes. It not only reminds us of the call to return to true Confucian values during the Tongzhi restoration (1861–1874), but also of recent calls for the return to an older socialist framework in Russia and parts of the former Soviet Union. The reaction against some current developments in Russia and the PRC may be for different reasons, but nostalgia for the relative certainties of the recent past come from a similar impulse. There is also the appeal of Confucianism and some traditional values. This may have begun as economic appeal, with the East Asian miracle of Japan and the Four Tigers, but it also has support among some PRC leaders for social, moral and even spiritual reasons, as seen in the recent foundation of the International Confucian Association.

As for the Taiwan issue, President Lee Teng Hui's quest for more international space has awakened the PRC leadership to its vulnerability in the face of growing admiration for Taiwan's 'national' achievements. How can the PRC contest that growing desire for sovereignty which economic success and democratic transformations have brought to more and more Taiwanese? This leads to the second question.

WHAT GIVES THIS LAYER OF NATIONALISM SO MUCH FORCE?

The modern history of restoration ideology provides some answers. I have referred to Sun Yat-sen's position in London and in the Xingzhong hui. That position had gone beyond the reformist drives for the Meiji Restoration (*ishin*, or *weixin*, that is, Renewal) in Japan and for Self-Strengthening during the Tongzhi *zhongxing*. The memory of the Taiping Rebellion, the examples of the American and French Revolutions and, during the decade before, the continued humiliations of the Qing court by the British, the French and the Japanese, had convinced the restorationists of the necessity to use violence to overthrow an apparently helpless regime. A common purpose was forged to place the restoration of national pride, power and prosperity above everything else.

In comparison, other restorations had no appeal. For example, the monarchical restoration of Yuan Shikai in 1915, and that of Qing imperial rule in 1917, met with no support. And, throughout the first two decades of the Republic, any talk of restoring Taiwan to Chinese rule was regarded as premature, if not hopelessly unrealistic. The various governments in China could not even handle the continuous and ever more threatening Japanese advances into Chinese territory on the mainland. Indeed, any suggestion that the Chinese governments had, during this period, abandoned the people of Taiwan and no longer cared for their future, simply reminds Chinese leaders that Taiwan's loss was a shameful part of the history of imperialism and gunboat treaties, of past humiliation and helplessness. It underlines the conviction that restoring Taiwan to China is the ultimate unfinished duty to restore China's self-respect and national pride to the full.

Only in the opaque area of restoring Confucianism did some leaders in the Nanjing government sense the possibility of success. But the Nationalist government's New Life Movement in the 1930s was poorly conceived and implemented (Israel 1966; Eastman 1974). When that failed, it merely proved that any attempt to resurrect Confucianism as a state ideology would meet with great resistance. The educated classes in the cities whose support the government most needed had by then been infected with enough Western modernity to treat such a return to tradition with deep suspicion.

In short, not all restorations are appealing, and none of the other restoration efforts mentioned could override the overarching one of the return to Han Chinese rule, the restoration of sovereign rights (cancelling the unequal treaties), and the struggle for independence, unity and reunification which Sun Yat-sen and his succession of political parties had stood for. The force which these causes lent to any group that would espouse them sustained the two revolutions of 1911 and 1949. Much of the work of restoration has now been done. The most striking of those remaining are that of reunification and that of the moral order (of which more later). Where reunification is concerned, after the return of Hong Kong and Macau in 1999, the leaders would have to choose between two courses: make Taiwan the exception, or stake their lives on its recovery.

External factors continue to be important. When Mao Zedong decided in 1949 on a policy to lean to the side of the Soviets, this led China into the Korean War and to the long-term American commitment to the support of the Nationalist government on Taiwan. Mao Zedong may well have believed that he was merely postponing the civil war against the Nationalists for a brief period, rather like, to use an historical analogy, the Qing waiting forty years to retake Taiwan in 1683. He did not expect to have to deal with Soviet threats by the early 1960s, least of all to have to lean towards the United States in the 1970s and have his successors, after his death, dismantle the centralised planned economy by the end of that decade.

Several diplomatic successes in the 1970s, supported indirectly by the United States, strengthened the PRC's international position, especially in the United Nations. But the economic achievements of Taiwan are obvious, and Taiwan's freedom to manoeuvre continues to improve. The leaders in Beijing must begin to wonder how they could ever reunify China. Many of them recognise that conventional notions of conquest and surrender are no longer applicable, but it will take courage and imagination among the leaders to produce a new formula that both sides think would last.

In facing this problem, in their puzzlement, there is enormous uncertainty which has led them back to restoration nationalism. My third question is:

WHAT WILL MAKE IT DANGEROUS, AND WHAT WILL DAMPEN IT?

As long as the restoration of China's sovereignty, prosperity and power appears to be impeded by external powers, there are historical analogies to show that this nationalism is easy to aggravate. When the nationalism was at its peak during the early years of the Republic of China, from 1912 to 1927, the strongest of emotions were aroused (Chow 1960; Chan and Etzold 1976; Waldron 1995). All players were led to aggrandise themselves by being seen as more nationalstic and thus more anti-imperialist than the others. In effect, each set of leaders had to be more virulently nationalistic than their rivals. Indeed, Chiang Kai-shek squandered his many advantages over the Communists by being seen as soft on the Japanese, and the Communist forces did well to portray themselves, despite their obviously foreign ideology, as true nationalists dedicated to restore China to greatness (Johnson 1962). The Japanese effort to restore Manchu dynastic rule in Manchuria after 1932 through their puppets reminded the Chinese people how far the country was from restoring self-respect to themselves. The failure of the Chinese leaders to unite against blatant Japanese encroachments was seen as a bitter lesson that later leaders could not ignore. With such a succession of failures on record, any appearance of external intervention in China's internal affairs would arouse the populace. When emotions run high, the leaders know that any tardiness at responding vigorously would be interpreted as dereliction, cowardice, or treachery. The only acceptable excuse would be that the military balance is weighted against immediate action or retaliation. Sadly and reluctantly, they would conclude that the reunification would have to be postponed — unless it can be done through peaceful negotiations.

The present revival of restoration nationalism has not been caused by conventional threats of foreign intervention. Where it has an external dimension, it has been provoked by the opening of the PRC to international relationships at all levels. This opening has been accompanied by an apparent weakening of central control over finances, revenues and key areas of decision-making in the face of rapid economic growth. This is a new experience for China. In the past, China's weakness came more from defeats in war than any other reason. During the Republican period before 1949, the weakness was more fundamental. There was simply no unified will or force for China to restore anything significant on its own.

The Nationalist government in Nanjing did face new kinds of intervention, forms of cultural imperialism from the West, some would say, for which they seemed to have had no answer. This was at the level of political ideology, educational and cultural values, and even hostile propaganda from the West. Another form came from the Soviet Union in its attempt to build and influence a rival political party and to mould a generation of radical revolutionaries that would subvert the nationalist ideals of the government. Through a combination of crude coercive policies and poor political management, the Nanjing government failed to contain the covert foreign activities that supported the Communist Party. There may be lessons in reverse here for the PRC leadership today. Many of them have reason to suspect that forces in the United States, who feel that U.S. hegemony may soon be challenged, are seeking to subvert the economic reforms that are enriching and strengthening China.

In any case, external aggravation as seen in the U.S.-China relationship today is only marginal to restoration nationalism and can be contained. Measures have been taken to identify sensitive areas of national concern in which foreign intervention would be resisted, for example, a range of illegal activities and extremist political and religious organisations, all matters pertaining to defence and security, the issue of Taiwan independence, and specific concessioned areas in the East and South China Seas.

More important are recent internal developments. The more successful the economic reforms, the more threats to the present political system. Deng Xiaoping's bold reforms have challenged the Communist Party to cleanse itself of rigidity and inefficiency, to move from the 'dead hand' of centralised planning to a new combination of the 'visible hand' and the 'invisible hand'. The loosening of controls has released more energy than expected. Growth has been uneven, with the favoured coastal areas developing much faster than the relatively neglected interior. Many divisions of government have failed to cope with the speed of change. This has benefited the enterprising and the bold, but unfortunately also the greedy and the corrupt. Thus the mood among the majority of ordinary people is for a stronger sense of direction, for greater checks on growth, and even nostalgia for the days when things were more certain and predictable.

All this encourages a different kind of restoration nationalism: that the country needs to be saved by a return to better planning and tighter controls over the immoral and the wicked. This includes correcting the growing imbalance between the interior and the coastal regions. It is manifested by the need for a restoration that is deeper both in time and space, that is, to restore the continental worldview that China has always had. According to this view, maritime interests have been narrow and self-serving, as proven by the behaviour of coastal Chinese throughout history. Mandarins and soldiers from the centre have always suspected the loyalties of enthusiastic merchants on the periphery. In modern times, the peasant revolutionaries' victory over the coastal Nationalist leadership point to an established pattern; so do many features of the Cultural Revolution. There is an inherent pull towards continental China's historic position, the wish to restore its supremacy over the dubious goals of richer maritime China, and this would include the extreme manifestations of wealth represented by Hong Kong and Taiwan.

Other appeals of restoration nationalism are easier to contain. The calls for traditional values to combat the rapid growth of failed Western ideas have been increasing (The debate over Hu Guoheng's [Henry K.H. Woo] new book, *Dugong Nanshan Shou Zhongguo* [1995], is an interesting extension of the ongoing restorationism of New Confucian Studies). It is doubtful, however, if combating foreign ways can be done simply by teaching classical literature and thought as a moral antidote to modern values. But as an alternate means to achieve clarity of purpose, much of the heritage could be presented afresh as tools that would enable Chinese to find their identity and restore their self-respect as worthy bearers of a great civilisation. Nationalism could be used to justify the use of the restored past to evaluate what is best in the modern. Some of the Chinese traditions that are being revaluated and modernised *outside* the PRC could serve as a start, especially the work that is being done by scholars familiar with changing conditions both inside and outside China (Tu Wei-ming 1991; Metzger 1996).

In fact, when a country is united and the leadership is strong, which is what nationalists say they want, there is little that people would need to restore. For the moment, the nationalism in the PRC is focused on restoring Taiwan to the motherland and reviving what is good in the Great Tradition. This leads me to my fourth question.

HOW VALID IS IT FOR ITS TIME, THAT IS, HOW JUSTIFIABLE IS THIS RESTORATION APPEAL NOW?

I began by saying that restoration nationalism is only one of the layers of nationalism experienced in modern China. To return to Sun Yat-sen's letter to Herbert Giles, several strands there have evolved and been modified over the past century. Driving out the Manchus had been followed by getting rid of all foreign imperialists. This was then extended to cover all issues of sovereignty, the inherited borders of the Qing empire, and the lost territories of Hong Kong and Taiwan. Reconstructing China (*zaizao Zhonghua*) was the next goal, in Sun Yat-sen's words. This represents a different layer of nationalism, one that emphasises the nation-building role of government. Here the successive phases of economic and political nationalism through the decades since Sun's death have produced advances in the rise of industry and commerce. These in turn have enabled the training of scientists and engineers, and the gradual modernisation of agriculture to feed nearly three times as many people as at the beginning of the century. In addition, such advances have supported efforts to promote health, increase life expectancy, eliminate illiteracy and improve other social benefits. All can claim many successes.

But this does not take into account the more sensitive layer of ethnonationalism which could threaten the idea of nation-building itself. The PRC understood this problem early and recognises 55 minority nationalities (*shaoshu minzu*) other than the majority Han Chinese (Dreyer 1976; Mackerras 1994). Most of these minority nationalities will not pose serious difficulties for the larger picture of nationhood, provided the government permits an interpretation of *minzu* that is inclusive and pluralistic. However, Tibet, Mongolia and the Muslim Turkic territories of Xinjiang are outstanding examples of where nation-building could still come unstuck, especially if external forces are tempted, or even invited, to intervene.

But note the next sentence in Sun's letter, "to restore the order of the Ancients and follow the ways of the West". Sun Yat-sen, of course, was not alone in talking about the restoration of the ancient order. That he did so in tandem with "following the ways of the West" also reflected the mood of many scholars and officials of his time. They had gone further than Feng Guifen and Zhang Zhidong in *not* giving priority to the Ancients over the modern West, but had not gone as far as those like Zheng Guanying, He Qi and Hu Lihuan in Hong Kong who were veering towards a greater degree of Westernisation (Chang Hao 1987). This moderate position of some kind of parity between Chinese and Western values was largely abandoned after the fall of the Qing dynasty. By 1919, with the May Fourth Movement, restoration of the finer points of "national essence" was challenged and more or less abandoned by all those who opposed the Nationalist government. A readiness to westernise completely had spread among the younger generation, well beyond what Sun Yat-sen had been willing to contemplate (Lin Yu-sheng 1979).

The Communist Party under Mao Zedong paid lip service to the various traditions still alive and meaningful to the ordinary people, but its main thrust was westernisation through Soviet Marxism. After forty years of indoctrination, few young Chinese today see the past order as something they really wish to restore. Despite the dismay at the ravages of capitalist values today, the voices for a restoration nationalism in the fields of ideas and values remain feeble. It is doubtful if any major campaign to restore the order of the Ancients is forthcoming, or whether it would receive much support if it was started. What is more viable is a return to a willingness to follow the ways of the West selectively as a means of modernising Chinese values and making Chinese civilisation great again. The area of contention, however, is whether the selection should be made with greater understanding of, and deeper reliance on, modern western ways, or only after efforts to produce a renaissance of the perennial Chinese values.

Underlying the call for selective restoration, a larger picture of restoration than that outlined by Sun Yat-sen is envisaged. This picture is founded on secure borders, increasing prosperity and a strong sense of national unity. Mao Zedong began in 1949 with many of the ingredients of such a restoration, but he was ambitious for China to regain preeminence in power and influence as quickly as possible. Nothing less than leading the world revolution would have satisfied him. This was restoration nationalism at its most romantic and Nietzschean, and it has not been wholly discarded. Among the PRC leaders and intellectuals, residual hopes have survived that the Chinese economic experiments today are not merely for regime-maintenance in China alone, but could be a model for other developing countries in the region, if not in the world (Wang Gungwu 1995).

It cannot be denied that this vision is part of the intellectual and political heritage of China. A separate and flourishing Taiwan stands in the way of the vision and an independent Taiwan would seriously undermine it. Thus the little restoration that incorporating Taiwan would represent is essential to the larger restoration that would satisfy the continuities of Chinese history. Relevant to this larger development are some countervailing trends which I shall now turn to.

I have referred to nationalist experiences outside the PRC. A new page was turned for all Chinese people in the 1950s in at least three respects. Firstly, the end of colonialism forced the Overseas Chinese (*huaqiao*) in Southeast Asia, where most of them were, to choose between being Chinese nationals or potential nationals of the new states created out of former European colonies. This had produced much anguish and indecision among those who wanted to remain in these new countries but who were unwilling to give up being Chinese, but the choice had to be made either sooner or later. Many of the young educated in Chinese schools voted for patriotism and returned to China. Others chose readily to naturalise locally. Some decided to remigrate to countries which seemed more tolerant of their loyalties to Chinese ways. One decisive factor for many was the perception that Nationalist China in Taiwan was a lost cause and identifying with the PRC meant being Communist. But for whatever reasons, including the willingness to be loyal to the new nation-states in which they had chosen to live, individual decisions were made that cut through what had been powerful symbols, including those of restoration nationalism. Once that massive defensive screen was breached, being Chinese in the region was never to be the same again (Wang Gungwu 1991).

Secondly, the gradual ending of racial categories in the immigration policies of the developed nations of the West, notably in the U.S., Canada and Australia, led to redefinitions of ethnic identities in multicultural, if not multinational, nations. This was something more subtle and harder to resist. New layers of nationalist consciousness that bore no relation to the modern Chinese heritage of restoration nationalism have been evolving. They were accompanied by relaxations of immigration regulations that permitted many more Chinese to enter such countries and eventually acquire local nationality. There was now an intermediate position, not simply either/or with permanent consequences following from each decision, but a stage in which shades of ethnic identifications were allowed if not actually encouraged. This was seen as part of a mature and confident nationalism in some Western countries that recognised political loyalty transference over time as both humane and wise. Such a recognition was in sharp contrast to what the Chinese had learnt to believe about nationalism (Wang Gungwu 1993). They were unaccustomed to any tolerance among foreign governments, and were initially skeptical, if not cynical or simply opportunistic. But one message was clear to everyone. Nationalism was not so exclusive and emotionally charged as it had been made out to be. There was freedom to change if the circumstances were justified. The story of how the Chinese reacted to these changes is yet to be told, but that there were feelings of relief among those who were brought up on a diet of restoration nationalism is entirely credible.

Thirdly, the survival of two polities who use the name of China, the People's Republic of China and the Republic of China in Taiwan, the only province it controls, posed new questions about national legitimacy. Indeed, both governments were sensitive to this from the start. Throughout the 1950s, the wooing of the Chinese overseas was taken seriously as a measure of the regime's "Mandate of Heaven". After that, when it was clear that most Chinese had taken other nationalities, various efforts were made to define and redefine what is meant by being Chinese. Despite that, the residual concern for all Chinese abroad to look to either the PRC or to Taiwan is still alive. And, in response to the new respectability gained by the market economy in the PRC, the wooing of foreign Chinese has been refuelled. As a counter-measure, the government in Taiwan too has revived its connections with such Chinese and intensified its campaign to regain their sympathies.

Here a major divergence of appeal has occurred. Restoration nationalism has much less meaning for the government in Taiwan once it was decided to abandon the idea of reconquering the mainland. All that remains would be the cultural symbols of legitimacy found in classical traditions, including the acceptance of the Confucian, Buddhist and Taoist heritage, and continuities with Sun Yat-sen's 1911 Revolution. With the PRC, however, the reverse is true. The theme of reunification is at the heart of restoration nationalism. Restoration is not only an essential part of the structure of legitimacy, the supremacy of continental interests. It is also the best defence against other threats to the sanctity of China's borders. The tense developments of 1995–1996 in cross-Straits relations testify to the emotional force that this view of its destiny can still generate.

Nevertheless, time has not stood still for the people of Taiwan. Their economic successes, accompanied by extensive political reforms, have led them further away from the broader ideas of Chinese nationalism (Moody 1992; Klintworth 1995). In their place have come explorations of the nature of nationhood and the processes in nation-building that might be relevant to Taiwan. The doubts about ultimate national and cultural identifications are now present. The pressures to play these down, and dampen any attempt to seek a new national identity, will remain very strong. But there is no denial that the historical appeal of something like restoration nationalism has greatly diminished in terms of polity and territory. Only in the area of cultural appreciation and renewal is the theme of restoration still viable. Sun Yat-sen's wish "to restore the order of the Ancients and follow the ways of the West" remains on the agenda [See the debate on China's division and unity held in Taipei in July 1994; Chung-kuo Li-shih shang ti Fen yu Ho 1995]. It is too early to conclude that this is more symbolic than real.

In all three respects briefly summarised above, Chinese nationalism was challenged and alternate nationalisms emerged for Chinese outside the PRC. Of course, as long as restoration nationalism is alive on the mainland, the majority view would be to arouse it from time to time in the national interest. But more and more, it will be seen that its appeal outside of the PRC is no longer potent, especially where Taiwan is concerned. Nevertheless, in the face of external pressures, it would not do to underestimate its invocative power.

In concluding, let me return to the external forces. Clearly, the smaller nations neighbouring the PRC would observe any Chinese expression of nationalism with great care. They would need to be continually reassured that the present forms of restoration nationalism will not be directed towards them. They would also want to assure the PRC that their efforts at regionalism, whether through ASEAN or APEC, or any others, are not aimed at the Chinese. There are other nationalisms to contend with, and the designs and ambitions of everybody's nation-building plans need to be as open as possible. Finally, for a long time to come, no region can do without the United States. The East Asian region needs to be assured that the U.S. will never be hegemonic in the region. But what will make the difference lies in the relations between the U.S. and the PRC. Restoration nationalism can be a positive force and feed hopes and bolster confidence when left in its historical frame. But if it is prodded out of place by calls for containment, by latent enmity and by near-hysteria, it too can generate emotions to match. No one, least of all the Chinese, will benefit from that displacement.

REFERENCES

Anderson, Benedict (1983). *Imagined Communities: Reflections on the Origin and Spread of Nationalism*. London: Verso Editions and New Left Books.

Barme, Geremie and Linda Jaivin, ed. (1992). *New Ghosts, Old Dreams: Chinese Rebel Voices*. New York: Random House.

Barme, Geremie R. (1996). "To Screw Foreigners Is Patriotic: China's Avant-Garde Nationalists" in Jonathan Unger, ed., *Chinese Nationalism*.

Chan, F. Gilbert and T.H. Etzold (1976). *China in the 1920s: Nationalism and Revolution*. New York: New Viewpoints.

Chang, Hao (1987). *Chinese Intellectuals in Crisis: Search for Order and Meaning, 1890–1911*. Berkeley: University of California Press.

Chow, Tse-tsung (1963). *The May Fourth Movement: Intellectual Revolution in Modern China*. Cambridge, MA.: Harvard University Press.

Chung-kuo Li-shih shang ti Fen yu Ho (1995). *Chung-kuo Li-shih shang ti Fen yu Ho Hsueh-shu Yen-t'ao Hui Lun-wen Chi*. Taipei: Lien-ching.

Deutsch, Karl (1953/1966). *Nationalism and Social Communication*. (second edition) Cambridge, MA: M.I.T. Press.

Dikotter, Frank (1992). *The Discourse of Race in Modern China*. Hong Kong: Hong Kong University Press.

Dreyer, J. T. (1976). *China's Forty Millions*. Cambridge, Mass.: Harvard University Press.

Eastman, Lloyd E. (1974). *The Abortive Revolution: China Under Nationalist Rule, 1927–1937*. Cambridge, MA: Harvard Universtiy Press.

Emerson, Rupert (1960). *From Empire to Nation*. Cambridge, Mass.: Harvard University Press.

Fazhi Ribao (1996). *Reports, National People's Congress*, by Tian Jiyun; Zhang Siqing; Ren Jianxin. 22 March.

Ge, Jianxiong (1996). "Minguo zhuyi shi jiuguo lingdan?", *Yazhou Zhoukan* [Asia Weekly], 21.4.1996, 14.

Gellner, Ernest (1983). *Nations and Nationalism*. Oxford: Basil Blackwell.

Guibernau, Montserrat (1996). *Nationalisms: The Nation-State and Nationalism in the twentieth Century*. Cambridge: Polity Press.

Hu, Guoheng [Henry K.H. Woo] (1995). *Dugong Nanshan Shou Zhongguo*. Hong Kong: Chinese University Press.

Hughes, Christopher Rene Hughes (1995). National Identity and Status in International Society: Taiwan in Chinese Nationalism. Ph.D. Thesis, London School of Economics.

Israel, John (1966). *Student Nationalism in China, 1927–1937*. Stanford U.P.

Johnson, Chalmers (1963). *Peasant nationalism and communist power.* Stanford: Stanford University Press.

Kamenka, Eugene, ed. (1976). *Nationalism, the Nature and Evolution of an Idea.* London: Edward Arnold.

Kedourie, E. (1960). *Nationalism.* (4th expanded edition, 1993). Oxford: Basil Blackwell.

Klintworth, Gary, ed. (1995). *New Taiwan, New China: Taiwan's Changing Role in the Asia-Pacific region.* Melbourne: Longman.

Kohn, Hans (1944). *The Idea of Nationalism.* New York: Collier.

Liang, Xiaosheng (1995). *Suishi choulou di Zhongguoren — Jiusan duanxiang.* Hong Kong: Cosmos Books.

Lin, Min (1995). "Moral Crusaders in China's Modernisation Process: The Case of Liang Xiaosheng", *Issues and Studies,* 31/10, October, 54–78.

Lin, Yu-sheng (1979). *The Crisis of Consciousness: Radical Antitraditionalism in the May Fourth Era.* Madison: The University of Wisconsin Press.

Mackerras, Colin (1994). *China's Minorities: integration and modernization in the Twentieth Century.* Hong Kong: Oxford University Press.

Metzger, Thomas A. (1996). *"Transcending the West": Mao's Vision of Socialism and the Legitmization of Teng Hsiao-p'ing's Modernization Program.* Hoover Essays No. 15. Stanford: Hoover Institution.

Moody, Peter R., Jr. (1992). *Political Change in Taiwan: a study of Ruling Party Adaptability.* New York, Praeger.

Nolan, Peter (1995). *China's Rise, Russia's Fall: Politics, Economics and Planning in the Transition from Stalinism.* London: Macmillan.

Peake, Cyrus H. (1932). *Nationalism and Education in Modern China.* New York: Columbia University Press.

Rezun, Miron (1992). *Nationalism and the Break-up of an Empire: Russia and its Periphery.* Westport, Conn.: Praeger.

Shakabpa, Tsepon W.D. (1967). *Tibet: A Political History.* New Haven: Yale University Press.

Shirk, Susan L. (1993). *The Political Logic of Economic Reform in China.* Berkeley: University of California Press.

Smith, A.D. (1971). *Theories of Nationalism.* London: Duckworth. 1971.

Smith, A.D. (1995). *Nations and Nationalism in a Global Era*. Cambridge: Polity Press.

Sun, Yat-sen (1981). *Sun Chung-shan quanji* (Complete Works), vol. I. Beijing: Zhonghua Shuju.

Tu, Wei-ming (1991). "Cultural China: The Periphery as the Center", *Daedalus*, Spring 1991, reprinted in Tu Wei-ming, ed., *The Living Tree: The Changing Meaning of Being Chinese Today*. Stanford: Stanford University Press, pp. 1–34.

Unger, Jonathan, ed. (1996). *Chinese Nationalism*. New York: M.E. Sharpe.

Wachman, Alan M. (1994). *Taiwan: National Identity and Democratisation*. New York: M.E. Sharpe.

Waldron, Arthur (1995). *From War to Nationalism: China's Turning Point, 1924–1925*. Cambridge: Cambridge University Press.

Wang, Gungwu (1991). *China and the Chinese Overseas*. Singapore: Times Academic Press.

Wang, Gungwu (1993). "Migration and Its Enemies", in Bruce Mazlish and Ralph Buultjens, eds., *Conceptualizing Global History*. Boulder, CO.: Westview Press, pp. 131–151.

Wang, Gungwu (1995). *The Chinese Way: China's Position in International Relations*. Oslo: Scandinavian University Press.

Wang, L. Ling-chi (1994). "Roots and the Changing Identity of the Chinese in the United States", in Tu Wei-ming, ed., *The Living Tree: The Changing Meaning of Being Chinese Today*. Stanford: Stanford University Press, pp. 185–212.

Wilbur, C. Martin (1976). *Sun Yat-sen: Frustrated Patriot*. New York: Columbia University Press.

Wu, Guoguang (1996). "Yi lixing minzuzhuyi kangheng 'weidu Zhongguo", *Ershiyi shiji* [Twenty First Century] (Hong Kong), no. 34, 25–33.

CHAPTER 6

RISE TO WEALTH 2008–2013:
TEN COMMENTS*

I have been asked to give lectures and talks on developments in China for many years. During the period 2008–2013, I wrote some short pieces on specific changes that I found interesting. Many were written for *The Straits Times* in Singapore. Of these, I have selected ten commentaries that illustrate a range of issues related to reform. They are included here as notes that reflect the themes of the volume. While they are consistent with China's changing interests as the country grows wealthier, they do not always show a China that is sensitive to the changes occurring around the world or to those in the neighbourhood.

Chinese Nationalism: Pride and Pitfalls

When Beijing bid for the 2008 Summer Olympics, it wanted to highlight China's successes over the past 30 years. Did it expect that others would do their utmost to highlight China's failures? It probably expected something from the usual suspects and made its preparations for that eventuality.

Nevertheless, it clearly did not expect riots in Tibet, which resulted in burnings and deaths. Once that happened, the chorus of voices already critical of Beijing rose to a crescendo. But what really surprised most people were the reactions of young Chinese to these foreign critics. They protested in the media and on the streets both inside and outside China. The explanations for

---

*The commentaries in this chapter were originally published in *The Straits Times* in Singapore.

this phenomenon have ranged from hurt national pride to dangerous, even rampant, nationalism.

The young voices came mostly from the *fenqing* or angry youth. It is hard to determine whether they were angrier inside or outside China. What astonished the international media was the fact that some of the protesters were students studying abroad, among the best-educated and most privileged in China. Certainly, whatever they may think of the Chinese Communist Party (CCP), these young people saw the attacks on China as attacks on the Chinese people.

Is this new? How did this form of nationalism come about?

The record shows that nationalism in China is truly modern. It began to grow only during the 20th century. There is no evidence that it arose from the Opium Wars of the mid-19th century, as some have suggested. Anger at foreign forces at the gate did lead to displays of xenophobia, but there was nothing new in that. That was the norm throughout Chinese history. For centuries, Chinese armies have fought ferociously against anyone who invaded their lands.

Others would date Chinese nationalism to the urgings of Sun Yat-sen, who lived long years abroad and was primarily educated in foreign schools. Yet others would link it to the Chinese students who went to Japan to learn the secrets of Japan's success, and to the *huaqiao* (Overseas Chinese) who had suffered discrimination at the hands of Europeans and Americans.

Certainly, all these contributed to the Chinese wanting a strong China that could restore its greatness. But the anger till the 1920s was never broad-based, nor was it ever directed against China's critics. Among educated leaders, it was often directed against abstractions like racism, imperialism and colonialism — and official historians then traced everything back to the Opium Wars.

What shaped the passionate nationalism that led the Chinese to identify a national enemy came from the conjunction of three events. The first was the rise of the Nationalist Party, the Kuomintang (KMT). By 1927, China was so divided and feeble that Japan intensified its efforts to take control of more Chinese territory. With Japanese advances into Manchuria and contiguous parts of North China, China's survival as a country was at stake.

The second followed from the succession of defeats the KMT inflicted on the CCP, which led the CCP to turn to nationalism to save itself and win support among peasants who never understood the tenets of Marxism-Leninism. That also attracted educated urban youth who doubted the KMT's willingness to fight the Japanese invaders, and they brought along with them their nationalism.

The final catalyst was the Sino-Japanese War of 1937–1945. In contrast to the first war of 1894–95, which occurred before the rise of nationalism, the second was a life-and-death struggle to save China. Both the KMT and the CCP drew strength from the emotions that sprang partly from anger at China's weakness but most of all from hatred of Japan's ambition to dominate the country. Both the KMT and the CCP became more nationalistic and devoted much energy to shaping nationalism to ensure their legitimacy.

Indeed, that competition continued even after the CCP established the People's Republic of China in 1949. It competed with the KMT in Taiwan for the hearts and minds of the *huaqiao* while at the same time highlighting its internationalist ideals. When internationalism failed, there remained only nationalism to bolster its right to lead the country.

What became of that nationalism after 1949? At one level, it manifested itself in China playing off the United States against the CCP's former comrades in the Soviet Union. At another level, it was evoked through memories of the patriotic war against Japan. No one could forget that it was the CCP's performance in that war that helped seal its success.

China's remarkable achievements since the reforms of 1978 and after have restored the pride of the Chinese people. As a result, now, when the government tries to please its foreign critics and adjust to their "universal" standards of correct behaviour, it could be perceived by the Chinese people to be unnecessarily weak. Furthermore, people who have benefited from the reforms feel that the continuing, sometimes carping and contemptuous, attacks on the regime are in fact aimed at China and the Chinese people. Hence their readiness to vent their anger towards the foreign critics.

But their passions should not obscure one undeniable fact: The source of their pride is now China's unity and potential power. There was sympathy for

China when it was divided and weak. That was lost when China became stronger. The government is aware of that change as it tries hard to assure neighbouring countries of its peaceful intentions.

It realises that the nationalism of small and weak states could be described as heroic. But the nationalism of a large, populous and technologically superior country, even if justified, would only generate fear and alarm.

Let us hope that the Games will end as Beijing hopes and millions around the world would cheer its success. That will be the time to ask if the Chinese people's pride in China's modernity cannot be celebrated without the need to resort to nationalism again.

6 August 2008

Taking China Beyond Global Economics

Banks lose billions in the United States and Europe. Millions lose jobs in Asia. No one can miss the effects of economic globalisation. The new batches of Chinese unemployed may hope that their condition is only temporary. But globalisation will not be. China will have to see its global future as a series of pluses and minuses it will have to live with and plan for.

For at least the last three decades, economic globalisation has been China's major concern. Foreign direct investment and the benefits of an export-oriented economy have transformed China into a manufacturing hub. Trade has become essential. Entrepreneurs now form a respected class and seem to have been given a place in society once reserved for scholarly mandarins.

The current financial crisis raises a question as to whether China's global economic future will continue to be at the centre of its national concerns. China had experienced long-distance trade for at least 2,000 years, a limited form of globalisation that never challenged the nature of its civilisation or the empire-state it had established.

Chinese ruling elites have traditionally recognised that they needed legitimacy, wisdom and a moral order to ensure the loyalty of their subjects. They secured the state against its enemies, not by military strength alone but by instituting a system of inter-state tributary relationships that afforded China safety and prestige. By such means, they limited the country's outreach and did not push towards the globalisation that enveloped the rest of Eurasia. Their vision of political globalisation remained focused on the primary needs of the Chinese state.

This vision was finally shattered during the second half of the 19th century when new kinds of national empires became global powers. After several military defeats, China saw that it had to accept the international system of nation-states in order to protect its sovereignty. But nothing could save the Manchu conquerors from the nationalism that the West aroused among a new generation of Chinese intellectuals.

The republic of 1911 marked the rise of a new nation-state based on the borders of the Qing empire and the ideal of a China consisting of many varieties of peoples. Such a state could be protected as long as China had the capacity to keep its borders intact. But the new competitive empires aggressively challenged those borders for nearly 40 years till the end of World War II.

After 1945, the victorious Americans and their allies devised a new political framework to regulate global power that was institutionalised in the United Nations. The privileged seat in the organisation given to China was denied to the Chinese Communist Party that seized power in 1949. For 22 years until its admission into the UN in 1971, this China remained outside the international system.

Since 1978, the People's Republic has opened itself to the global economy and worked to become a status quo power within the UN system. But just as it becomes comfortable with globalisation, it now encounters the vital test that is confronting the international economy. How can China help to repair the economic damage the world faces?

The Chinese have always prided themselves as being the bearers of universal ideals. Since the early 20th century, they have struggled to learn how to learn and master the most progressive values. They adopted the principles of science as the foundations of modernity. They accepted new standards of health, aesthetics, sport and lifestyle. But, in the realm of universal political ideals, the revolutionaries who believed in "creative destruction" won the battle. However, they destroyed much and failed to be creative. In an unprecedented reversal of policy, their leaders changed course in the late 1970s, after the death of Mao Zedong.

Those hostile to what China might stand for are not satisfied. They insist on higher "universal norms" that China has yet to accept: ideals of individual freedom, democracy and human rights protected by the rule of law. Until it does so, its dramatic economic achievements seem to be directed at strengthening an authoritarian state capitalism to keep the current regime indefinitely in power.

The West expects further progress in China to conform to what is considered appropriate for the global future. But China's sense of itself questions the validity of these Western demands. The Chinese leaders want to reach their own selection of what they need for their multinational state to be prosperous, safe and civilised. They would like to do it in their own way and at their own speed.

This is now more possible than before. The current financial crisis in the West, the turmoil in the Middle East and a string of failures in Africa have given China more time and space. Given China's history, both ancient and modern, its priorities are likely to be as follows:

The Chinese will continue to treat the economic globalisation as a means to a greater end, not an end in itself. They see the need to redefine universalist values for China — accept whatever is necessary to sustain civilised living, and integrate modern ideas with the best of its own heritage.

However, for the long haul, Chinese leaders will concentrate on what they have always thought to be central: the security and stability of a unified state and a harmonious society, something that only good governance can ensure. Achieving this in the uncertain environment of potentially turbulent globalisation is China's greatest challenge.

19 March 2009

China in G-2: Avoid a Rhetorical Trap

How much China has risen or re-risen has led to many exaggerations. Some have matched China as a superpower with the United States. Among the more dubious labels is the one characterising the bilateral meetings between U.S. and Chinese officials as G-2 gatherings. The label is eye-catching. US-China bilateral meetings are now bound to generate even more hyperbolic assertions about Chinese power. But does the label bear scrutiny?

The Chinese have emphasised that the meetings are simply to allow the two countries to discuss many common concerns. The use of the G-2 label, however, invokes a different perspective. It reminds one of the great capitalist powers that met first as a Group of Six, then Seven (G-7), about 35 years ago. That group consisted of the US, France, Britain, Germany, Japan, Italy and Canada. After the Soviet Union collapsed, a chastened Russia was admitted in 1997, and the G-7 became the G-8. China was not considered ready for membership.

Over the years, other countries have been invited to attend and, in 2005, the G-8 plus 5 was formalised. This time, China was invited. But there is still uncertainty as to which countries really qualify.

At one level, all these meetings affirm that the major economic powers are looking for ways to deal with global problems. The United Nations, the World Bank, the International Monetary Fund and other agencies, all seem unable to cope with recent changes. Over the past decade, China has adapted as quickly as it could to the current international system and has rarely complained about it as other powers have done.

Once the G-7 was seen as a helpful institution, its significance moved from symbolic to real. Since the 1990s, the trend has been towards more inclusive membership structures in key international institutions, and China patiently waited its turn to join. The Chinese sent their finance ministers to meet their counterparts in a gathering called the G-20. Then, last year, with the global financial crisis upon us, the G-20 became a summit gathering. G-20 heads of government met again in April this year, and there will be more such meetings.

But the media has stressed the fact that China is rising. And in the midst of the gloom and alarm of the global economic crisis, bilateral US-China meetings were promoted to G-2 gatherings. A country that was only formally admitted in 2005 into the G-8 plus 5, and seemingly content to be a part of the G-20, is being portrayed as the reason why the expansive process that led from the G-6 to the G-20 is now being reversed to just the G-2. Some Europeans have even wondered whether the European Union should not try to join this G-2 and make it G-3.

What does all this mean?

The range of terms — from G-7 to G-20 to G-2 — highlights a pervasive restlessness about the current international system. We know this system evolved out of the relations between European nation-states after the 17th century Treaty of Westphalia. The whole world was thereafter dominated by the Great Powers. Under the leadership of the national empires of Britain and France, the system was adjusted to suit their imperial relationships. The system failed to prevent World War I, so it was redesigned as the United Nations by the victors of World War II.

This new system proclaimed the equality of all nation-states, though veto powers were awarded to five privileged members of the UN's Security Council. The reality was actually simple, and for over 40 years, world politics was shaped by the balance between two superpowers, the US and the Soviet Union. Then that world ended in the early 1990s, when the Soviet Union collapsed and the US emerged as the victor of the Cold War.

Over the past 200 years, China declined from a resilient Confucian state with an ancient civilisation to a weak new republic fighting for survival. Even as it recovered over the past 50 years, it remained for decades a disgruntled outsider contained by greater powers. Only in the 1980s did it pull itself out of a self-destructive isolation to find a place in the international system.

Climbing a steep learning curve, Chinese leaders mastered the rules of the global market economy. It is still arguable whether they succeeded by mastering the international system that emerged in 1945 or whether they did so despite the system. In recent years, when calls were made to revise the system to reflect new international realities, Beijing made it clear that it was not pushing for change.

It is in this context that being identified with the US as the other member of the G-2 combine is so anomalous. There may be some Chinese who are flattered by what might be seen as a great compliment. But their leaders must be bemused by this swift promotion to superpowerdom.

They are likely to see the label as a rhetorical trap that could eventually be used to delineate China as the replacement for the Soviet Union and to be no less feared. Given the massive problems within the country that they still face, Chinese leaders can do without that.

8 July 2009

Top Students Offer New Promise for China

I was recently in China and met some very ambitious and intellectually curious students from some of its best universities. They came from different academic disciplines but shared a keen interest in Chinese traditional values. It surprised me to see so many engineering and business undergraduates asking searching questions about ancient Chinese history.

After two sessions with them, I was led to think of some of the contradictions China faces today in higher education. On the one hand, there is amazing progress in tertiary institutions, with more than four million students graduating last summer with qualifications in technical, business and other practical subjects. Hundreds of thousands are still looking for work that would match their qualifications.

On the other hand, competition for entry into the top universities is greater than ever and university fees are rising. Millions of high school students have been left behind and some now wonder whether going to universities is worth the investment of time and money.

Some university leaders confirm that they are often torn between wanting their best universities to be world class, comparable to the best in the West, and hoping that bright high school students will all get a chance to study at their universities.

The current gap in access is striking. More than half the total expenditure devoted to higher education is spent in the three great cities of Beijing, Shanghai and Tianjin and the seven coastal provinces, and less than a quarter in the 10 provinces in the western half of the country.

It is widely accepted that Peking and Tsinghua Universities, both located in the capital Beijing, are outstanding universities — they are certainly among the best 100 in the world. Some suggest that another 50 or so will become outstanding within a few years. The remaining 1,500 or so will continue to train skilled manpower for local and provincial service.

Despite the cries of unfairness in the distribution of resources for education, there is evidence that most of the brightest students are getting to the best universities. This owes much to the national examination for university entry, which many consider to be a horrendous exercise that does not necessarily bring out the best in the candidates. Nevertheless, it stands for open competition and is generally thought to be fair.

Ever since this "annual obstacle race" was introduced after the end of the Cultural Revolution some 30 years ago, it has offered the best opportunity for students of all classes to get into the leading tertiary institutions. I first encountered this examination in 1978 when the backlog of students who had missed out on an opportunity for a tertiary education in the 10 preceding years seized the chance to study again with determination and gratitude. They performed extremely well.

Over the years, I have seen professors, locked up on university campuses, spending several summer weeks grading anonymous answer books for this examination.

Over the years, I have also met many of the successful candidates who gained admittance to the top universities in Beijing, Shanghai, Guangzhou and elsewhere. I still remember what I thought when I first met them: these students did not need much teaching. The keenness of mind and the confidence they exhibited suggested that they could learn anything they wished. All they needed was the environment to meet scholars and have access to libraries and laboratories.

The top universities still have the pick of the best candidates, especially those in the fields of science and technology. Their annual undergraduate intakes have not increased by much over the years, so it does not surprise me that their students are brighter with each passing year.

What has surprised me, however, is that many among them are not content with their chosen disciplines. When the best universities began to offer a wider choice of humanities and social science courses, the number of engineering students who asked to take these courses — and did very well in them — was remarkably high.

Hence the exciting time I had last week with the lively students I met — in two sessions of 30 each from two successive freshman classes, selected mainly from among budding engineers and scientists. What astonished me was that both groups had signed up for two years of courses that included the reading of Chinese classical and historical texts.

These courses, carefully structured to harmonise with China's desire for modernity in business, technology and culture, were additional to their normal classes. They had to be taken during weekends.

I had been told that Chinese universities embarked on such courses so as to introduce their students to traditional values. Meeting these students convinced me that this is more than a cultural exercise, more than a minor attempt to broaden their minds. The students had volunteered to be allowed to take the courses and were all intensely committed.

If such courses continued to attract the best students for another generation, higher education would have shaped another dimension of modernity for China.

20 October 2009

China Talks Tough But Policy Unchanged

Relations between China and the United States seemed to have worsened because of the US arms sale to Taiwan and a host of other issues. In the US, support for President Barack Obama's programmes appears to have weakened. Has that encouraged the Chinese to talk tough? Are there developments within China that have led its leaders to move away from low-key responses and take higher profiles abroad?

Certainly Beijing's tone and the words it has used in public exchanges have been stronger than usual. Does this come from a shift in Chinese thinking?

I believe that China is not obsessive about what the US thinks, but it has always looked around in every direction. So I thought I should go through my checklist of what would appear to be the core global issues from the Chinese perspective.

China has carefully studied the rise and fall of modern great powers from the time they sprang out of the aggressive political cultures of the 15th and 16th centuries and re-configured the course of Atlantic history to the present. Although the empires of the Western powers reached the Indian and Pacific Oceans, the real struggle among them remained in the Atlantic. It was not till late in the 20th century, after the empires were finally dismantled, that the centre of gravity of great power conflicts moved eastwards to Asia.

Chinese leaders know that China's greatest mistake from the 15th to the 20th centuries was to remain with its continental mindset while a fundamental shift had taken place in the world. Chinese leaders are still struggling to find the right balance between their overland concerns and the threats to their maritime borders. But they know a great deal about nuclear weapons and are learning fast about cyberspace. On the whole, they now find it easier to understand what is necessary in order to ensure their security.

Recent geopolitical changes have occurred because China's rise has produced the view in the West that China is the only power that can resist Euro-American global hegemony. Other pockets of resistance in Africa, Latin America and the Middle East can be handled as local operations. Thus the attempts to induce, if not force, China to conform to the dominant norms.

The Chinese see this as a continuation of the ideological thrust that has been challenging China's sovereignty for the past 150 years. Their leaders note that this could ultimately be aimed at another regime change.

To them, the obvious manifestation of this thrust is the coming together of the US, Japan and India in the name of shared democratic values. This is feasible because modern military and communication technology has ensured that the Indian and Pacific Oceans are no longer too big for political cultures and patterns — the tussle between democracies and non-democracies, for example — once confined to the Mediterranean to replicate themselves in Asia. China realises that it has to be more watchful of such rivalries, for they may well threaten it.

In this context, China finds comfort in Asean's reluctance to join the ideological game. In its own interest, Asean has played a valuable role in reducing the sense of threat among the major protagonists involved in the region. Its efforts to minimise ideological thinking emphasising differences have been reassuring. China wants to help promote policies that can knit together those with similar goals in both the Pacific and Indian oceans.

In contrast to South-east Asia, China sees the regions to its north and west as posing persistent and intractable problems for its security and is determined to strengthen its defences along its borders with these regions.

My checklist of China's core interests becomes simpler when it comes to the country's internal goals. The hierarchy of its concerns has changed little over recent decades. The highest priority is still rapid economic development.

Two developments have pushed for change internally: the financial crisis in the West, where China's main markets are; and the damaging environmental degradation within the country. But China will change its policies gradually; the changes will not be panic-driven.

Beijing's concerns with internal stability remain unchanged. National attention has been directed at achieving social harmony, a clear admission that rapid economic development has led to inequalities beyond what can be tolerated by the Chinese people. The authorities know that there is widespread anger at the rampant corruption in official circles. Judicial and political reforms will continue, but the stress will be on caution. All future moves will continue to be deliberate and controlled.

China's key concern over the past century has been its sovereignty. The legitimacy of any Chinese government depends on its capacity to unify the country and preserve its borders.

Many lessons have been learnt from the period of turmoil that the Chinese people experienced, the most important being the country will always need development and order. Thus, the US and China may be talking less softly to each other today, but nothing fundamental in Chinese policy has changed to explain this shift.

24 February 2010

Six Cities, All Clones of One Another

During my most recent trip to China, I visited six cities in the Yangtze delta. They were of different sizes, but what I saw made me wonder if the changes they have undergone could be explained simply by the urge to modernise.

On my earlier visits to China, I focused more on the cities in north China, followed by some cities in the south, not to mention the ancient port city of Guangzhou. In comparison, my visits to the Yangtze cities were brief.

But that was not how my experience of China began. When I was young, it was Shanghai and the Yangtze cities that left a deep impression on me.

As a small-town boy from Ipoh, I was impressed by Singapore when we passed through the city in 1936 on our way to China. But when we arrived in Shanghai, I was told that this was truly a city.

The Chinese word for city refers back to market towns or market sectors within walled Chinese capitals. Shanghai was an urban centre built to deal with trade and industry, and was by the 1930s the most modern city in Asia. The city was not based on the old walled *yamen*, where government officials determined how much commerce was allowed and how every transaction should be conducted.

Some 10 years later, I returned to the Yangtze delta to study in Nanjing, then the national capital. I loved the walls that surrounded it, though they were symbols of the traditional official-dominated Chinese capital city that commercial Shanghai was not. I regret, however, that I did not pay closer attention to its ambience and administrative structure before much of the city was transformed following the communist victory of 1949. Everything was changed afterwards in the name of industrial urbanisation.

The Chinese idea of an authority centre controlled by bureaucrats and military personnel has been carefully described in the historical records. Changing prefectures, counties, districts and towns into cities dedicated to industry and commerce was something new in Chinese history. By the middle of the Cultural Revolution (1966 to 1976), a series of three volumes about the Chinese city, from the late imperial period through several transitions to the communist era, was published, and the urbanising processes in China came to be better understood.

When it became possible for me to visit the People's Republic in 1973, I found that the changes that had occurred in China's urban areas were indeed profound. Although our delegation members were not free to wander far from our hotels, we saw that there were only bicycles and a few official and military vehicles on the wide new roads. The few narrow cobbled streets that remained were equally silent and dark at night. In the briefings we received, ambitious goals were outlined of each city's progress, but the presentations seemed perfunctory.

What happened when Deng Xiaoping assumed power in 1978 can be told as a fairy tale about inspired organisation and visionary entrepreneurship on a scale never before seen in China. Stories of rapid urban industrial growth, including the upgrading of small towns into large cities, have been repeated endlessly in just about every corner of the country.

My last visit has confirmed that cities at every level are growing at the expense of neighbouring rural areas and that such expansions have gained great momentum. The most striking fact is that everything is now centred on cities without walls and dedicated to economic development.

The former designation of an urban centre has given way to the ideal of the developmental cities. Only if cities achieve that status can their officials be assured that their cities have made progress — and that their performance in running them is recognised.

In the scramble to attain the name of city, there are now three layers of administration which all use the same word: the largest four cities, which report directly to the central government; the 230 or so cities which report to provincial governments; and the 430 or more smaller towns, all claiming to be cities, coming under various lower jurisdictions.

Older names like counties and townships have virtually disappeared. All formerly rural areas close to urban centres have been systematically incorporated into the centres, and the boundaries between cities have been continuously redrawn.

What is unmistakable, however, is that the cities have yet to become cities of trade and industry supported by an active citizenry. Instead, they remain Chinese cities insofar as they remain under official control and are governed by the party and the bureaucracy, with each level of authority firmly tied to the authority above it.

As a result, the six cities I visited have become remarkably alike — indeed, so alike that they seek to attract tourists in precisely the same way: by tearing down old towns and constructing wide boulevards and then building standard replicas of what are described as "Old Streets" or "Streets of the Ming and Qing Dynasties".

It is hard to imagine what tourists will admire about them.

28 April 2010

Change of Political Weather

There are so many levels of fascination in what is happening in the Arab world today. Expectations of revolution, fear of instability, the survival of secular governance over theocracy, the future of democracy, the power of Facebook and Twitter — the list is long. Media reports have been excitable and it is too early to digest all the implications of the historic event.

One aspect of the reports deserves attention: These noted that China's media kept its reporting of the events in Cairo low-key and that the word "Egypt" was kept off the Internet. Ever since the middle of last month, when the Tunisian President fell, the Western media has noted what the Chinese press has failed to report.

In China, the stress has been on concerns for stability. The range of emotions on display in Cairo's Tahrir — or Liberation — Square was largely downplayed. Not surprisingly, words such as freedom, democracy and revolution were not to be found in Chinese reports.

However, in anticipation of President Hosni Mubarak's departure, Chinese blogs did compare Liberation Square with Tiananmen. The consensus was that China was different from Egypt but that there were lessons to be learnt.

At one extreme, as one might expect, there were voices calling on the Chinese people to see what the Egyptian people had achieved and thus not be afraid. At the other, there were sober assessments of the damage done to Egypt's economy.

Among the many comments in between were reminders that the income inequality in China had become more obvious, that efforts to limit widespread corruption were superficial, and that political reform had not been pursued as promised. Others chose to emphasise the need for China's economy to grow further.

Wherever possible, people were finding reasons to say why China was different from Egypt, although much remained to be done in China. Underlying all the commentary was the idea that change was normal and always to be expected. Nothing can remain the same for long.

That belief comes from the classic of change, the Yijing 易经, and is an idea that the Chinese people have lived with and believed in since their civilisation emerged over 3,000 years ago.

But the popular word for change is not *yi* 易 but *bian* 变, now a powerful word employed in many contexts. One of its recent uses is captured in the term *biantian* 变天, a changed sky or heaven.

This is derived from innocent references to sudden changes in the weather. Especially in our era of global warming and climate change, it is a term appropriate for describing the sudden snowfalls and unseasonable floods and droughts that have been reported everywhere.

But *biantian* has also been used in the language of politics, notably for regime change. The term is notoriously imprecise. It was first applied to the overthrow of reactionary rulers. Mao Zedong approved its use for the fall of the Manchu "bureaucratic state" as well as of the inept and corrupt Kuomintang regime, but the word did not become popular.

Probably in retaliation, Taiwanese politicians popularised a variation of the term, *bianse* 变色, using change to refer to changes of colour — for example, from blue to red, a reference to when the "red" communists won on the mainland in 1949, overthrowing the "blue" Kuomintang.

Recently, the word has also been used in Taiwan to describe dramatic changes via the ballot box — as in blue to green when Mr Chen Shui-bian won the Taiwanese presidency in 2000, and back from green to blue when Mr Ma Ying-jeou won eight years later.

For such changes, no matter how dramatic, words such as revolution and liberation do not apply. *Biantian* can represent change without violence and bloodshed. Thus the word has even been applied to the election of Mr Barack Obama as President of the United States, a dramatic and once unthinkable event that put an African-American in the White House.

This term has since been used to describe what has happened in Tunisia and Egypt. The blogs using the word reflect the hope that peaceful *biantian* can occur in China in ways that will not threaten stability.

By implication, this suggests that the Chinese leadership need not fear instability when it responds more tangibly to the people's wishes for justice and respect.

But will the usage of the word in this context be accepted in China? The Chinese language is wonderfully plastic.

Biantian once had astrological connotations, alluding to the victory of the yang of light over the yin of darkness that led to the creation of all things.

In modern times, it came to refer to dramatic weather changes but also, following Mao, to the act of replacing a reactionary system with a progressive one. Today, it still captures the idea of regime change for the better.

In the word *tian* 天, heaven or sky, many Chinese would also think of change that receives Heaven's blessing and is thus a righteous cause. And as major Chinese philosophers since Confucius and Mencius have all proclaimed: The mandate to rule comes from seeing the people's wellbeing as the source of social harmony.

China is not Egypt, and *biantian* — making changes to meet Heaven's wishes — is not something that any Chinese should fear.

16 February 2011

90 Years, 80 Million Strong

The Chinese Communist Party (CCP) celebrated its 90th birthday on July 1. There is joy but also soul-searching in China. Many are incredulous that the party can claim "four generations under one roof" and is 80 million strong.

The party insists that people are its primary concern. It even goes further, in arguing that China's future and progress depends on the people. Thus, it is the Chinese people who make the country admired or feared. They can make China an advanced country that evokes admiration and respect. Or they can attract attention to themselves as being concerned only for wealth and power, at once self-centred and arrogant.

The emphasis on support from the people was part of the party's earliest history. The CCP began in 1921 with men of ideas who were inspired by the Russian revolution four years earlier. The Chinese had an earlier revolution in 1912, but that faltered badly, with its ideas criticised for being incoherent and its leaders hobbled by elitist tradition.

The young men who met in Shanghai to start the CCP thought that the model of an armed party disciplined enough to gain support from the working classes was the answer to the country's woes.

At that time, China had many enemies, and the first priority was to unite the country by any means possible. The young CCP helped the Kuomintang against warlords but were treacherously betrayed on the eve of victory. Its members were driven to the countryside where they fought desperately to survive. Fortunately for them, the Japanese invasion distracted the Nanjing regime and the two erst-while comrades were persuaded to come together to defend the country.

The CCP sent its army out to keep the Japanese invaders busy through guerilla raids but it also used the opportunity to sharpen its ideological focus.

Under Mao Zedong and his comrades, it emerged after 1945 ready for the civil war they knew they still had to fight. By any account, their final victory against the Nationalist government was well deserved.

But it needed new ideas to translate victory in the battlefield into success in uniting people and managing a broken economy. The party turned to the Soviet Union for help. Together, they confronted their Cold War enemies led by the United States. In turn, China's socialist partners extracted a heavy price by drawing China into the Korean War.

The toughest test, however, came from within the party, which was split on the key issue of whether it should focus on rebuilding a prosperous China or whether it should have grander ambitions to be the vanguard of world revolution.

To Mao Zedong, the world was the new *tian xia*, "All under Heaven", and he hoped to prepare a socialist China to lead that world. Not everyone agreed and the inner party struggles began.

The party came to invest too much power in one man — Mao. His absolute power and rigid ideas led the party to unprecedented mistakes. For more than 20 years — through the Great Leap forward that caused famine and the Cultural Revolution that victimised the "bourgeois" and the educated class — millions of talented people with independent minds were ousted and many more millions lost their lives. By the 1970s, the party was bereft of ideals and in tatters.

Deng Xiaoping led the reversal of what Mao had done and gave the party a second chance. The people were tired of being revolutionary and poor; that was not the socialism they died for. Deng mobilised the Chinese people's pragmatism and entrepreneurship that had made them bold and inventive in the past. He opened the country to the outside world and offered the Chinese people freedoms they had not had for decades, and access to new ideas.

The CCP's 90-year history shows it has the capacity to reform itself, and to take decisive action to do so. It has survived internal ideological battles and a challenging external environment. It has been able to open the economy to foreign investment, allowing its people the opportunity to learn from advanced economies. Its policy of opening up the economy has brought the country spectacular success.

But when it feels threatened, the CCP is still wont to take one or two steps back for every step forward. It still believes that it is the only institution that can empower China and save it from disorder or dreaded collapse.

What is next for the party in its 90th year? It faces new challenges.

Rapid development has created new problems, most notably widespread corruption aggravated by secretive institutions. As standards of living rise, gross inequalities have become obvious. And while the country has produced more lawyers and judges, the justice system remains suspect.

Not many people seem satisfied by the party's own call for more democracy within its ranks. The party, which has prided itself on the strength of its ideological appeal, will need fresh ideas to bring it into its 10th decade. To do so, it needs to attract and motivate talented young people and induct them into its socialist heritage.

China today has returned to the leading position in the world that it enjoyed at the end of the 18th century. But that powerful position did not save the country then from succumbing too quickly to division and ruin.

Today's success cannot guarantee safety. For China, this is not the time for complacency. The party wants members not only to celebrate its past 90 years but also learn from the mistakes that generations of Chinese leaders have made.

This is a wise reminder.

13 July 2011

Drawing Lines in the Sea

The region has certainly had an uncomfortable time in recent years with disputes concerning the South China Sea.

Several concepts have dominated the heated debates, with words like sovereignty, borders, maps, islands and rocks, international law and Unclos (United Nations Convention on the Law of the Sea), EEZ (exclusive economic zones), fishing and exploration rights, and stop and search powers, just to name a few.

Most of these terms are of recent vintage and many countries still have difficulty with the definitions and legal implications of some of the terms used. In Asia, the problems are particularly acute, especially on the issue of maritime borders. The leaders of the first post-colonial nations, since the 1950s and 1960s, were engrossed in their own nation-building projects and not in a hurry to define any of the terms more precisely, if they thought about them at all.

Indeed, if all the terms were legally clear and their interpretation obvious, there would be far less turbulence today. Alternately, if national interests did not overlap and fishing and energy resources were evenly distributed or divided to satisfy the peoples concerned, there might be no disputes at all. Since neither is the case, the problems of maritime borders have unleashed strong emotions everywhere.

We need to be reminded that countries in Asia have never, in the past, had the concept of sovereignty and permanent and legal borders, even on land. As for the sea dividing kingdoms and empires, the problem never seemed to have arisen before the coming of the Europeans. When that issue first arose, sovereign disputes referred to those between different European nations and empires which needed to draw lines to match the ideas of law, rights, borders and economic interests that they had brought with them.

The story began with the Treaty of Tordesillas of 1494 when the Spanish and Portuguese rulers divided newly discovered lands to the west and south of their respective countries. This was sanctioned by the Pope and extended by the Treaty of Zaragoza 35 years later to cover the world, including the Indian and Pacific oceans.

In our region, that meant that some vague line was drawn that placed the Philippines in Spanish hands and left bits of the Moluccas (Maluku) to the Portuguese.

Over the next four centuries, more borders were drawn by the imperial powers or by organs set up by European empires, and some of these became the borders of new nation-states after 1945.

The other famous treaty that focused on maritime borders was the Anglo-Dutch Treaty of 1824, which divided two large parts of the Malay archipelago along the Strait of Malacca. Indeed, the idea of sovereignty was easily grasped for landed territories, but extending the concept to cover the waters around islands was never understood in Asia.

After 1945, the world was transformed and, for the very first time in history, all states, including former colonies, were legally equal and new rules of the game came into play. The victors of the World War II, with the best of intentions, established the United Nations organisation to entrench new legal ideas and limitations in international affairs to prevent future wars.

Among other things, scores of new states were recognised and, since then, atlases have had to be redrawn many times.

Land borders were drawn and sometimes renegotiated, mostly with success, but the sea remained problematical. Hence the need for Unclos, a massive work in progress, with gaps of interpretation still to be tested. And until recently, the countries in our region seemed to have recognised how complicated the negotiations have been and have been patient to work out the principles over time. So why the flurry of aggravations in the South China Sea during the past few years?

It is clear that the pressures for urgent action are not because of the desire for peace, or the concern to affirm principles of international law, or from some breakthrough in ways to resolve the issue of sovereignty and maritime borders.

The urgency has been brought about by two major factors: first, the drive to exploit each country's undersea energy resources and, second, the reports depicting a rising China about to use naval muscle to get its way in waters that are not recognised as its own, which some think triggered the American "pivot" to Asia.

Both issues touched on the one question that Unclos was never meant to resolve, that is, what does sovereignty mean where maritime borders are concerned? Sovereignty has historically been a matter between claimant nations, and disputants draw maps usually to mark their prime negotiation positions. Unclos negotiators found it too hard and turned to other measures to minimise conflict, effectively leaving sovereignty matters for the states concerned to deal with.

It would appear then that the old adage applies: Possession is nine points of the law. The country in possession keeps what it has and would seek to acquire the power to hold on to it. If that is the position in the South China Sea, the alternatives are clear. If sovereignty is the key issue, both sides should exercise patience and look for peaceful ways to demarcate their maritime borders.

If, however, the need for resources cannot wait, then practical terms have to be negotiated by the interested parties to share their respective interests. But, if patience is not possible and economic negotiations still depend on who is sovereign, what should be done?

The countries in the region face dilemmas for which nothing in their respective histories has prepared them. They depend on a framework of international law that they have been taught to use only recently and no one is confident that they fully understand how that would work for them in the long run.

With each incident, countries can turn to their diplomats to find new ways of drawing lines on the waters. The diplomats would have to be at their best. If they fail, maritime borders will either stay in the too-hard basket or be determined by ships armed to confront one another at sea.

11 July 2011

Getting China to Play by the Rules

The danger of another Sino-Japanese war has set alarm bells ringing for the past several weeks. Comparisons have been made to the start of World War I. China's assertiveness has reminded some of upstart Germany or Japan and their imperial ambitions earlier in the 20th century. All these are misleading. What many of the headlines are trying to do is to warn China to back off from what it is doing in the South and East China seas and conform to the current international system — or be treated as a threat to world order the way Germany and Japan had been.

The modern system of international relations evolved during the past century from its base in the North Atlantic. At its peak, countries such as Britain, France and the United States dominated it. Earlier in the 20th century, Germany had twice wanted to share power in the system. But its challenges were repulsed and its power finally destroyed after two world wars.

In Asia, leaders in Japan tried to come up with their share of the system in order for them to dominate the Asian continent and the Western Pacific islands but they too were eventually defeated. Today, they calculate that their future place must depend on using the same global system to counter a rising China.

One could add revolutionary Russia after the 1940s as another power that also had a turn at trying to undermine the Atlantic system. Its efforts were global during the Cold War but its overreach ultimately undermined its ability to challenge the US.

Today, the US appears to think that the only country that has the capacity to compete with it is China. Other Asian countries are the products of years of tutelage under Western colonial officials. In any case, after decolonisation, none of the new nation states can act like Germany or Japan. They accept the existing international system and have readily used it to serve their own interests. Such support has strengthened the system's claim to universality.

China's traditional system was the last in Asia to fall. It was fortunate that rivalries among the Great Powers prevented it from being dismembered. Its two revolutions — in 1911 and 1949 — were both inspired by European models, and they put China on the road to participate in what the West had established. In addition, after 1978, Deng Xiaoping used the system cleverly to help China's economic reforms and this has ensured China's high level of dependence ever since.

The Chinese are now discovering that full membership of the system exacts a high price. Behind the economic benefits it provides is a structure of laws and analyses that guide diplomatic and strategic thinking and action today. China has been wise to attend to that structure systematically. But its focus has been largely on shaping an environment that will allow the country to develop. There is little evidence it would engage in activities that go beyond that goal. Chinese leaders realise that they do not have an alternative system to sustain future development. They know that their country is not Germany or Japan, and have carefully studied how to avoid the mistakes that led both to disaster. But there are analysts in the region and beyond who remain sceptical and still fear that China could follow the examples of the two expansionist powers.

Given such circumstances, China has to reconsider the way it handles the current international system. National pride and a deep sense of duty demand that it defend its right to remain sovereign and distinctively Chinese. But when the country is also beset by corruption, injustice, environmental degradation and growing discontent within, the struggle to develop in peace could become more difficult.

Chinese history has warned of dangers when both internal unrest or nei-luan 内乱, and external turbulence, waihuan 外患, are present. China may, sooner than it likes, face that condition again. But it is no longer a matter of dealing with smaller neighbours one at a time. What their leaders face is a powerful rule-based system that most countries are prepared to accept.

China has so far been able to use the system to serve its interests. But it is more demanding than what China has been ready to give in return. The game requires that it submit to principles that are being codified as universal, some of which Chinese leaders are not yet able to accept.

Here is China's challenge. The guardians of the international system project a rising China that is unwilling to be more open and free. They imply that when China becomes more powerful, it will be harder to make it play by their rules. Whether justified or not, using the German and Japanese analogies will help them suggest that China is a potential threat to world order.

It is in this context that Japan is joining those that are similarly concerned about China's rising power, to encourage the American pivot or rebalance in Asia. Chinese leaders are aware of this danger to its image and its future role in the region. If China's leaders and diplomats fail to counter the current efforts to paint the country onto the German and Japanese template, there will be even more strategies to contain China, strategies that would disrupt the economic progress it still needs.

The problem the region faces is not China's rise to power or even the mistakes that China is seen to be making. It stems from the sense of urgency among some countries to make China conform to a system that still needs American power to enforce its will. Thus it is not only China's own initiatives that really matter. It is also what the US is willing to do to further empower that system and how much it understands China's need to protect its distinctive place in the world.

12 February 2013

CHAPTER 7

FACING SOUTH: CHANGING PERSPECTIVES

Sixty years ago, when the People's Republic of China was established, the new state could see that the lands to its south were being radically transformed. It was clear that China and the region called Southeast Asia would have to make adjustments to their relationship. The process was far from straightforward. The Cold War divided the region, with China and the Soviet Union supporting the region's communist parties and most governments more or less ready to take sides against communism. When the Cold War ended in 1991, the ten countries in the region put aside their differences to enable the Association of Southeast Nations (ASEAN) to become inclusive. They thus stepped onto a new stage of its history and both China and ASEAN are aware that they will have new kinds of relationships. Both are aware how complex they are and how difficult it will be to achieve a stability that would satisfy both sides. The world is global and many more players have stakes in both China and the region. To begin to understand what is involved, it is important to remember that the relationships between China and its southern neighbours have a long history.

From early times, the Southeast Asian region consisted of a dynamic and volatile group of mainland and island states that had undergone many kinds of changes. During centuries of continual relationships, the Chinese perspective of developments there was more or less consistent. There was a difference between what was based on contacts by land and those by sea. Those overland were limited because of the difficult terrain in Southwest China where most of the indigenous peoples still controlled their own tribal kingdoms and chiefdoms. The contacts off the coast of southern China, however, were built on a flourishing trade that foreign merchants had initiated to reach the markets of a wealthy and technically advanced Chinese empire. The officials of that empire established key entry points at the Chinese ports that were designated to deal with all foreign relations.

The ruling classes in the region and the many different peoples who serviced the interregional trade between the Indian and Pacific Oceans kept a keen interest in what was happening in China. Depending on the proximity of their ports to China and the extent of their commercial dependence on the trade, the merchants and their sponsors developed different policies and attitudes. Everything began to change after the coming of the West to the region. By the 19th century, there was a new global maritime order that undermined traditional Sino-Southeast Asian relations. Inevitably, this has influenced the way China must now look at the region and, no less, the region's understanding of its future relationship with China. In particular, the desire for regional solidarity in the face of the re-emergence of a powerful China warrants close attention, not least by the leaders of a more confident China. It would be useful to examine the historical forces that led to the present situation.

The research done by archaeologists and ethnologists over the past century has given us a new picture of how the region was settled. There were several strands. An ancient one from the Indian sub-continent came mainly by sea across the Bay of Bengal. Another, involving larger numbers of people, came overland from the southern and southwestern areas of China and they spread south down the valleys of great river systems like those of the Mekong and the Salween, as well as the smaller rivers of the Irrawaddy and the Menam, until they reached the respective river deltas. Other overlanders stayed in the uplands and maintained their distinct ways of life down to recent times. A third strand that also came by sea were speakers of Austronesian languages who came across the Taiwan Straits and the South China Sea; the most adventurous among them went well beyond Southeast Asia, westwards across the Indian Ocean and east and southwards to the South Pacific.

By the 1st century A.D., the Chinese Han Empire had consolidated its power over one corner of the region in what is now northern Vietnam. By that time, the settled populations of the larger peninsula lands and the archipelago had established kingdoms and port cities that drew traders from India and Persia, not least those who wanted to reach further east to the markets of China. Some of those who accompanied the traders coming from ports west of the region brought their religious ideas and practices, concepts of kingship and feudal governance, even networks of political and commercial relationships that invigorated the long-distance trade. When the Chinese also embraced Buddhism and discovered the sea-route to India, the home of the Buddha, the trade in and through the Nanhai grew even more attractive and profitable. For this early period of the first millennium, the Chinese records we still have, mostly based on official documents, are fuller than all other literate sources. They have been invaluable in the reconstruction of the early history of the region and thus contributed significantly to a Sinocentric perspective on the region's history. It is this perspective that has governed much of Chinese thinking about Southeast Asia throughout history and one that is being challenged by the events of the last century.

Over the centuries, the growth of trading systems enabled larger political entities to be established. From the first to the 14th century, there were the powerful polities of Funan and Champa, of Chenla and the Angkorian Empire on the mainland. The maritime empires of Sri Vijaya and later of Majapahit exercised control over large tracts of the seas around the extended archipelago. These kingdoms and port cities not only provided local hubs for all regional activity but also became the centres for a regular and flourishing inter-regional trade that linked the Indian Ocean with the Western Pacific, especially the China coasts.

During the early period, the institutional changes throughout the region were gradual. China and its southern ports were content to be the eastern terminus of a trade largely carried in foreign ships. It was not until the tenth century that Chinese merchants began to participate actively in tandem with those from India and the Muslim world. By the 14th century, however, Chinese shipping was the most active in the region. This enabled two Ming emperors, Yongle and his grandson Xuande, to preside over the seven naval expeditions to the Indian Ocean from 1403 till 1435. Even after the fleets were withdrawn and private overseas trade by Chinese was banned or carefully restricted, Ming China continued to manage a tributary system through which foreign countries could determine for themselves how much they wanted to trade with China. Chinese official interest in maritime relations with the region steadily diminished. For the next four centuries, there were only informal, often illegal, contacts and it was largely the risk-taking merchants of Fujian and Guangdong provinces who maintained them. As a result, the Chinese mandarins saw no reason to alter the Sinocentric perspective that guided their policies towards their neighbours across the South China Sea. If anything, Chinese wealth and power underlined a relationship that only required, from time to time, minor adjustments in the way the foreign states and port cities were dealt with. If those states saw China differently through their own local perspectives of China, that view seems not to have been registered in any of the surviving documents. We have to assume that the Chinese did not pay attention to views that were contrary to their own.

This remained true even after the coming of the Europeans to the region. There is nothing in the local and Chinese records to suggest that the arrival of European ships beyond Malacca after 1511 marked any awareness of significant change for anyone. It is understandable why no Chinese officials saw that as marking the beginning of a power shift that would ultimately transform the region's relations with China. The mandarins were satisfied that the Portuguese who arrived on the China coast were not strong enough to threaten imperial interests. The private Chinese merchants there adapted to this new foreign presence. They took note of the new kinds of products brought to Macau and further east and readily supplied the different range of goods that attracted Portuguese interest. When Jesuit missionaries followed and brought new knowledge to the Chinese literati, there was keen interest among some of their more alert members. But there was no change in policy towards foreign contacts. Later, when the Dutch built a base in southern Taiwan, the Ming court was by that time busy defending its northern borders and was in no position to show concern. Indeed, coastal Chinese adventurers participated in extending Dutch trade to Ryukyu and Japan.

The new dynasty after 1644, the Qing, continued to pay scant attention to the fact that Europeans in larger numbers were coming to the China coast. To the victorious Manchu and Mongol elites and their armies from beyond the Great Wall, the European traders could be tolerated as long as they accepted the conditions set by their empire. The coastal authorities were aware that these heavily armed merchants from Europe were different from the kinds of Southeast Asian, Arab and Indian merchants who had come in the past. They knew that the Europeans were keen to trade and some had found Chinese partners to help them expand their China trade, but these officials made no effort to intervene as long as imperial interests were not affected. For them, the traditional China-centred perspective remained sound and they believed that it could safely remain unchanged.

By the 18th century, the Europeans had established mercantile empires that linked the region to the economies of the rest of the world. The industrial revolution followed by the rise of powerful European nation-states led to new kinds of empires being built in which the overseas Chinese communities resident in their colonies and ports also played important roles. These were maritime powers that systematically pushed beyond the Malay Archipelago to force China to open its ports to trade. Their successes were dramatic and inspired the Japanese empire to imitate them and modernize its own forces. Very quickly, it gained the capacity to destroy the foundations of imperial China and even thrust deep into Chinese territory. After two World Wars, in part spurred by Japanese invasions, the whole region was transformed from a conduit in the larger Asian trade to become a set of decolonized new nations that emerged with their own distinct identities. By this time, it was clear to everyone that maritime power had helped to bring China down and a new regional order was being shaped off the Chinese coasts.

When the People's Republic was established in 1949, its leaders saw that nationalist leaders in Southeast Asia were fighting for freedom and independence and building their new nations. Some were already thinking of their countries sharing common political, economic and security interests with one another. After being divided for centuries as small rival kingdoms and port cities, their new leaders could see how important it was for their countries to share a regional identity. For the first time in history, they were in a position to build a structure of relationships that could affirm such an identity, and that would enhance their place in Asia and beyond. In 1967, five of them, Indonesia, Thailand, Malaysia, Philippines and Singapore, came together to form its own regional group, ASEAN, one that was to be independent of external powers.

In short, the new China after 1949 faced a global environment that challenged the old Sinocentric worldview. The emerging nation-states to its south in turn discovered that they had a fresh perspective from which to re-examine their relations with China. But they were not immediately able to focus on the issue in a peaceful environment. For over forty years from the 1948 to 1991, China and Southeast Asia were divided by the Cold War between the post-war superpowers, the Soviet Union and the United States. In China, that division manifested itself in the tensions between the People's Republic and the Republic of China in Taiwan. In Southeast Asia, battle lines were drawn between the former French Indochina and the rest. For countries in the region's north, Vietnam, Laos and Burma shared a long border with China's southern provinces of Yunnan and Guangxi. For the coastal states, there were the disputed waters and islands of the South China Sea where China's claims included the Paracels and Spratlys, marked by eleven dotted lines on its maps from 1947. The Cold War reinforced the global maritime perspective that the European powers had brought to Asia, but with one major difference. Power in the region was no longer about commercial and imperial relations. The new alignment of forces was based on secular ideologies like capitalism and communism that claimed to be universal, something that replaced the older religious divisions between the Chinese and most of the peoples of Southeast Asia.

During the Cold War years, liberal capitalist, Marxist communist, or a variety of neutral socialist perspectives competed for attention in the politics of the region. For China and Southeast Asia, the major contests were represented, on the one hand, by a land-based expansion of revolutionary ideas through China to mainland Southeast Asia and, on the other, by ocean-based forces that controlled the coastal waters south from Taiwan to the Philippines,

Malaysia, Thailand and what had been Indochina. Since the Cold War ended, continuous efforts have been made to end the divisions by uniting Southeast Asia as a single region. It is envisaged that, with ASEAN, such a regional community would be able to deal with both a continental China and the maritime alliances of the Indian and Pacific Oceans with its own independent vision, something that it had never had throughout the region's history.

In short, in the space of less than a century, the region has seen the eclipse of the Sinocentric worldview and the rise of national rewritings of history. At the same time, it also experienced the struggle of two modern power centres in the United States and the Soviet Union with their competing claims to be universal. These three perspectives, the Sinocentric, the nationalist and the universal, have competed for preeminence in the evolving region. How that will influence future relationships will depend on the answers to the following questions. Will the liberal capitalist project determine the shape of a permanent international world order? Will a new civilization in China seek to bypass the emerging national and regional identities and return to a reconstituted all-under-Heaven (tianxia) with China as centre? Will the new region stay united so that external rivalries can be harnessed to enable a distinctive community of nations to remain free and inclusive?

I have set out the background to some of the issues that China now faces to its south. All three questions posed above are important, but I shall leave the first and third questions for another time. Here I shall only try to answer the second: will a new civilization in China wish to return to a Sinocentric worldview or will Chinese leaders see that the time is past for such a perspective?

In 2012, a conference was held in Singapore on Imperial China and its southern neighbours. It highlighted China's early experiences with the peoples in the south, comparing the period before the Qin unification with those of imperial China after the 3rd century B.C. The Chinese kept records of trade and tributary relations pertaining to Southeast Asia and provided a continuous story that has dominated the narratives prior to the modern period. In comparison, Southeast Asia's own chronicles and stories have been dispersed and fragmentary. It is only in modern times that these scattered accounts have been threaded together with the help of archaeological finds and the use of modern anthropological, philological and historical methods. For recent centuries, there also records kept by the Portuguese, Spanish, Dutch, English, French and American merchants and officials. Some of the more curious and learned also collected and examined cultural artifacts and reconstructed local histories, and many went on to fit the new materials into the new world history.

What is clear now is that, for the PRC today, as it formulates policies towards its southern neighbours, it has to face three distinct narratives that have been developed from separate sources but may be seen as inextricably intertwined. The first is the Sinocentric Chinese perspective, looking southwards from the capitals in the north, whether in Nanjing or Beijng or elsewhere. The second comes from the opposite direction, looking north from the maritime states around the South China Sea and the mainland states bordering Yunnan. The third is a more distant perspective from the west of Southeast Asia. Its earliest manifestation was South Asian Hindu-Buddhist contacts; it was supplemented by Middle East and Islamic influences; and that has been added to by the worldview of Atlantic trading fleets coming around the coasts of Africa and across the Pacific. With the scientific and technological advances that created global commerce and the modern economy, this third perspective has inspired new approaches to universal history. The three narratives have elements in common: they are linked to people who made history and show the power this history has on people's imagination. They are the products of those who decided how history should be written and used, and can help to determine which narrative should be dominant.

THE SINOCENTRIC PERSPECTIVE

During the past six decades, the changes in China and the littoral states of Southeast Asia require us to re-examine this perspective. China is now an economic powerhouse seen as the second largest economy in the world. ASEAN has been surprisingly successful in building a cooperative framework that strengthens its regional self-image. It is now in a position to make itself the heart of a larger region that connects South Asia and Oceania with China and the other states of East Asia. The historical research done during the past five decades has unearthed evidence of underlying commonalities that further supports a new confidence among ASEAN leaders. In addition, there is increasing interest among scholars and officials within China to deepen its links with the region. Key institutions, including academies, universities and think tanks, have been asked to pay special attention to the rise of this new regional entity to China's south. To many in the region, it is increasingly important to know what can advance understanding in China about the polities and peoples to its south.

As Asia regains its historic place in global affairs, China and the region may have to look again at the existing paradigm of inter-state, inter-regional and international relationships. In that paradigm, two kinds of relationships between China and its overland neighbours stand out. One consists of the historical narratives of the many wars between Vietnam and China since ancient times. Related to that but described differently, and in less Confucian terms, are accounts of persistent turbulence on the borders separating Yunnan from Burma and the Shan/Lao/Thai chiefdoms. The other relationship is connected to maritime polities, and these have always stressed a wide range of commercial links. With the coming of Islam and the Christian and capitalist Europeans, the narrative began to shift. Faced with new protagonists, China was torn between adopting attitudes of passivity and permitting private entrepreneurship. That uncertainty about what to do left the initiative to those powers that were alert to what Southeast Asia could offer to an expanding economic system. The Chinese were thus poorly prepared for the onslaught when the European powers overwhelmed Southeast Asia during the 19th century.

Modern Chinese scholars acknowledge that imperial China adhered to a singular perspective about the south for most of its history. Even when the Manchu conquerors were aware of the European gunboats off the coast of southern China, they thought that Sinocentrism was the appropriate framework to confirm their legitimacy with their Han Chinese subjects. Sinocentrism reached its peak during the 18th century about the time when European empires became global.

After two revolutions during the 20th century, Chinese leaders no longer think only in Sinocentric terms. They know that a Eurocentric worldview is dominant and that even those who want a more genuine world history have yet to find a narrative that would replace it. Under the circumstances, it is not possible to see how, even with wealth and power shifting back to China, a new Sinocentrism towards the region can be justified. It would be more desirable for China and the region to its south to look afresh at their relationship in the larger global context.

The Sinocentric perspective reminds us that the process of becoming Chinese in the south is still work in progress. Until today, there are large numbers of peoples in China's southwest who remain wedded to their own ways distinct from the culture of the Han majority. Of course, with modern direct interventions from a powerful central government and the advantages of having a shared national identity, that process may be speeded up and those who still resist it may find it more difficult to do so. Whatever happens will be likely to affect the Sinocentric story. As Chinese historians confront other historical perspectives, the new story will surely have to be told differently.

THE REGION'S NORTHWARD PERSPECTIVE

Most Southeast Asian rulers through the centuries would have been familiar with the Sinocentric perspective if they paid it any attention at all. What was significant in modern times was that republican China in the 20th century seemed to find Sinocentrism useful as the basis of a nationalist narrative, and therefore a necessary part of national revival. That perspective remained central to the defense of a weak and divided China fighting Western power and the Japanese invasion of the 1930s. In Southeast Asia, nationalism also became the norm when new leaders admired Japan for its successes against the West. But most countries in the region were also conscious of the thousands if not millions of Chinese in their midst who were expected to subscribe to the Sinocentric perspective. They were taught to see Chinese history and culture only from within, as the starting-point from which to understand China's neighbours and to be used to explain what the western world had done, and was still doing, to China.

However, for Southeast Asians who were being educated at this time, they were also introduced to the history of their respective European rulers. That education helped them to reject the Chinese viewpoint by seeing that

Europeans had a totally different perspective. The latter was drawn from its own ancient origins in the Mediterranean. Although the Spanish, Dutch, British and French stressed very different factors in their respective national histories, their starting-points were always from within their countries before looking outwards. In short, the modern norm began with the national narrative and that took precedence over the economic, social and cultural institutions that many countries might believe they had in common.

It is true that, from an indigenous perspective, the region did not do much about recording the past. It is therefore not surprising that there are few references to relations with China. Throughout history, China's southern neighbours, except for the Vietnamese, countered any Sinocentric historical narrative largely with silence. There was no shared or sustained perspective towards China and very few local records extant could tell us what the southern neighbours thought of China. This shows that the Hindu-Buddhist and Islamic polities of Southeast Asia were content with economic relations but had no other interest in China. It also suggests that the powerful and prosperous empire to their north had little impact on their politics, society and culture.

Indirect material can be found in some Chinese reports that note what the native peoples thought about China's power and some of their experiences with Chinese officialdom. There are examples that mention wars and conflicts in which Chinese were involved — those that touch on changes in tribute-paying conditions, and others concerning culture-contacts with Chinese by people in the northern regions of Vietnam, Laos and Myanmar as well as some of the littoral kingdoms of the South China Sea. The first full Chinese account that has good examples is the *Man Shu* of Fan Zhuo, a record of the state of Nan Zhao in Yunnan and northern Burma in the 9th century. Another was Zhou Daguan's *Zhenla fengtuji* written four centuries later. There were others that have summaries or fragments of lost works that carried material on local thinking. But none can be said to represent the northward perspectives of China from the region, merely what Chinese officials thought were worth noting of some of their views.

Vietnam was exceptional. After a thousand years under Chinese administration, their historians were deeply influenced by Chinese records. After independence in the 10th century, they selected materials from early Chinese official accounts in order to recapture their ancient past. They re-interpreted Chinese accounts in distinctive ways wherever possible and also used that framework to account for their rulers' relations with China. Consequently, that provided the Vietnamese people with a proto-nationalist perspective not only about the Chinese empire but also a Vietnam-centric perspective of their southern neighbours. After the coming of the West, new narratives were introduced by Christian missionaries and French colonial historians. The Vietnam-centric view has now been replaced by modern nationalist historiography. Between the rejection of Sinocentrism and the adoption of nationalism, it is difficult to determine if there is an indigenous perspective.

As for Thai and Burmese court chronicles, references to China were largely limited to the intermittent official contacts that they had. In the Malayo-Javanese written records, it is remarkable how little has so far been found about relations with China, whether diplomatic or commercial. It is possible to speculate what the rulers and officials of these kingdoms might have thought of China. For example, reading Chinese records "against the grain", that is, by discarding Chinese viewpoints and interpretations and focusing on what the records tell us about local events and personalities, as some Southeast Asian historians have done with colonial records, is one way we might find glimpses of what northward perspectives might have been like. But it is unlikely that there will be a rich haul.

From the 16th century onwards, there are European historical notes that portray some of the experiences that Southeast Asian rulers and traders expected of the Chinese and these often included descriptions of how local protagonists dealt with Chinese merchants. But, on the whole, except for the relationship with Vietnam, it was rare to find imperial China directly present in the region. It was only during the 20th century, in part through the eyes of the Europeans, that different countries in the region each now have a northward perspective towards China. That is a start and a regional view will surely emerge in order that ASEAN can adjust fully to the rising power to its north. Although it is still work in progress, it is great leap from the centuries of silence that had been the norm.

MODERN PERSPECTIVES

A powerful perspective today comes from the narrative developed by the nation-states of the West that is being modified to provide a basis for writing world history. As has been shown above, China's southern neighbours do not have strong historical tradition with which to construct a distinctive view of their place in world history. They are, however, finding the national approach helpful to them for creating new vistas of the past. When they first encountered the call for "Christians and Gold" that inspired the Portuguese to trade and fight in Asia, that gave them a glimpse of a new worldview. The call came from a Europe-based knowledge system that produced a narrative that strengthened the confidence of the nation-states. When these national empires of Western Europe expanded their capitalist economies in the 19th century to become truly global, they shaped the new paradigm of universal history. The colonized Southeast Asians were soon made aware that this ideal of universal history was based on strong national narratives, notably those with French, German and Anglo-American imperial roots.

For new nation-states, this universal history founded on national histories is attractive. It has a historiographical pedigree traced back to the histories of Herodotus and Thucydides and the rich accounts of the Greek and Roman empires. Later on, the salvation faiths of the Jews, Christians and Muslims gave that history a linear and progressive time-line that provided post-Renaissance Europe with a master narrative, and this was adapted to serve the needs of the secular nation-state. Finally, the success of these modern states in defending their interests and expanding across the globe made the model irresistible to all those they conquered. This impact can be seen in the speed at which various Asian leaders used that framework to re-write their own histories. The Japanese had taken the lead in the late 19th century and they inspired the Chinese, Koreans and others to do the same, including the nationalists of the states in China's south.

Thus, when former colonies became new nations after the Second World War and emulated the states of the West, it is understandable why they adopted the master narrative that the West had brought with them to their shores. Two main strategies are now being used to firm up this narrative for the region, first by reading the colonial records, as I mentioned above, "against the grain" to reconstruct local history; secondly, by digging into each country's past for authentic traditions that could help define the modern nation. By doing this, their historians can also serve to re-interpret their relations with China. Two examples show how the re-interpretations can now influence future relations. One draws attention to China's traditional tributary system and treats it as an early muted form of imperialism. The hierarchical system used by Chinese emperors has been made to appear like imperial domination and used to foster alarm. The other is prompted by proponents of capitalism and private enterprise. They fear that an authoritarian Chinese state might become a successful model of state-sponsored capitalism. A strong and centralized state, reminiscent of the imperial Chinese bureaucratic state, could bring an end to what many believe has been the engine of progress in modern history.

The master narrative of world history is based on the sovereignty and legitimacy of nation-states. The origins of each state were traced back to the past to suggest that the state was destined to become the nation it is today. That approach draws on political judgments made to determine which parts of the past can be used to support the national ideal that is central to the country's survival. This approach can serve to bolster a people's sense of belonging and support the desire to be comfortable in a collective identity. When that is secured, nations can work together to support a global order to ensure peace and prosperity.

This nation-based narrative is indeed contrary to the Sinocentric perspective, but it is also one that promotes the modern Chinese nation-state and, in so doing, could bring about a revival of some degree of Sinocentrism. When nationalist leaders drew on the deep roots of Chinese history to construct their new narratives, especially when the Chinese people felt gravely threatened by Japanese invasion, some Sinocentric slogans were actively promoted. Members of the opposition Communist Party were initially drawn to an idealistic proletarian internationalism but even they accepted the nationalist programme to fight against the Japanese. After the communist victory in 1949, nationalism was officially rejected in favour of a global ideology, but the Maoist millenarian challenge to Soviet leadership also appealed to a strong pride in being Chinese. It was not until Deng Xiaoping returned to power in 1978 to rescue the Party from near destruction that all talk of revolutionary internationalism was finally abandoned. China began to take a fresh look at the national narrative as it seeks ways to re-design a new kind of multinational state.

Thus China and the countries to its south are at a new phase in their relationship. The nations of Southeast Asia have found a new basis for looking northwards. While adjusting to a China that is regaining its position as a modern and dynamic power, the countries in the region realize that a collective perspective common to all its members is invaluable. In turn, China has formally discarded the Sinocentric perspective and is finding its place in a world based on nation-states. In this new relationship, China has to adjust to the new lens that its neighbours are using and be alert for interpretations and representations that could lead to misunderstanding and strife. It is unclear how China and the region will see their role together in the new international world order, but it will help if they factor in the changing historical perspectives that both sides have experienced.

CHAPTER 8

THE SEARCH FOR FRIENDS*

The remarkable record of China's economic development during the past two decades has created a new role for China to play in the 21st century. By any standards, the transition from a centrally planned system to one that encourages private enterprise is extraordinary and, compared with the madness of the Great Proletarian Cultural Revolution, what happened was incredible. As a result, the region in particular, and the world in general, are looking at China as a future great power.

All sorts of projections have been made about when, and not if, China will be the dominant power in East and Southeast Asia. These projections have led to prominence being given to the issue of China as a potential threat to its neighbours, as a regional hegemon, as a possible expansionist empire. This has cast a shadow on China's role in the region and is likely to influence the way the Chinese themselves see that role in a suspicious if not hostile world. Given the strength of this perception of China, it would be realistic to tackle the subject directly. I propose to do so by focusing on firstly, the external perspective of the China threat and then, on how China sees itself, especially in the context of being regarded as a threat. Both have a vital bearing on the role China is likely to play in the 21st century.

I shall approach China's own perspective from different angles. The two questions I will ask in this connection are: Will China see its role in terms of a nation-state in a world of nation-states, and use its emerging power as an extra-large nation-state? How will China's cultural heritage be revived or

---

*This article was first published as *China's Place in the Region: The Search for Allies and Friends*, The 1997 Panglaykim Memorial Lecture, Center for Strategic and International Studies, Jakarta, 1997.

transformed to meet the new threat projections, and what impact would that have on China's place in the region?

THE CHINA THREAT

First, the external perspectives of the China threat. There are several major reasons for seeing China as a threat. One is based on a reading of China's history as a dominant empire in Asia. Another is based on estimates of the wealth and power that China will wield if its economic development continues. Others are concerned with the two questions I asked about how China sees itself, and I will deal with that later.

A recurring theme is the restoration of China's traditional tributary system in the region, albeit in modern guise. It suggests that the fear of China stems from a reading of Chinese history. This leads us to ask, What is the evidence for an expansionist China during the three millennia of formation, establishment and consolidation of the empire? What is the function of the tributary system that has led it to be seen as the basis of a "Chinese world order"?

During the first two millennia to the 10th century A.D., there were two distinctive developments. The northern and western borders were porous and virtually indefensible. A movable frontier divided the sedentary agricultural regions of the Yellow River valley from the steppe lands of the nomadic tribes. Eastwards and southwards, there was room for expansion towards the sea. That expansion had begun with trade, but state formation during the first millennium, B.C., led to continuous internal conflict that lasted for at least 300 years and ended with the unification of all the Warring States of North and Central China by the Qin empire in the 3rd century, B.C. The conquest of South China was part of the momentum of Qin armies marching into the territories of the very large Chu state to its south. But once the imperial armies reached the coast, the expansion stopped.

After that, the peoples in southern China were gradually sinicised through trading relations and Han Chinese migrations. The migrations were stimulated in part by foreign nomadic invasions of the North China plains and the economic disruptions that ensued. Independent "empires" in the south flourished and trade with foreign kingdoms was highly developed, including diplomatic and naval visitations. The Chinese described these largely trading relationships in terms of a feudal rhetoric of gifts and exchanges which evolved into a tributary system. The system was very much the projection of a continental mentality that anchored itself to deal with northern enemies and remained uninterested in maritime ventures. During the Tang dynasty (618–907), southern China had become an integral part of Chinese civilisation. But there was no expansion of territory southwards. If anything, China lost territory when Vietnam detached itself to become an independent empire during the 10th century.

During the last thousand years, from the 11th to the 20th century, China has been on the whole defensive, constrained and inward-looking. For 350 of those years, China was wholly conquered by northern nomadic tribal confederations, that of the Mongols and then, after a break of 276 years, that of the Manchus. And for more than 500 years, the northern half of China was never free from non-Han Chinese rule. During the Qing dynasty (1644–1911), the land borders were extended, but largely into areas which had previously been inside, or on the landward peripheries of, earlier Chinese dynasties. Notably, there were conquests in Mongolia and Xinjiang. This was partly in response to Russian advances into Central Asia and Siberia, and partly defensive efforts to strengthen the less stable borders in the north and west. Less direct were the claims to suzerainty over Tibet, but these claims were consolidated in the 18th century. Elsewhere, the borders were pushed south into Yunnan during the Yuan (1279–1368) and the Ming (1368–1644) dynasties, and, in view of the anti-Manchu threat from Zheng Chenggong (better known as Koxinga), the Qing extended its rule across the Straits to Taiwan in the 17th century.

Throughout the period, all foreign relations were conducted through the tributary system, which remained useful as a means for both controlling foreign trade and ensuring minimum security on the borders. The system was never used for territorial expansion, only for extending influence and affirming China's interpretation of its central place in the universe. The system provided one of the ways of reminding China's neighbours of its view of its own centrality. In essence, the system was used to stabilise the status quo. This was particularly true for the coastal regions where there had never been any serious threats to the empire, and was the key to the special relationship between China and both Vietnam and Korea. But despite the long history of that relationship, today's China has accepted the independence of both those countries, following brief periods when Korea was part of the Japanese empire, and Vietnam part of the French empire. In addition, the PRC has acknowledged the independence of the Mongolian republic.

During the 19th century, China's borders actually shrank in Mongolia, Manchuria, and Xinjiang. Largely due to defeats in war, China lost territory to Russia; also, in 1895, the defeat by Japan (followed soon after by Japan's victory over Russia in 1904) weakened China's position much further. China continued to be divided and weak until the reunification in 1949 and the establishment of the People's Republic. With the exception of Mongolia, the borders were similar to those of the Qing empire. Hong Kong has now been returned to China and Macau will follow suit in 1999.

The only outstanding issues within China's borders are,

(a) Taiwan: this could be described as a leftover from the Civil War, but it is a critical problem for China. It is a residual question of reunification, but because of some 48 years of division, the subject has far-reaching ramifications involving China's international relations with the U.S. as well as Japan.

(b) Tibet: this is not a matter so much of disputed territory as a question of minority rights. It is likely to continue to be a cultural and moral dilemma for China, but it is not a question of expansion outside accepted Chinese borders.

In short, Chinese history does not provide any convincing argument for an expansionist China. References to a return to some sort of tributary system not only misrepresent the system to imply dominance and potential expansionism, but are also totally anachronistic. The world has changed enormously. Given the international system of nation-states and the interdependent networks of a market economy, any return to a system largely based on feudalistic relationships simply will not be acceptable, not even to the Chinese.

However, there are new issues, all involving maritime disputes, something traditional China has never been interested in the past. I refer to the disputes over the Paracels, the Spratlys and the Diaoyutai islands in the South and East

China Seas. This new interest in the sea stems from the painful lessons learnt from having neglected coastal and ocean-going matters for centuries, neglect which resulted in China's defeat by the British in the Opium Wars and the century of humiliation which followed. Any consideration of these new disputes should take into account that the issues have no precedents in Chinese history. They are modern problems of international relations, and China must deal with them in terms acceptable to the rest of the world.

The Diaoyutai protests in 1972 and in 1996 show how easily this issue can be contained if both China and Japan want to do so. It is not itself of importance and would only surface if other much more substantial matters cause Sino-Japanese relations to break down. Similarly with the Paracels, which is a residual dispute which China and Vietnam could sort out without disrupting regional relationships. Calls for the United States, or Japan, or the Association of Southeast Asian Nations (ASEAN), to take vigorous action against China because Vietnam must be right and China must be wrong would be counter-productive.

As for the Spratlys, there are genuine disputes here. This is the most sensitive matter for China's relations with Southeast Asia. The point here is that, in terms of disputed territory, the Spratlys is the only one which is serious, and on which there is no agreement about the claims made. None of the claimants have convincing cases that have been confirmed by historical records or by international courts. Hence the uncertainty, and the need for careful negotiations among those directly involved about each individual claim. If badly handled, these could strain relations in the region, but the disputes in themselves do not represent any threat against any of China's neighbours. If, however, outside powers decide unilaterally that other claimants have better claims and try to interfere on their behalf against China, that would raise the stakes considerably. Anything that looks like a strategic ganging up against China would seriously destabilise the region.

WEALTH AND POWER

The second reason why there are perceptions of a future China Threat stems from estimates of the wealth and power that China will wield if its economic development continues. Will economic growth lead China to become the world's largest economy, from no. 3 to no. 1, sometime towards the middle of the 21st century?

The projections that point to this are misleading. They fail to highlight the enormous problems the country faces in trying to straddle a Leninist political structure and a market economy at the same time. The great inequalities in income and the uneven distribution of wealth and development across the vast country are well-documented. There is considerable unemployment or under-employment, and many bottlenecks in the economy which are vulnerable, espe-cially structural reforms pertaining to the state-owned enterprises. The country will continue to depend on large inflows of foreign direct investment (especially from HK and Taiwan). It will also increasingly be open to uncertainties on China's borders, including many matters that are beyond its control.

There is therefore every reason for China to be extremely careful about preserving favourable conditions for economic growth — and this means ensuring a peaceful environment as long as possible. That same environment would also mean that China's neighbours will be able to enjoy opportunities to develop strongly, and keep up with China's economic growth. If the rela-tivities remain about the same, there will be less reason for conflicts to occur. This is a very big "if", but it has more to do with good management both in China and among its neighbours and a Chinese leadership that is prepared to go through further reforms, and very little to do with China being a threat to its neighbours.

What about the military buildup, the modernization of the People's Liberation Army? All studies show rapid growth in the military budget and the updating of defensive hardware has been going apace. In addition, there has been continuous upgrading of skills and training. Of course this had all begun from a low base, especially if we note that the PLA still has mostly outdated military equipment and weaponry.

This matter obviously needs continuous monitoring, but nothing has been alarming to the neighbourhood so far largely because of overwhelming U.S. military superiority and the continued U.S. presence in the Asia-Pacific region. Obviously, all countries must look to their defences and do everything they can to ensure security. If everyone did so in a more or less open manner, including China, and recent trends point in that direction, it would reduce unnecessary fear and anxiety, and thus ultimately lower the risks of open conflict.

I do not want to over-simplify here. There are potential areas of tension in the relations between China and its neighbours, and between China and the U.S. There will always be the need for vigilance. But an arms race accompanied by belligerent or alarmist rhetoric is not the solution. In the region itself, the institutions that have been created by ASEAN, notably the ASEAN Regional Forum, are good examples of what can be done to reduce misunderstandings. The APEC Forum can also serve as another means of promoting relationships that encourage mutual respect and exchange of sensitive and strategic information.

No less important are regular contacts between China and powers like the United States and Japan, and also between China and neighbours like India, Russia, and the Muslim states in Central Asia. If the European Union, or at least some of its major member-states, also increase their involvement in Asian development, the involvement of a larger number of long-distance and international players would greatly strengthen the security networks which the region is building up. The use of multilateral linkages that are built upon the system of nation-states accepted by most countries would ease the burdens that the U.S. has had to carry, and it would do so in a way that does not threaten any single country.

A NORMAL NATION-STATE

Let me turn to the question of how China sees itself. Will China use its emerging power as an extra-large and domineering nation-state to threaten other nation-states?

China has often been accused of not behaving as a normal nation-state and has been described as a Civilization-State. What does this mean? Old Confucian imperial states were based on the idea of a universal ideology and a high degree of cultural homogeneity — and there was a unique mixture of Confucianism, Buddhism and Taoism for the majority, which is not true for at least provinces like Tibet, Qinghai, Xinjiang, Ningxia, and Inner Mongolia. Using that traditional way of defining the civilization, that majority mix of moral and religious values and social institutions should make Korean and Vietnamese cultures more in common with those of Han China than those of some border provinces.

The present leaders are not influenced by such a view. We have seen official Confucianism rejected after the May Fourth Movement that started in 1919. During the first three decades of the PRC, both Buddhism and Taoism were also rejected. There was almost nothing from ancient Chinese civilization that the Maoist revolutionary government would accept. In recent years, however, there is evidence that, by turning away from an earlier internationalism (as represented by the Communist International), even the communist theorists have agreed that modern nationalism is once again a powerful force to be reckoned with and one that can be useful to China.

How does an imperial state become a nation-state? The modern nation-state spread widely from western Europe and became the political form which all former European colonies chose to emulate. Even non-colonies in Asia like Japan, Thailand and Iran, late in the 19th century, accepted that the modern world would have to be based on nation-states. But not all countries or former colonies are natural nation-states. A most important exception, for example, was India. When it became independent, it was clear that, if nations were defined narrowly as in most of Europe, India was really a state of many possible nations, something like a multinational state.

Modern China inherited a deep-rooted empire in which an agrarian Han majority lived for centuries with scores of nomadic peoples, hill tribes and forest minorities. Over the centuries, the Han had increased enormously in numbers, while the minority groups strengthened their various homelands. In this way, the transformation into a republic made 20th century China like another kind of multinational state. This China is not like the Union of India which behaves almost like a federal state, with the centre retaining considerable reserve powers to intervene. China, on the other hand, preserved the highly centralised state that had always sought to control everything within its borders. After Deng Xiaoping introduced his economic reforms in the late 1970s, this position has undergone major changes. Centralisation has been much weakened. The complex centre-provinces relationships may appear familiar, but they are very subtle and multi-layered. They are not dependent on legal and constitutional definitions but partly on communist party discipline and partly on personal and informal linkages. The relationships are still evolving and may change and take different shapes in different parts of the country.

Would a federal structure for such a large country work better? Is there any prospect for federalism? Official and formal federalism is out of the question. It goes too much against the grain, against at least two thousand years of history. But something like the kinds of compromise necessary to facilitate local and provincial decision-making, especially where it concerns wealth-production, seem definitely practicable. The political and administrative ramifications of these developments are still unfolding. One thing appears certain. They are not pointing to an imminent break-up of China, as in the Soviet Union, nor to a new era of warlordism. This is important given China's future place in the region.

What about nationalism as a force for nation-building? There has recently been a rash of writings that refer to a new spirit of "nationalism" that is readily replacing communism among some people. Given the conditions of relative openness to the world, of rapid change within Chinese society, as well as of severe economic restructuring, this is not difficult to understand. The lack of strong idealism and the loss of the earlier ideological underpinnings have led to anxiety, even fear. And, for those who are not adapting to the new competitive market system, the uncertainty may be even greater. Nevertheless, it is debatable if the new nationalism is aroused by internal factors. The most popular books that seek to represent the neo-nationalism are more concerned that China is once again being bullied by a foreign power, in this case, the United States. It is doubtful if they genuinely reflect popular feelings today, but if there should be evidence of unjustified foreign hostility towards China, this nationalism would certainly become an important factor in future policy-making by PRC leaders.

We would expect such nationalist awareness to produce growing interest in the sort of nation that China is going to become. The dominance of the Han majority (well over 90% of the total population) is clear. But the PRC has always claimed to have policies that respect the minorities. Officially, there are

55 minority groups. In the constitution, different levels of autonomous entities and administrations have been established. There is no assimilation policy, even though minority children are expected to learn the Chinese language and are largely taught with Chinese as the medium of instruction at the secondary and tertiary levels. Thus, in practice, China is a kind of multicultural, multilinguistic, and multinational country. Any further development of modern nationalism will have to take this into account, and guard against it becoming a source of conflict and instability between the majority and minority peoples.

The most testing case for the PRC has already raised its head. Xinjiang is the most sensitive border province because of the volatility of the Central Asian Muslim republics that have become independent from Russia. The Uighurs there not only share a common history and culture with the neighbouring Turkic-speaking countries, but also have in Islam a universal and all-embracing faith. The religion does not stop at the Xinjiang border, nor is it likely to allow its believers to be content to be marginal Chinese. It is here that nationalism acts as a double-edged sword. How Beijing's Han Chinese leaders can pacify their Xinjiang minorities and win them to a commitment towards China will be a major test of whether the modern nationalism of a normal nation-state is viable in China as a unifying rather than a divisive force.

Finally a brief word about restoring all of China's territories. This has been focused on Hong Kong for the past decade and a half and Macau is next. Hong Kong is the first place where restoration to China has been peacefully negotiated. That should have an impact on future negotiations over Taiwan, the last area awaiting restoration. But Taiwan is a much more complicated issue that needs a long-term view. Its integration with the mainland certainly cannot be rushed. On the other hand, there are great dangers here, perhaps as much arising from political pressures within Taipei as with countervailing forces in Beijing. And the international dimension involving the U.S. and Japan can never be ignored. There is much room for miscalculation, especially if emotional forces play their part in factional politics and in the formation of Chinese policy on Taiwan.

Possibly the most difficult, however, would be the question of Taiwanese nationalism and a future nation-state in Taiwan. This would conflict directly with the historical heritage that stresses ethnicity and civilizational identity. The idea of a modern Taiwan nation combined with the national minorities question would greatly trouble China's progress towards a nation-state. Intractable problems like these will drive the Chinese leaders back to a greater emphasis on the supremacy of the state in a multinational China. Early this century, both Guomindang and Communist leaders had discovered the power of the modern national state. Facing the problem of Taiwan, the government in Beijing will seek to restore more of the central power that it had had during its first three decades. A country in which the state takes such precedence would be a serious constraint for any liberal and democratic urges that its peoples may have. In this context, the issue of Taiwan and what it stands for is not only one of reunification with or without the use of force. It also has the potential to challenge the very self-image of China as a modern nation-state and stir up forces which would be difficult for Beijing to control.

THE CULTURAL HERITAGE

Let me now turn to the second of the ways that China sees itself. I have asked the question, how will China's cultural heritage be revived or transformed to meet the new threat perceptions, either of threat by China or threat to China? What impact would that heritage have on allies and friends?

The background is clear. The years of reform have been astonishingly successful. There is now the likelihood of significant cultural change. This includes both a readiness to learn from the capitalist world and a return to respect for Chinese history and China's past achievements. Between restoration and revolution, the former dominates the policies and goals today. Beneath the rhetoric, a deeper and more permanent revolution in values is taking place. If that, however, is not encumbered by visions of future threats by powerful neighbours or clusters of neighbours, it is likely to be an irreversible set of changes.

The lack of a strong and unified ideology may be a weakness in a society accustomed to having one, but such a lack is a refreshing change and may also be a blessing. What would cause concern is for the Chinese people to go on for much longer without a cultural core, a system of moral values which they could all identify with. On the surface, there is intense debate among those torn between those who are still true to socialism and those who are ready to go the whole way with capitalism. But, of increasing interest is the way a mix of moral-spiritual and materialist values rooted within China is being pit against a set of foreign but modern values which have begun to attract general and intellectual appreciation.

For all the talk about Confucianism recovering part of its traditional position as a state ideology, wide acceptance of such a development by the Chinese people is unlikely, if not impossible. Large numbers of people are seeking a personal autonomy to find and practise their own faith, including millions of those who have rediscovered Buddhism and Taoism, or are practising Muslims. The small Christian congregations in China may never match the other groupings in size and distribution, but the intensity of faith that they represent will serve as a reminder that there are alternative world-views outside China which deserve respect. Among them are those who have also found the austere and demanding Confucian ideals surprisingly satisfactory at a personal level. Increasingly, these practices and ideals will find genuine religious or semi-religious expression, and restore a more spiritual life to individuals and their families than has been possible for decades.

It has been reported that, without a moral core in a society that is changing rapidly in uncertain directions, there is some nostalgia for Mao Zedong. There are even mentions of Neo-Maoism. But such desultory and scattered nostalgia for a Maoist past is superficial, more pathetic than giving cause for alarm. Without a similar Mao-like or Deng-like leader today, the new leaders have to adjust to more mundane changes, especially those demanded of them by the sustained evolution of the market economy. At best, they will try to keep as much of the present forms and structures as long as possible, and gradually jettison those that are no longer effective. If they fail to do the latter when developments require them to, it could lead to an erosion of credibility and moral authority and that would seriously undermine the role that China hopes eventually to play.

The combined force of liberal democracy and modern nationalism could make a contribution to the new set of cultural norms. The former could in time moderate the possible excesses of the latter, while nationalism could give liberal democracy more vigour and a more focused sense of direction. Has this form of democracy got a chance in China? All the evidence suggests that it does not, at least not for a long time. The often-mentioned reason for this is that the present leaders want to stay on in power, and liberal democracy is dangerous to them. What has not been given enough weight is the view that a poor developing country of this size, with the largest population in the world, cannot afford a risky experiment in the midst of one of the most remarkable transformations in modern history. And, there is also the view that good government by strong leaders is more important for rapid economic development. Many countries in Asia attest to this conclusion, although there are many negative examples of strong leaders leading bad governments. Nevertheless, there is greater freedom in China today, not only in business and competition, but also in discourse and learning, than anyone could have expected two decades ago. That freedom, taken together with greater economic development, offers an alternative route to cultural change. Whether or not that change will shape a new and distinctive role for China to play in the 21st century will depend on how it is used to create a new world of allies and friends.

CHINA IN THE REGION

There are norms and rules governing the idea of allies and friends in political relationships. The Chinese understand from their history that alliances and friendships between polities do require degrees of cultural harmony. These are likely to be more precarious when there is cultural dissonance. Many countries in Asia are increasingly conscious that the norms of behaviour and discourse in such relationships today have been established by the West. These norms come from a distinct political culture that was evolved in Europe from a particular state-system. The system was then spread around the world by the aggressive and expansionist power of 19th century Western civilisation.

I have suggested earlier that China understands and accepts these norms as a means to protect its sovereignty and national integrity. It has tried to model its international behaviour on the Great Powers and has moved away from the hierarchical view that underlies the tributary relationships of the past. But the state-system of the Great Powers has itself been evolving. International relations theory changes with new realities. Most recently, the end of the Cold War has removed what had been the central balance managed by two superpowers. China has been deeply affected by this change, especially by the idea that the world will be dominated by, if not dependent on, one superpower, the United States. They are reminded from their own history that, when many states struggle for power and wealth, one must guard against a hegemon emerging to dominate all the others. They are not sure that the present situation is analogous to the past, but they have found the idea helpful in their own analysis of future relations with the United States.

The Chinese had enjoyed the happy years of the 1980s before the Tiananmen tragedy of 1989, when relations between China and the United States could not have been better. The Chinese leaders were bewildered when American public opinion turned hostile because of their use of the People's Liberation Army against unarmed students in order to restore order. While the leaders recognise the tragedy as a setback, they see it as largely a temporary failure in good management. Lessons have been learnt and the mistake is not to be repeated. They are, therefore, genuinely surprised at how unforgiving some influential American leaders have been about this whole matter.

Many Chinese leaders now think that this change in attitude towards China is really part of a grand strategy to keep China poor and destabilised in order to preserve U.S. dominance in Asia. They do not always accept that the U.S. does not need to do that to remain preeminent in the region. Their understanding of the modern state-system recognises that, in a world that is getting smaller and more interdependent, there are informal empires of clients, satellites and dependencies that are bound together by the superior forces of modern communications technology. Some Chinese are inclined to believe that the U.S. will try to consolidate alliances along such lines. And it will take time for them to reassure themselves that such a system will not end with China being bounded by a chain of countries that are allied and friendly to a hostile power.

To most Chinese leaders, it is a measure of a world at disequilibrium if China does not have a place of respect commensurate with its size and history.

After years of ideological correctness, China now has a pragmatic and flexible approach in its relations with its neighbours. Today, the most important goal of China's foreign policy in the region is to make friends and find real allies there. If they can do so while continuing with its successful economic reforms, this would be ideal. If they can do so without incurring United States suspicion that China seeks to replace them as the dominant regional power, that would be even better.

Thus the priorities are clear: economic growth and political stability within the country would provide the foundations for secure borders and stable relationships with China's neighbours. Three of the danger points are obvious: attempts to internationalise the Taiwan question; the Korean peninsula and the uncertain outcome of any attempt at reunification; and any effort to exploit differences between China and the ASEAN states. With each of them, the respective roles of the United States and Japan have been given maximum attention.

Let me quickly examine these points before I conclude. I have already mentioned the Taiwan issue in the context of the China threat to peace in the region. No less significant is the threat to the sovereignty and integrity of China if powers like the United States and Japan intervene either directly or indirectly in Taiwan's active quest for international space. It would be dangerous to underestimate how much external interference could threaten regional stability here. Despite the protestations of both the U.S. and Japan that their defence arrangements are not intended to apply to the Taiwan area, the Chinese remain convinced that the arrangements will spill over easily. If it does, it will disrupt efforts to keep the issue as one between two sets of Chinese political actors.

As for the Korean peninsula, China has maintained a subdued presence. Considering how close both protagonists are to China, and not only territorially, you may find it surprising that China has not been more active in reducing tension between the two. The situation is, however, full of contradictions for China. It had fought in the Korean War and sided fully with the north for nearly 30 years. It then turned to the south for close economic relations and abandoned the closed door approach that the north still insists on. Its position is so delicate that the diplomatic skill required of China is extremely demanding. If anything, it demonstrates that when China needs to focus its mind, it can do so with great sensitivity. Whether this is due more to a traditional appreciation of the Sino-Korean relationship, or whether it is evidence of the Chinese mastery of modern state-system diplomacy, is difficult to determine at this stage. The subtlety of the methods employed to avoid tension and conflict points to two things. China has a keen sense of danger to its borders and its security. It also has the will to tread warily in the search for long-term and peaceful solutions to intractable problems.

China's ability to cooperate with all the powers concerned suggests that China's recent diplomatic activities in Southeast Asia could develop along the same lines. If it continues to act with great attention to international niceties, this will help China to win friends and allies in the region. Already, its performance at APEC and ASEAN Regional Forum (ARF) meetings has quietened many of its strongest critics. As for bilateral relations with each country, there are reports that the Chinese have shown sensitivity in dealing with matters pertaining to sovereignty and cultural dignity. If this sensitivity persists, it suggests that China will be willing to commit itself to support and strengthen the international norms laid down by the modern state-system, and contribute to the adaptation of that system to regional conditions.

China will always be large and potentially rich and powerful. Therefore, its neighbours would need to construct the necessary checks and balances to ensure mutual respect. They have shown that the best way to do so is by engaging China as much as possible in a whole range of regional activity. And participation together with ASEAN in extra-regional matters involving the Western Pacific, or the rest of Asia, or Europe, or the Americas, seems to be paying off. ASEAN member states are now in a position to play a role in easing the much more difficult relationships that China has with the United States and Japan. They also seem to realise that it is in their interest to do so. If successful, it would help China to accept the parameters of the international system and encourage it to play an even larger and more positive part in world affairs.

CHAPTER 9

NEW BEGINNINGS IN SOUTHEAST ASIA*

At the outset of the 21st century, Southeast Asia's relations with China appear to be the best in at least half a century. In some countries, "China fever" seems to be replacing "China fear" and many look forward to the new "strategic partnership" and Free Trade Area being forged between China and ASEAN. Although this turn of events is significant, future relationships do not depend only on contemporary developments, but they must also be placed in the larger historical context.

On the surface, China's relations with the region's new nations have been totally transformed since the end of the Second World War. Two thousand years of history, however, have established a deeply ingrained pattern that it would be difficult to dismiss as irrelevant. During most of that time, Southeast Asia was part of China's larger circle of relationships, especially those of trade and tribute zones divided between polities that sent their envoys by sea and those that did so overland. Even that division fails to capture the differences between the lands that bordered South China from the Han dynasty and those that came into China's ken much later on. For example, the areas that became Vietnam had a different relationship with China from states like Burma and Laos which became neighbours only after Yunnan was made a province of the empire more than a thousand years later.[1] As for the maritime

---

*This article was first published as "China and Southeast Asia: The Context of a New Beginning", in *Power Shift: China and Asia's New Dynamics*, edited by David Shambaugh, (c) 2006 by the Regents of the University of California, Berkeley: University of California Press, 2006, pp. 187–204.
[1] This contrast becomes clear during the Ming dynasty (1368–1644). Wang Gungwu, "Early Ming Relations with Southeast Asia: a background essay", in John K. Fairbank

port kingdoms of Southeast Asia, the Chinese rarely differentiated them from those in what we would today call East Asia and South Asia. Up until the 19th century, many Chinese mandarins subscribed to the view that there existed an East-West division, with the Philippines, Borneo and the islands east of Java part of the "Eastern Ocean", and the rest of the Malay Archipelago part of the "Western Ocean", a geographical concept that encompassed not only the lands of the Indian Ocean to the Red Sea but also, between the 16th and 19th centuries, the European kingdoms of the Atlantic coasts. Also, in contrast with overland relations, which were invariably linked with political and territorial tensions, relationships with the seafaring peoples to the southeast were focused on trade and considered on the whole unthreatening before the 19th century.[2]

Much of the political landscape was changed during the 20th century. But the shadow of what had been a tributary system remained a long one, one that has often been anachronistically interpreted as a kind of imperial dominance comparable to the modern phenomenon. When Western powers began to decolonize after the Japanese had failed to build its Co-Prosperity Sphere in Southeast Asia, it coincided with the near unification of China by the Chinese Communist Party in 1949. The spectre of future Chinese dominance after the West retreated was raised in the larger context of the Cold War. John King Fairbank even spoke of a "Chinese World Order" although he stressed what was relatively benign and defensive in his description of that network of "feudal" relationships.[3] Others, however, portrayed that prospect as similar to Western imperialism and this interpretation was used by many Western

---

(ed.) *The Chinese World Order: Traditional China's Foreign Relations.* (Cambridge, MA: Harvard University Press, 1968), pp. 34–62, 293–299; and "Ming Foreign Relations: Southeast Asia", in Denis Twitchett and Frederick W. Mote (eds.) *The Cambridge History of China, Volume 8. The Ming Dynasty, 1368–1644, Part 2.* (Cambridge: Cambridge University Press, 1998), pp. 301–332.

[2] The distinction was systematically employed after the 16th century, Zhang Xie, *Dong Xi yang kao* (On the Eastern and Western Oceans). Preface 1618. (Beijing: Zhonghua shuju, 1981). The contrast with overland relations is brought out sharply in essays by Joseph F. Fletcher in Fairbank, *Chinese World Order*, pp. 206–224; and Morris Rossabi in *Cambridge History, Ming Dynasty*, pp. 221–271.

[3] Fairbank, *Chinese World Order*, pp. 1–19.

analysts and Southeast Asian leaders in their anti-communist propaganda from the 1950s until the 1990s.

Recent changes have eased concerns about the future of China's policy but they have not erased the memories of Cold War propaganda.[4] A major question is, how much weight should now be given to the facts of geography and the heritage of history. In that context, China's perspectives of the region as unintegrated but broadly divided into three parts remains important: namely, Vietnam and its immediate neighbours, Myanmar bordering the strategic Chinese province of Yunnan and the Tibetan world, and the fluid and changeable formations among the maritime states.[5] In describing Southeast Asia holistically, China's relations with the postcolonial nations could be regarded as a new beginning. There was one exception. China had a relationship with Thailand that was adjusted from the ancient one whereby the kingdom of Siam dealt with a Confucian state, to one that became, from 1912 to 1949, a modern diplomatic relationship with Republican China. This fact of Thailand's independence throughout the colonial period has helped to make the country a pivot for Southeast Asia in the strategic thinking of China and countries like the United States and Japan, that would like to limit China's influence in the region.[6] As for the other nine countries in

---

[4] These concerns are addressed in the essays by Robert Sutter; Zhang Yunling and Tang Shiping; and Bates Gill in David Shanbaugh (ed.), *Power Shift: China and Asia's New Dynamics.* (Berkeley: University of California Press, 2005), pp. 289–305; pp. 48–68; and pp. 247–265.

[5] First, Vietnam and the ancient kingdoms of the Cham and the Khmer peoples now within the modern states of Vietnam, Cambodia and Central Thailand. It would include some of the inland kingdoms that now form the states of Laos and northern Thailand. Second, Myanmar and the lands straddling Southwest China (Yunnan and eastern Tibet) and India, where many speakers of Thai and Tibeto-Burman languages now live. Third, the island world of the speakers of Austronesian languages related to Malay that extend from Taiwan to the northern tip of Sumatra, and to the eastern end of the Philippines and parts of New Guinea. On the mainland, this includes the whole length of the Malay Peninsula.

[6] The two research reports by Khien Theeravit draw interesting comparisons after the Vietnam War: *Japan in Thai Perspective* and *China in Thai Perspective.* (Bangkok: Chulalongkorn Asian Studies Monographs, nos. 26 and 27, 1980). More details about the changing course of the China connection is given in R.K. Jain (ed.) *China and Thailand, 1949–1983* (London: Sangam, 1987). A more recent review that brings out Thailand's central position is Gerrit W. Gong (ed.) *Southeast Asia's*

Southeast Asia, China has had to face the products of colonial state-build-ing, new countries that the Spanish, Dutch, British, French and Americans had done much to transform en route to modernity.[7] The British and French tried to do even more to protect their interests when they returned to their colonies in 1945 after three and a half years of Japanese occupation, but the end of their rule was never in doubt. China, however, was in no position to take advantage of their withdrawal. For one thing, as the strug-gling government in Nanjing prepared for the new states to emerge from the decolonisation process, it had to face a bitter civil war. No sustained diplomatic negotiation was possible and by 1949 a revolutionary regime was established in Beijing under the shadow of an internationalist commu-nist order.[8]

As a result, decolonisation in Southeast Asia became less one of local nationalist leaders determining the kind of nations they wanted and more one of finding out which set of powers these leaders could count on to enable them to establish independent sovereign states. In the developments that followed, China could only play a subordinate and marginal part. The Nationalist government, first in Nanjing, then in Taipei, was more concerned with its legitimacy and concentrated on asking all compatriots in the region to confirm their loyalty to China. The new communist

---

Changing Landscape: Implications for U.S.-Japan Relations on the Eve of the Twenty-first Century (Washington D.C.: Center for Strategic and International Studies, 1999), pp. 29–38; 67–82.

[7] The limits to state-building and decolonization are closely examined in Marc Frey, Ronald W. Pruessen, and Tan Tai Yong (eds.) *The Transformation of Southeast Asia: International Perspective on Decolonization* (Armonk, N.Y.: M.E. Sharpe, 2003), essays by Hugues Tertrais, Karl Hack and Robert J McMahon, pp. 80–82, 122–126 and 213–225.

[8] Diplomatic relations were established early with countries that either considered themselves neutral and refused to take sides between the Western allies and the Soviet bloc, like Indonesia (1950) and Myanmar (1950), or who needed comradely sup-port, like the Vietnamese government of Ho Chi Minh (1950). When Thailand and the Philippines did not follow suit, that laid the foundations for a tense superpower rivalry for the next two decades. A valuable contemporary record is George McT, Kahin (ed.) *Governments and Politics in Southeast Asia* (Ithaca, N.Y.: Cornell University Press, 1959). A longer view is outlined in C.P. FitzGerald, *China and Southeast Asia since 1945* (Camberwell, Vic: Longman, 1973).

government in Beijing countered this policy by encouraging these same overseas Chinese to support the forces of anti-colonialism and work against the representatives of Western imperialism. Beijing's policy was actually counter-productive and ultimately contributed little to the shape of the new regional system now emerging. The mixed experiences of the nine new countries (apart from Thailand), whether communist, capitalist, or neutralist, have left their legacy. Although they all looked to the system of United Nations-based states, they found that the system by itself was inadequate to protect their new-won sovereignty. They all needed powerful allies in an unstable and volatile world. This was also true for the regimes in Beijing and Taipei for whom sovereignty was no less insecure in the midst of superpower rivalry.[9] By 1975, the Vietnam War had demonstrated that fresh diplomatic starts were necessary for all.

China's adjustments to the changing circumstances of the 1970s did not evoke the same responses from the ten Southeast Asian states. It is, therefore, still useful to recall the older relationships between China and its overland neighbours and those across the South China Sea. On land, the Chinese state had consolidated its power along the borders of Yunnan province, putting great pressure on the kingdoms of Burma and Vietnam during the 18th and 19th centuries.[10] Elsewhere, however, China was relatively passive. Its coastal defence forces had been adequate only for dealing with local piracy. In its

---

[9] All post-colonial states were left with untidy boundaries and multiple ethnic communities and many in Southeast Asia had to fight territorial claims from neighbours and secessionist groups as soon as the colonial powers departed, for example, between Malaysia and the Philippines, Thailand and Cambodia, China and Myanmar and various claims in the South China Sea. The initial faith in post-Westphalian ideals has been diluted by many new challenges, not least the pressures of economic globalization. There is renewed interest in the region in the new efforts to re-examine the concept itself: see Stephen D. Krasner (ed.) *Problematic Sovereignty: contested rules and political possibilities* (New York: Columbia University Press, 2001) and Daniel Philpott. *Revolutions in Sovereignty: how ideas shaped modern international relations* (Princeton: Princeton University Press, 2001).

[10] Trung Buu Lam, "Intervention versus Tribute in Sino-Vietnamese Relations, 1788–1790", in Fairbank, *Chinese World Order*, pp. 165–179; G.H. Luce, "Chinese Invasions of Burma in the Eighteenth Century", *Journal of the Burma Research Society*, vol. xv (1925), pp. 115–128.

trading relations, it was often the littoral states from Japan to the Indian Ocean that took the initiative. Foreign ships had come to China for over a thousand years before enterprising Chinese began to extend the trade for themselves. Official policy required that trade be conducted behind a framework based on tribute and security concerns, but enterprising merchants made their own connections, notably from the middle of the 16th century down to the 19th.[11]

In the following pages, China's relations with Southeast Asia are examined in four parts. The first two cover Vietnam (with Laos) and Myanmar separately while the third focuses on Thailand and the region's heartland. The fourth part examines the archipelago world where the Chinese are very conscious of the differences between the Philippines and Indonesia, and the exceptional countries of Malaysia and Singapore. But it is also along this archipelagic arc that ASEAN was born. China's awareness of the sets of relationships and institutions that have been created to override the region's immediate interests is a major landmark in the new beginning for China that this volume of essays seeks to describe.

VIETNAM, WITH LAOS

Vietnam clearly stands as a special case, based on two thousand years of a close but unequal relationship. Although the French ended Vietnam's tributary relations with China and, for about seventy years, offered a kind of liberation, it was one that ultimately humiliated its people. The French tried to keep the Vietnamese separated from the Chinese, but they could not prevent close associations between the political leaders on both sides. Since the Chinese invasion of February 1979, the Vietnamese have learnt that help from any faraway power, for example, the Soviet Union, cannot provide

---

[11] Wang Gungwu, *The Nanhai Trade: Early Chinese Trade in the South China Sea.* (Singapore: Eastern Universities Press, Second Edition, 2003), pp. 136–142, 151–155; and "Merchants without Empires: the Hokkien Sojourning Communities", in James D. Tracy (ed.), *The Rise of Merchant Empires: Long-distance Trade in the Early Modern World, 1350–1750* (Cambridge: Cambridge University Press, 1990), pp. 400–421.

guarantees of national security, especially if China is strong and Vietnam itself is seen as ambitious. Ultimately, a good relationship with China and other neighbours is the answer.[12] The presence of a prosperous and united China has clear consequences. The fact that the Vietnam and China share a political system has made it easier for their leaders to appeal for common policies by using familiar rhetoric and devices to ameliorate the problems left over from the past. This includes regular meetings of senior party and government leaders in Beijing and Hanoi, encouraging freer trade and settling border disputes in an orderly way. Within a few years, the Vietnamese have recovered their ability to express their different identities from the Chinese without discarding similarities in political culture.

Nevertheless, Vietnam needs ASEAN to help affirm its national independence as much as ASEAN needs Vietnam to help forge a meaningful presence next door to China. This does not ease Vietnam's position in its older historical relationship with China. But its problems with China should not be exaggerated, nor should its long-term success in dealing with a powerful neighbour be underestimated. While the new Vietnam finds comfort in the ASEAN framework, it does not depend on that alone. It has also cultivated close bilateral relations with China, especially where trade and ethnic affairs along its long border with China are concerned.[13] Between them, there is also the question of their relations with Laos, an area in which feudal kingdoms and shifting populations have established a modern state. China and Vietnam are both sensitive to the local dynamics that is integrating the economies across the borders, especially key sections of the Mekong valley that link China and Myanmar with Laos, Thailand,

---

[12] Stephen J. Hood, *Dragons Entangled: Indochina and the China-Vietnam War* (Armonk, N.Y.: M.E. Sharpe, 1992, pp. 155–160). Vietnam's actions in Cambodia were seen as expansionist and the Treaty with the Soviet Union was threatening not only to China but also to the region.

[13] From 1991 onwards, officials at all levels of the respective communist parties and the government have had regular meetings; Gu Xiaosong and Brantly Womack, "Border Cooperation between China and Vietnam in the 1990s", *Asian Survey*, vol. 40, no. 6 (2000), pp. 1042–1058. A fuller analysis of the relationship in the 1970s is Brantly Womack, "Asymmetry and Systemic Misperception: China, Vietnam and Cambodia during the 1970s", *Journal of Strategic Studies*, vol. 26, no. 2, pp. 92–119.

Cambodia and finally, the Vietnam delta provinces. Although progress is slow, all the countries involved agreed to cooperate to bring interested international players to join the Mekong Valley Development, and limit the damage that conflicts over human and natural resources would produce.[14]

China's interests, whether in improving transportation lines to its south or in re-establishing normal relations, are clear. But for ASEAN, the picture is less clear. Its existing mechanisms for regional economic cooperation are not well equipped to move quickly on issues at the region's periphery. Vietnam and Laos have found that the best way to make progress in their links with Southwest China is to find high-level support from agencies of the central authorities in Beijing wherever possible. ASEAN can provide back-up support that emphasises a responsibility to consult and not harm the common interests of its members, and this would normally be protection enough. Under that umbrella, other sources of international assistance could play an important part in infrastructure development, and there is evidence that China would welcome that as something from which local Chinese organisations could also benefit.[15]

---

[14] A study that traces the efforts down to the late 1990s is Nguyen Thi Dieu, *The Mekong River and the Struggle for Indochina: Water, War, and Peace.* (Westport, CT: Praeger, 1999), with a useful summary on the Greater Mekong Region, pp. 199–227. Also Nick J. Freeman, "Greater Mekong Sub-Region and the "Asian Crisis: Caught between Scylla and Charybdis", *Southeast Asian Affairs 1999* (Singapore: Institute of Southeast Asian Studies, 1999), pp. 32–51. Since the late 1980s, many national and international agencies have tried to cooperate on the development of the Mekong Valley, and there are numerous reports, especially on the sections in Laos, Cambodia and Thailand. ADB, UNESCO, UNDP, and the WHO have all been active, but there have also been national efforts to cooperate in that development. The renewal of interest following the "Kunming Initiative" in 1999 has prompted India to be more active, notably with its Mekong-Ganga Project. But the ADB's Greater Mekong Subregion Economic Cooperation Program was refreshed in Dali in November 2003 following a meeting of the six heads of states most directly concerned. The six seemed to have a strong China focus that had not been obvious before; "Mekong versus Metookong", 13 November 2003 (http://www.asiasource. org/trade/fifteen.cfm)

[15] China has several projects involving the waters of upper reaches of what the Chinese call the Lanchang River and attention is being paid to their ramifications on downstream countries, for example, Qinghua University and the Geographical Research

The key here is that China knows Vietnam well and the Vietnamese have a rich store of experience in dealing with Chinese authorities that enables them to play a distinctive role in China-ASEAN relations if and when necessary. This includes the knotty problems of the South China Sea. Much has been made of China's claims to sovereignty over all the islands, shoals and reefs down to the northern coast of the island of Borneo and the eastern coasts of the Philippines. These claims stem mainly from an earlier nationalist response to French and British claims before the Second World War. The issues now have a totally different focus and good relations with ASEAN have minimized the dangers of open conflict. What remain difficult, however, are the disputes between China and Vietnam over the Paracels and certain parts of the Spratlys. Vietnam finds the support of ASEAN reassuring, but it has always known that ultimately this is a matter that can only be settled directly with China. The regular bilateral talks going on all remaining disputes for the past decade have made steady progress and China's recent policies should be even more helpful.[16]

The isolation of Myanmar

Myanmar's traditional ties with China were cut off by the British in the 1880s. Unlike the rulers of Vietnam, the Burmese kings have never been under close scrutiny by Chinese mandarins. China, in turn, has never had great expectations of Theravada Buddhist Myanmar, a polity outside the

---

Institute of the province of Yunnan have been asked to develop a support system for the upper reaches of the valley; *People's Daily*, 17 November 2001.

[16] After the Vietnamese withdrew completely from Cambodia, Hanoi was invited to join ASEAN, after which tensions with China began to lighten. Gradually their leaders met more regularly, increasingly on a bilateral basis. One of the most significant was that of Premier Zhu Rongji to Hanoi in 1999 to announce that the two countries had resolved their outstanding land boundary disputes; *People's Daily*, 4 December 1999. When Nong Duc Manh was appointed the new General Secretary of the Communist Party of Vietnam in 2001, his visit to Beijing was hailed and Jiang Zemin called on him in Hanoi soon afterwards; *People's Daily*, 28 February 2002. In 2003, Nong visited Beijing to congratulate the election of the new President of China, Hu Jintao, and again this was acclaimed as another strong step in bilateral relations; *People's Daily*, 8 April, 2003. General Secretary Nong also made highly publicised visits to Japan and India, but no other country in Southeast Asia received as much attention by the most senior leaders of China since 1999.

Confucian ken. But the decision by the British to administer Burma largely from New Delhi as part of their Indian empire led to much bitterness among the Burmese. The nationalist Burmese elites after independence spurned membership in the British Commonwealth and forged a go-it-alone neutralist stance. China's support for Burma's communist rebels only pushed the country into a deeper isolation. Then followed the Cultural Revolution, and the ideas that the Chinese tried to export to Burma between 1966–1976, in particular, were disastrous for bilateral relations.[17] It was only after the beginning of the economic reforms of Deng Xiaoping in the early 1980s that the leaders of Myanmar began to build up a new level of trust. By that time, the military junta had become unpopular and a national opposition had coalesced to fight for democracy. The sympathy generated for its leader, Aung San Suu Kyi, and the fierce criticisms by the West of the regime drove the leadership even further away from normal diplomatic relations.

Thus, the invitation to Myanmar to join ASEAN came at a time when China was one of Myanmar's few friends. The fact that China understood Myanmar's desire to become a member of ASEAN is important and marks the fresh awareness of ASEAN's potential as a friendly grouping for China. ASEAN was strengthened by having all countries in the region inside the organisation. China realised that the eclectic membership of ASEAN reduced the chances of unfriendly forces ganging up to its south. The Western hostility towards Myanmar over questions of democracy and human rights is so intense that some ASEAN members are embarrassed by the negative attention the region has received. But with its strict policy of non-intervention in each other's internal politics, ASEAN has continued to give Myanmar ample time to resolve the question of political normalcy.

China is not committed to the ASEAN position, though it too has affirmed the principle of non-interference in the internal affairs of other countries. It sees the attacks on Myanmar by the West differently. For its own

---

[17] Ralph Pettman, *China in Burma's foreign policy.* (Canberra: Australian National University Press, 1973), Contemporary China Papers, no. 7.

political and economic reasons, it has cultivated a special relationship with Myanmar for at least two decades, especially after 1988, when China finally stopped supporting the pro-Beijing faction of the Burmese Communist Party.[18] The Beijing government is aware that, from outside the region, there is concern that Myanmar has become one of China's "client states" and that this is strategically important if China is to become active in the Indian Ocean.[19] As a member of ASEAN, Myanmar could be less dependent on China but, if the country continues to be ostracised by too many countries, Myanmar could also be even more of an ally of China within the ASEAN system. In this context, India's recent efforts to have closer relations with ASEAN and to cultivate Myanmar are clearly justified.[20]

THE THAI HEARTLAND

For more than a century, the heartland of the Hindu-Buddhist world of mainland Southeast Asia was divided. French incursions into Cochin-China and Cambodia and British advances in Lower Burma, plus an Anglo-French understanding to leave the Kingdom of Siam as a buffer zone between their respective empires, masked the deep fissures that had grown between the ancient Khmer and Burmese polities between the Mekong and the Salween and the

---

[18] Liang Chi-shad, "Burma's Relations with the People's Republic of China: from Delicate Friendship to Genuine Co-operation", in Peter Carey (ed.) *Burma: the Challenge of Change in a Divided Society* (London & New York: Macmillan; St. Martin's Press, 1997), pp. 77–90.

[19] Tin Maung Maung Than, "Myanmar and China: a Special Relationship?", *Southeast Asian Affairs 2003* (Singapore: Institute of Southeast Asian Studies, 2003), pp. 189–210; David I. Steinberg, "Myanmar: Regional Relationships and Internal Concerns", *Southeast Asian Affairs 1998* (Singapore: Institute of Southeast Asian Affairs, 1998), pp. 179–188.

[20] John W. Garver, *Protracted Contest: Sino-Indian Rivalry in the Twentieth Century* (Seattle: University of Washington Press, 2001), has two excellent chapters that sum up the issues that have led to some recent Indian actions, "Burma: The backdoor to China", and "The Indian Ocean in Sino-Indian Relations", pp. 243–274; 275–312; S.D. Muni, *China's strategic engagement with the new ASEAN: an Exploratory Study of China's Post-Cold War Political, Strategic and Economic Relations with Myanmar, Laos, Cambodia and Vietnam* (Singapore: Institute of Defence and Strategic Studies, Nanyang Technological University, 2002), pp. 77–88; 119–133.

Thai forces that had swept steadily southwards since the 13th century. French rule helped to save the weakened kingdom of Cambodia, the centre of an extended Khmer empire, but it also heightened the historic rivalries between the Khmers and their neighbours. The Thais had destroyed their empire and sought to absorb the territories west of the Mekong. From the north, Vietnam had steadily moved south at the expense of the Cham kingdom to take all the lands east of the Mekong. The Cambodian state was saved by the French intervention. With their departure after 1954, that state was given a new chance to restore itself. For fifty years, Prince Sihanouk managed, with great difficulty, to provide symbolic unity for the country's survival.[21] Among the measures available to him was a traditional turn to Beijing where his complaints fell on willing ears. These complaints included not only fears of a Thailand that sided with the capitalist enemies of communist China but also of China's communist comrades in Vietnam. Despite Sihanouk's political agility, his weakness was accompanied by the rise of the Khmer Rouge and the tragic years of the killing fields. Nevertheless, his durability has been a factor in the country's ability to survive, no less in obtaining support from China, the United States, Japan and Australia during the 1980s.[22] It is too early to say how soon Cambodia will regain prosperity with international help, but it is clear that, preferably through ASEAN, Cambodia is likely to strengthen its links with China.

Recent developments highlight the central position of the lands between the Mekong and the Salween in Southeast Asian history. They also underline the vital importance of Thailand in any regional development. The record shows that it was no accident that Britain and France recognised its buffer function in the 19th century, that Japan persuaded the Thai military regime to lean to its side early in the 20th, and that the United States found Bangkok crucial during the Vietnam War.[23] Since the Second World War, the region has

[21] Marie Alexandrine Martin, *Cambodia, a shattered society,* translated by Mark W. McLeod (Berkeley: University of California Press, Rev & updated ed., 1994), pp. 61–77, 110–120, 135–138. On the beginning of his dependence on China, pp. 88–95; Milton Osborne, *Sihanouk: prince of light, prince of darkness* (St Leonards, N.S.W.: Allen & Unwin, 1994), pp. 72–84; 151–155.

[22] Osborne, *Sihanouk*, pp. 248–263.

[23] Kobkua Suwannathat-Pian, *Thailand's durable Premier: Phibun through three*

often swivelled on a Thai-based diplomatic axle, and China since the 1970s has increasingly appreciated the dynamic role that Thailand can play in the region and beyond.[24] This is not a question of merely acting the dependent ally, or as a temporarily useful instrument of foreign political manoeuvres but one of having a steady hand to provide a sense of direction in a complex and fluid situation. With that background, the region has come to see that Thai moves towards or away from China may provide a valuable indicator of how to read the future. For example, Thailand under its present Prime Minister Thaksin Shinawatra has demonstrated that he knows how to find a comfortable position between the United States and China.[25] That both China and the US appreciate this suggests that factors of history and geography will be an important factor in political and strategic calculations in the region. One of the reasons for this success is the way Thailand has been managed by skilful diplomats whose work has been an inspiration for their younger regional counterparts. Thailand's success was by no means inevitable. It was hard-won and has contributed to the forging of a valuable instrument for regional cooperation.[26]

---

decades, 1932–1957 (Kuala Lumpur & New York: Oxford University Press, 1995), pp. 240–243, 283–291; Daniel Fineman, *Special Relationship: The United States and Military Government in Thailand, 1947–1958* (Honolulu: University of Hawaii Press, 1997), pp. 259–263.

[24] Sukhumbhand Paribatra, *From enmity to alignment: Thailand's evolving relations with China* (Bangkok: Institute of Security and International Studies, Chulalongkorn University, 1987), pp. 34–49; Arne Kislenko, "Bending with the Wind: the Continuity and Flexibility of Thai Foreign Policy", *International Journal*, vol. 57, no. 4 (2002), pp. 537–561. But, rather as with China, being in the centre also means that it is vulnerable and its policies seen to be ineffective; Chayachoke Chulasiriwongs, "Thailand's Relations with the New ASEAN members: Solving Problems and Creating Images", *Southeast Asian Affairs 2001* (Singapore: Institute of Southeast Asian Affairs, 2001), pp. 337–354.

[25] Michael R.J. Vatikiotis, "Catching the Dragon's Tail: China and Southeast Asia in the 21st Century", *Contemporary Southeast Asia*, vol. 25, no. 1 (2003), pp. 77. In 2003, the United States re-confirmed Thailand's partner status while Prime Minister Thaksin carefully re-affirmed its "strategic cooperation" with China (as in The China-Thailand Joint Communique, 29 August 2001); *The Straits Times*, 19 October 2003. Rapid progress followed immediately with a free trade agreement with India in October.

[26] Thailand's diplomatic contributions to the ASEAN way began with one of the founding foreign ministers in 1967, Thanat Khoman, "Foreword: ASEAN: Conception and Evolution", in K.S. Sandhu *et al.* (comp.) *The ASEAN Reader*

It also explains why China recognises that Thailand has the potential to serve as the anchor for a new Southeast Asian identity.

ISLAND SOUTHEAST ASIA AND ASEAN REGIONALISM

In contrast, China's maritime relations with Southeast Asia did not have the same importance until the 20th century. The continuous pressure since the end of the 19th century, however, on China's coastal provinces to respond to new dangers and opportunities has been a spur to review its policies about its long-neglected navy. This has been further heightened by United States support for Taiwan since 1949, something that China sees as a challenge to its sovereignty. In response, the Chinese has turned more attention to maritime power and this has ramifications for island Southeast Asia.[27] Nevertheless, this perspective from the China coasts does not mesh with the one from Yunnan and Guangxi provinces and makes it difficult for China to see Southeast Asia as an integrated region. Maritime Southeast Asia is more like an extended periphery, part of the arc that begins with Japan, and includes all the Malay archipelago nations through the Straits of Malacca and the Sunda Straits into the Indian Ocean.[28] In that context, this outer ring of Southeast Asia is an important sector of a larger Asia that China finds easier to connect closely to East Asia and have it also serve as a sea-link to South Asia and beyond.

The historical background supports such a prospect. Formal relations between the Malay states and the Ming and Qing dynasties had ended

---

(Singapore: Institute of Southeast Asian Studies, 1992), pp. xvii–xxii. They have been well-sustained into the 1990s; John Funston, "Thai Foreign Policy: Seeking Influence", *Southeast Asian Affairs 1998* (Singapore: Institute of Southeast Asian Affairs, 1998), pp. 292–306.

[27] Lee Jae-Hyung, "China's Expanding Maritime Ambitions in the Western Pacific and the Indian Ocean", *Contemporary Southeast Asia*, vol. 24, no. 3 (2002), pp. 557–564.

[28] The historical evolution of this maritime periphery has been described in two stimulating studies work by Hamashita Takeshi, "The Intra-regional System in East Asia in Modern Times", in Peter J. Katzenstein and Takashi Shiraishi, (eds.) *Network power: Japan and Asia*. Ithaca, (N.Y.: Cornell University Press, 1996), pp. 113–135; and "The Tribute Trade System and Modern Asia", in A.J.H. Latham and Heita Kawakatsu (eds.) *Japanese industrialization and the Asian economy* (London and New York: Routledge, 1994). pp. 91–107.

centuries earlier. In the case of Malacca and other Malay states, including those in Java, relations had stopped since the early 16th century. These differences mattered little at the time. The Qing rulers paid little attention to affairs to the south of their empire and the first two emperors in the 19th century were genuinely surprised by British power off the China coast. What did become clear was that, while the mainland states like Burma and Vietnam provided something of a defence bulwark for China, the port kingdoms were wide open to European dominance.[29] In the island world, local Malay rulers and their European partners were conscious that Chinese private traders and their ships played a useful part in helping European trading fleets establish their economic dominance. But the Qing rulers were either unaware of the role of those Chinese or cared too little to try to influence what they were doing. Their only concern was that these Chinese who defied the ban to trade overseas did not bring their illegal ventures back to China's own ports.

The gulf that grew between China and much of this maritime world extends also to cultural spheres. Buddhism and the Indian linkages of that religion had provided some common values when the first contacts were recorded. This was no longer true for the Malay world, notably after a sinicized Buddhism had drawn China away from the religion's Indian roots and when Islam advanced into the archipelago after the 13th century. As a result, the wide range of links across the South China Sea that once thrived on the religious and cultural connection was further weakened. In contrast, Theravada Buddhism spread from Sri Lanka to the mainland kingdoms up to the borders of the Song and Yuan empires and helped to ease relations with the Chinese state as Chinese traders and settlers moved towards those land borders. Although religious policy has never been its strength, China remains sensitive to the differences in faith that have grown over the centuries in the island

---

[29] They were wide open insofar that an assumption of "mare liberum" (free seas) seemed to have been taken for granted by the Malay seafaring peoples and their trading partners. Hugo Grotius thought through the legal principle as "a navigable body of water, such as a sea, that is open to navigation by vessels of all nations"; Hugo Grotius, *The Freedom of the Seas; or, The Right which belongs to the Dutch to take part in the East Indian Trade*, tr. by Ralph Van Deman Magoflin and edited by James Brown Scot (New York: Oxford University Press, 1916).

world. China pays close attention to common Islamic concerns in countries like Malaysia, Indonesia and Brunei.

Nevertheless, China's maritime relations in Southeast Asia became less marginal when both China and the region shared the experience of post-industrial European expansion. Because of the dramatic impact of the West, China has now re-evaluated the significance of the region as the passageway towards its southern coast, its soft underbelly. Its leaders have learnt the hard lesson that weak and unstable polities in the region could allow foreign powers to threaten China.

It is important to highlight how far China has transformed its relations with this maritime world during this past century. Until the end of the 19th century, port cities and riverine kingdoms were rarely able to sustain themselves for long as stable states. Now the archipelago has five (East Timor is excluded here) that have successfully weathered decades of nation-building.[30] Although none can be said to have assumed a definite final form, China knows that the heritage of colonial methods of state formation has given them the means to affirm their respective sovereignty. Chinese officials have also learnt what a mixed group these states are. The two with clear Muslim majority populations, Brunei and Indonesia, are totally unlike each other. The one that is based on Christian communities, the Philippines, strains at understanding its neighbours. Malaysia is an exceptional kind of Muslim monarchy, with its Malay majority divided between modernisers and the tradition-bound, whereas Singapore that might have acted as a balancer member of the Malaysian Federation now serves as the only genuinely secular state. It is therefore not surprising that none of the five see China in the same way, and that, in its recent bilateral relations, China has worked very hard to respond to the varying needs and expectations of each of these states.[31]

---

[30] The nation-building history project at the Institute of Southeast Asian Studies has stressed that the task begun some 50 years earlier is far from done, but at least two generations of leaders and officials have learnt what the most difficult problems are; Wang Gungwu, "Introduction", in Cheah Boon Kheng, *Malaysia: the Making of a Nation* (Singapore: Institute of Southeast Asian Studies, 2002), pp. xi–xviii. This is the first of a five-volume series on Malaysia, Indonesia, the Philippines, Thailand and Singapore.

[31] Brunei is a monarchy of 360,000 people while the Indonesian republic has a population of 235 million; Philippines is a well-established democracy of over

China has also learnt a sharp lesson from its early dealings with the region's largest country, Indonesia. The country was created in 1945–1950 out of revolution and had hoped that China would be an ally in a neutralist world. The Bandung Conference in 1955 was a landmark for that cause as President Sukarno wanted real independence from the capitalist West. China's keen support for that ambition, however, was to cost the Chinese dearly. The president's flirting with the Parti Kommunis Indonesia, the October 1st coup in 1965 and the killings of "communists" that followed, and the rise of President Suharto soon afterwards, were followed by 25 years of Indonesian hostility and suspicion.[32] That turnaround gave a major impetus to the establishment of ASEAN, with Indonesia acting as the organisation's anchor. Accompanied by the country's impressive economic development for the next thirty years, this initial grouping of five nations (later six, with the addition of Brunei) gave the region a common sense of purpose that no one had predicted was possible. Indonesia was helped in its axial role by the mature monarchy of Thailand and the relatively stable Philippines state. Together, in 1967, they provided a protective shield for a riot-torn Malaysia and the former colony of Singapore that Malaysia had just shed to become the region's newest republic.[33]

---

80 million Christians out of a total of 85 million; and the 13 states of Malaysia form a special kind of Islam-based federation with nine sultans acting as heads of state in rotation. Singapore is unique as the only state in the world in which immigrant Chinese form a 75% majority of its people. During the past two decades, China has published dozens of books on Southeast Asia and scores of articles on relations with ASEAN and each of its member countries; Liu Yongzhuo, *Zongguo dongnanya yanjiu de huigu yu qianzhan.* [*Southeast Asian Studies in China: Retrospect and Prospect*] (Guangzhou: Guangdong Remin Chubanshe, 1994). This is updated by Liu Hong, "Southeast Asian Studies in Greater China", *Kyoto Review of Southeast Asia* (Issue No. 3, March 2003) kyotoreview.cseas.kyoto-u.ac.jp.

[32] On the 1965 upheaval, John Hughes, *The end of Sukarno: a coup that misfired, a purge that ran wild* (London: Angus & Robertson, 1968); Benedict R. O'G. Anderson and Ruth McVey, *A preliminary analysis of the October 1, 1965 coup in Indonesia* (Ithaca, N.Y.: Modern Indonesia Project, Cornell University, 1971). For Suharto's policy towards China, Rizal Sukma, *Indonesia and China: the Politics of a Troubled Relationship* (New York: Routledge, 1999), pp. 104–165; Leo Suryadinata, *Indonesia's Foreign Policy under Suharto: Aspiring to International Leadership* (Singapore: Times Academic Press, 1996), pp. 101–121.

[33] For the most hopeful and difficult formative years, Michael Leifer, *ASEAN and the Security of South-East Asia* (London, New York: Routledge, 1989); Roger Irvine,

Despite the strong support from the United States, Britain and Australia, the formation of ASEAN was far from convincing at the time, and, insofar as it was seen as a grouping directed against China, it was certainly not something the Chinese wanted to succeed. But China was in a poor position to deal with the new organisation. It was then in the grip of the Cultural Revolution. Its foreign policy was incomprehensible even to China's friends and its Foreign Ministry was dysfunctional for years. No one, in any case, anticipated that ASEAN would later provide a framework for the kind of communication and interaction that began to change the region's political and security environment.[34] ASEAN members in turn did not know how desperate China had become when it faced a hostile Soviet Union during the height of the Vietnam War. It took the bold steps by President Nixon and Secretary of State Kissinger to cut through the hard curtains that divided Asia at the time.

The ramifications of that ideological war in the Southeast Asian jungles and padi-fields have been great. The war changed the expectations that most Asian leaders had of the benefits of decolonisation, the ideal that independent nations should be free of any kind of external interference. The fact that this was somewhat utopian and unrealistic could be ignored during the struggle for sovereign freedoms. By the start of the war in Indo-China in the mid-1960s, however, no one could pretend that each nation could shape its own destiny all by itself. The twenty years of development from the 1970s to the 1990s for both China and Southeast Asia have created completely new conditions for the future. This was even more striking after the start of the economic reforms in China, followed by the end of the Cold War and the disintegration of the Soviet Union.

"The Formative Years of ASEAN: 1967–1975", in Alison Broinowski (ed.) *Understanding ASEAN* (London: Macmillan in association with the Australian Institute of International Affairs, 1982), pp. 8–36. Seen in longer perspective, Shaun Narine, *Explaining ASEAN: Regionalism in Southeast Asia* (Boulder, CO: Lynne Rienner Publishers, 2002), with a short introduction on the organisation's formation, pp. 9–38.

[34] Sharon Siddique and Sree Kumar (comp.) *The 2nd ASEAN Reader* (Singapore: Institute of Southeast Asian Studies, 2003), Sections V, pp. 263–309. Frank Frost, "Introduction: ASEAN since 1967 — Origins, Evolution and Recent Developments", in Alison Broinowski (ed.) *ASEAN into the 1990s* (New York: St. Martin's Press, 1990), pp. 10–28.

The decades of moving towards interdependence in the world have reached a phase when a new generation of leaders have come on the scene both in China and Southeast Asia. Most notably, the financial crisis that led to the fall of President Suharto was accompanied by experiments in democracy, a succession of transitional leaders, and sharp challenges to Indonesia's commitment to secularism. This has weakened the thrusting advances that ASEAN had achieved before 1997.[35] Fortunately, leadership in the other original member-states remained strong under President Fidel Ramos of the Philippines, Prime Ministers Mahathir Mohamad of Malaysia and Goh Chok Tong of Singapore. Thailand now has a strong leader in Prime Minister Thaksin Shinawatra and new leaders in Malaysia and Singapore are ready to be tested.[36] All this coincides with the emergence of a technocratic Politburo in Beijing under President Hu Jintao. Since the late 1990s, China has engaged the region through the ARF, not only on matters of trade and investment, but also increasingly on security issues.[37] These initiatives have

---

[35] Siddique and Kumar (comp.) *2nd ASEAN Reader*, Section VIII, pp. 471–508; Simon S.C. Tay, "Institutions and Processes: Dilemmas and Possibilities", in Simon S.C. Tay, Jesus P. Estanislao, Hadi Soesastro (eds.) *Reinventing ASEAN* (Singapore: Institute of Southeast Asian Studies, 2001), pp. 243–255, 261–269. Narine, *Explaining ASEAN*, pp. 193–209; Amitav Acharya, *Seeking security in the dragon's shadow: China and Southeast Asia in the emerging Asian order* (Singapore: Institute of Defence and Strategic Studies, 2003).

[36] All four leaders named here kept close relations with China through making regular visits to China and inviting senior Chinese leaders to visit their respective countries. President Ramos continued to maintain his China links after retirement. One of the warmest relationships in recent years has been the visit of the new leader of Malaysia, Prime Minister Abdullah Ahmad Badawi, in September 2003, on the eve of his taking over from Dr Mahathir Mohamad; Karim Raslan, "Engagement with China", http://www.inq7.net/opi/2003/oct/01/opi_commentary1-1.htm. Lee Hsien Loong of Singapore, of course, is well known in China not only as the son of Senior Minister Lee Kuan Yew but also in his own right, http://fpeng.peopledaily.com. cn/200010/21/eng20001021_53217.html

[37] Joseph Y. S. Cheng, "China's ASEAN Policy in the 1990s: Pushing for Regional Multipolarity", *Contemporary Southeast Asia*, vol. 21, no. 2 (1999), pp. 183–200. The move towards an ASEAN-China Free Trade Agreement began in Manila in 1999, was pursued further in Singapore in 2000, and endorsed in Brunei in November 2001; Kevin G. Cai, "The ASEAN-China Free Trade Agreement and East Asian Regional Grouping", *Contemporary Southeast Asia*, vol. 25, no. 3 (2003), pp. 387–402.

begun to bear fruit, not least in giving fresh vigour to ASEAN in the larger context of East Asian regionalism. That body now has the opportunity to consolidate both its economic and security concerns as well as explore what it can do beyond Eastern Asia in a larger Asia.

Have these recent changes fundamentally rewritten the script for both China and ASEAN? Will the new regionalism lead to a different kind of sharing altogether, or will it ultimately revert to older patterns of relationships? On the one hand, there is a near reunified China, almost a return to China of the Qing dynasty in 1911. On the other, there is a clearly incomplete regional effort to integrate the ten countries of Southeast Asia into ASEAN. This has evoked many different responses. For many leaders, this is an unequal relationship, but a united ASEAN should do much better than each country having to face China alone. To others, ASEAN was first brought together by fear of a common enemy, international communism, and would need a common enemy to bind four new countries to the original members. That condition is no longer there, and it is unlikely that China will allow itself to be portrayed as a potential enemy in the future. Yet others see a new regionalism as a challenge to make ASEAN one of its big players. This would be possible if it can help to shape the larger regionalism that promises to bring prosperity all round.[38] If that succeeds, it could seek to act as something of a bridge between power groups in the Asia-Pacific and Indian Ocean worlds. In getting China to sign the Treaty of Amity and Cooperation in Bali in 2003, ASEAN has certainly made a major breakthrough.[39]

---

[38] Following the Final Report of the East Asia Study Group presented to the ASEAN + 3 summit in Phnom Penh, November 4, 2002, rapid moves were made in 2003 to deepen the relationships of ASEAN + 3 (China, Japan and South Korea) and work towards regional integration and a economic community. East Asia Study Group Report and the Phnom Penh Communique of ASEAN Foreign Ministers of 17 June 2003: http://www.aseansec.org/14833.htm and http://www.mofa.go.jp/region/asia-paci/asean/pmv0211/report.pdf

[39] Chinese initiatives at the Bali Summit in October 2003 were widely reported, notably China's signing of the Instrument of Accession to the Treaty of Amity and Cooperation in Southeast Asia. Also significant was the Joint Declaration of the Heads of State/Government of the Association of Southeast Asian Nations and the People's Republic of China on Strategic Partnership for Peace and Prosperity, October 8, 2003, signed in Bali at the Ninth ASEAN Summit, http://www.aseansec.

This brings us back to the context of the larger region in which China has invariably seen itself as placed at the centre. There are two perspectives here. From the point of view of its Southeast Asian neighbours, there is historical baggage for all to carry. The proximity of Vietnam, Laos and Myanmar to the politics of both Southwest China and the metropolis of traditional China, and the almost continuous trade and tribute diplomacy between Thailand and China for centuries, cannot be easily set aside. The special local reasons for Cambodia to look beyond its immediate neighbours for support of its independence remain relevant to its future. This collection of relationships was severely disrupted during the past century but it has not been broken. Some national leaders expect parts of the old relationships to be revived whether they like it or not. Others, notably the archipelagic countries, believe that long-distance interventions from outside the region may protect them from any possible Chinese ambitions. Yet others know that they need to be flexible in arranging their bilateral and multilateral links if they are to survive the rapidly globalizing world.

China's larger perspective contains some of the same ingredients. It is not only Southeast Asian countries that are challenged in ways never encountered before. China's decisive moves to engage them as ASEAN form part of an effort to set new parameters for a new Asia in which China hopes it may act as a responsible Great Power. As several other essays in this volume show, China still faces powerful neighbours, unstable states and potentially unfriendly alliances in almost every direction around its long land and sea boundaries. Although this phenomenon of being the target of external forces has been a familiar one since ancient times, China has learnt over the last thousands of years that, at every stage of growth, the power and determination of their neighbours have been harder to deal with. Most of all, the Chinese know, at each succeeding stage, how their past economic and technological advantages has been reduced. As each set of neighbours mastered whatever the Chinese had developed, the dangers to the "centre" have been all the greater.

---

org/15265.htm. The framework agreement for comprehensive economic co-operation with India and that for comprehensive economic partnership with Japan were signed on the same day.

There are now no illusions about what advantages some of its neighbours have over China and how much these can override considerations of history and geography. As China sees its position today, a hard-headed realism, free from outdated rhetoric, is necessary until China feels secure and confident enough to redefine itself distinctively in ways that the modern world would respect. From that perspective, Southeast Asia has its rightful place as a cornerstone of a larger East Asian arc of safety that stretches into the Indian Ocean. If the ASEAN way can enable the region to be the first part of that arc to make China feel safe after more than a century of turmoil and anguish, it is likely that future Chinese leaders will remember the debt that they owe to the initiatives ASEAN first took in the later half of the 20th century.

CHAPTER 10

US AND CHINA: RESPECT AND EQUALITY

In a world of hierarchies and league tables, the equality of nations is an ideal that is often nominal but nevertheless it has symbolic value. How can that translate into mutual respect between the United States and the People's Republic of China? At another level, with education and literacy standards rising and the reach of information knowledge increasingly borderless, will that lead to greater mutual respect among the peoples of the two countries? These are not questions central to the concerns of experts in international relations theory or strategic thinkers. I ask them because they are pertinent to perceptions and emotions that peoples have of one another and are questions that have not been given enough attention in current analyses. The questions here are framed in the context that the PRC is not the equal of the US and that their peoples have different ideas about what they most respect. I shall argue that attitudes towards the pursuit of equality, and judgments about what deserves respect, are important for both countries and their peoples. In the longer run, how they manage concepts like equality and respect could seriously affect hopes for peace and stability in the Asia-Pacific region.

In 2005, the idea of a Group of Two (G-2) surfaced to highlight the rise of Chinese economic power and it was thought that treating China as equal to the US in that context could be a useful way to place the relationship between the US and China on a new footing. Zbigniew Brzezinski, who had played a key part in establishing diplomatic relations between the two countries in 1979, strongly advocated such an approach when he met Chinese leaders in 2009 and, together with a few others, went so far as to suggest that, alongside the Group of Eight (G-8) or the new Group of Twenty (G-20), the Group of Two could enable the two countries to work together to deal with some larger global problems. Given the obvious inequality between the two countries, it was surprising how much that idea dominated some of the media during much of the year 2010.

The G-2 idea was subjected to many interpretations. To some, this was but a just recognition of China's new status in world affairs. As an offer on the part of the Americans for some kind of partnership with the other stake-holder in global wellbeing, it was visionary and constructive and showed a new respect for China that China should welcome. Others were more skeptical. The reasons ranged from distrust of the motives of the US to all kinds of fears about China's ambitions, to serious doubts about the established alliances and even to mockery of American naivete. Some Chinese leaders were puzzled how there could be respect without equality on key matters of political and military power. Yet others suspected that the media attention was directed towards scaring readers into believing that a second not so benign superpower was on the horizon, rather like telling ghost stories to try to banish terrors of the night. The heavy coverage in the media did not point to any real equality between the two nations. What emerged was the scant respect that the media of each country showed for the other.

As we know, a week is a long time in politics and a month can be like eternity. The yearlong obsession with a possible G-2 relationship was soon taken off the map and, by early 2011, the headlines had all turned to new configurations in the old hot spots of the Middle East, from the Arab spring to new uncertainties in Syria. There was even talk of a similar China spring that would immediately downgrade the PRC to the level of the dictators that the West had supported for decades. Unrelated to these developments, attention shifted in Southeast Asia to the US return to Asia, what has also been described as the US pivot or re-balance. Much speculation has followed to assess whether this return is temporary or permanent, rhetorical or substantive, and comments have ranged from counting more ships in Asian waters to more boots on the ground.

How does this affect the way we see the future of US-China relations? We could remind ourselves how unpredictable the world still is and how meaningless words like equality and respect can become. Do the events like the Arab equivalent of a colour revolution that no one had predicted for the Middle East point to the need for the US and China to recalibrate their relations yet again? It is to be expected that relations between China and the US would capture the front pages again, but the subject is now unlikely to come back as a G-2 syndrome, or anything as simple as confrontation or partnership. What seems more likely is that, whichever way that relationship evolves in the future, the underlying issues of equality and respect will remain enduring and important.

For a clearer view of future relations between the US and China, it is instructive to review some of the references to G-2 as a development that might characterize a new power structure in the Asia-Pacific. From the start, there were different responses to the very idea of G-2. For some, it appeared that the Americans who initiated the idea and kept talking it up were insincere. They seemed to have used the term as a wishful device either to get the Chinese to share the world's burdens before they are ready, or lure them to so much self-congratulation that they would let their guard down. Many Chinese were flattered, but it soon became clear that their leaders were realistic and showed their deep suspicions of the dubious honour conferred upon China. Of course, economists are more likely to agree that, if China's economic growth rate is maintained, it would not be long before China really became Number Two in the world in the political sphere as well. In that case, it would be better if the US and China could work together rather than to spin off in opposite directions towards hostility and bitter competition.

In any case, each county also has politically conscious people who responded differently to the idea that equality in any form would bring about respect. For example, no one in the US seriously believes that China is its equal and I would be surprised if there are many American political leaders and thinkers who believe that the Chinese state deserves their respect. Transnational capitalists may think it useful to engage China as an equal in commercial and industrial development and even show some respect for Chinese technical ingenuity. Strategic thinkers may need China to be seen as an equal in order to plan their worst-case scenarios for the Asia-Pacific region, but there is scant respect for China's military capacity in global terms.

Similarly, no one in China thinks that China is equal to the US in terms of power and wealth, though many would consider that prospect attractive in the longer run. In the traditional areas of culture and social values, even Chinese who are very proud of their heritage would acknowledge that the US, as the leader of Western learning today, is superior in all scientific fields, including in the social sciences, at least for quite a while longer. Consequently, there is respect for American core achievements as the spearhead of Western civilization. In short, the combination of equality and respect that we might expect to find in the idea of a G-2 partnership of two major countries destined to help the world become more peaceful and prosperous is an ambiguously mixed one. Nevertheless, both countries cannot turn away from the perceptions and attitudes linked to persistent inequality and stubborn disrespect.

THE PURSUIT OF EQUALITY

The pursuit of national equality has often been misunderstood. In both China and the US, this is sometimes portrayed as a matter between the two countries. This fails to take into account the history of the pursuit of equality by generations of Chinese leaders since the 19th century. This pursuit began by focusing on acquiring new knowledge to enable China to develop and become secure. That had begun when two powerful maritime empires, the British and the French, successively defeated China along the China coasts. Both demonstrated overwhelming superiority and were increasingly contemptuous towards the disintegrating Qing dynasty. In comparison, the US at that time seemed respectful. Their representatives confined their demands in China to commensurate trading terms and conditions, and also to the right of their missionaries to help the Chinese people. The work of the latter that led to the building of useful institutions like schools, colleges and hospitals was particularly impressive. For decades, the US displayed a willingness to offer a helping hand while the Europeans remained haughty and condescending. It was truly remarkable that, within a decade of the Treaty of Peking of 1860, the Chinese had agreed to send young students to study in schools and colleges in New England and the young boys were well received by American educators, if only as potential Christians.

The point that needs emphasizing is that no idea of national equality was involved. The Qing officials saw the Americans as softer, friendlier Westerners who could teach them what they wanted without arrogance. As students and followers of European learning, the Americans could show the Chinese how to learn from the powerful Europeans. The Chinese saw this country of the New World as merely a few steps ahead of the Chinese in their pursuit of being treated as equals, if not respect, by superior Europeans. Similarly, even after being defeated by the Japanese in 1895, the Qing sent their best students to Japan to study from people who had studied from the West so successfully. There was no question of national equality with Japan either. They were simply fellow students of the advanced nations of the West.

All that was to change after the fall of the Qing and the establishment of the Republic. New expectations were aroused, especially after Japan achieved equality with European empires and began to behave with the same arrogance towards a China destroyed by its quarreling warlords and civil wars. National equality thus became a powerful issue and the desire to be united and strong became China's most urgent national goal. At the same time, the US as a nation also changed in Chinese eyes. At the end of the First World War, it had become another European power that was equal to Britain and France. It stood with the other powers at the Versailles Conference where China as a nation (and not the decrepit Manchu empire) was openly humiliated. For the first time, all Chinese, whether literati, merchant, labourer or peasant, realized that their country was seen by Westerners as sick and feeble and unworthy of respect.

A few years later, in 1922, at the Washington Naval Conference, this was confirmed when the US, Japan and Britain, without Chinese participation, sorted out new naval power dispositions on China's coasts. It was obvious thereafter that China was no longer equal in the eyes of the imperial nations. The pursuit of equality by all means became uppermost as the Chinese began to learn about nationalism in earnest when the Japanese thrust into the Manchurian provinces and Mongolian feudal lands in the Republic of China inevitably led to the Second Sino-Japanese War.

One product of these changes was the re-reading of modern history. It was after the Versailles Conference that Chinese politicians dated China's loss of equality, as well as sovereignty, to the now renamed "Unequal Treaties", the various treaties signed after the Opium Wars of the 1840–1860 period. The recovery of equality thus became a national duty and two generations of Chinese diplomats devoted themselves obsessively to this task until the end of the Second World War. The ability to eliminate inequality became the litmus test for all political leaders. From then to the victory of the Chinese Communist Party and the establishment of the Peoples' Republic, Chinese nationalist leaders chose to see the US as the country that could help China become equal to the imperial powers like Britain and Japan. Ironically, later in the early 1970s, they even thought that the US was essential in their quest for equality against their erstwhile ideological comrades, the Soviet Union. As some historians in China saw it, America's experience as a colony that was liberated from another empire placed it on the same side as China. Thus, throughout most of the century after the forced opening of China in the 1840s, the US was portrayed as the most successful student of Western European power and wealth who remained benign and could show China the way forward.

The context changed after 1949 when the bitter rivalry between the US and the Soviet Union, now called superpowers instead of imperial powers, made the question of national equality irrelevant. Nominally, the new international structure of the UN in 1945 had made it appear that all countries were equal. At the time, Nationalist China was fortunate that, with US support, it was among the five more-than-equal nations in the organization's Security Council. At least in theory, there was equality among five nations in the world and Guomindang China was more than content with that. For a poor and divided country in 1945, what more could it ask for?

In Chinese eyes, the end of the Cold War in 1990s has confirmed that the US inherited the mantle of the British Empire at its height, as the most powerful country in the world. If the comparison is taken further, it too could also decline as the earlier empire had done after a century or so. To avoid doing that, should the US find another enemy or take a powerful partner?

Either way, China would have to be conferred some degree of equality whether China likes it or not. This is the context of the G-2 syndrome. If that meant that China had to choose whether to be enemy or partner, is that the kind of equality it wants?

Of course, equality is also an evocative idea that has little to do with nations. For individuals to be equal before God or Allah has always been a great comfort but it is not a proposition that can be demonstrated. A more tangible aim is for people to be equal before the law but the idea of being equal in an international court is still being tested. However, the ideal of all humans having equal rights is perhaps the highest expression of equality. And it is this idea that has captured the imagination of everyone. Here China has a different heritage, one that assumes that hierarchy is a worldly norm. But that has not prevented Chinese dissenters over the past 2,000 years from promoting various kinds of egalitarianism for which millions of rebels have fought and sought to implement. As recent examples, one can point to the rhetoric used by some of the supporters of Mao Zedong during the Cultural Revolution, but the consequences were so dire that the Chinese people have foresworn such calls for egalitarianism altogether. And there are hundreds of others in jail or in exile who sought basic legal and political equalities that the regime is still unwilling to give. Today, with increasing dissatisfaction, the majority of Chinese have to live with a kind of inequality of wealth and status that has rarely been seen even in its imperial past.

Thus the Chinese have always had a mixed picture of the US. Their textbooks still refer to the time when Americans in the goldfields and elsewhere showed their contempt for Chinese immigrants and humiliated them relentlessly. That was a time when China was given lessons in diplomatic equality while the Chinese as people were clearly treated as inferior. Also, the Qing government seemed not to have cared much because Manchu aristocrats and Han mandarins were shown official respect even while anti-Chinese exclusion acts were being passed by the US Congress. What is significant during the past thirty years is that the Chinese have learnt how much the US has changed. They observe that the relative inequality in the US is set at a higher level where equality of opportunity is institutionalized and very few are desperately poor. This is something they can admire. In fact, such a realizable ideal of equal opportunity is something they are committed to establishing in their own society.

Linked to the idea of equality are other comparisons. Many people have forgotten that China had been politically and economically superior in much of Asia for centuries up until the 18th century. There is now a growing literature about China re-emerging with images of the country being restored to its earlier greatness. Economic historians in the west agree that, up to the 18th century, the Qing empire was one of the richest countries in the world. Some predict that the current China will regain that position by the second half of this century. On this issue, there are some in China who think that the pursuit of equality with the US is too modest. The country should expect ultimately to recover its primacy beyond Asia, not by challenging US military power but surpassing the US in terms of the social morality and cultural splendour that is the key to China's heritage.

In that context, China's economic performance since the 1980s would be but a prelude to what will happen in the 21st century. But primacy is not equality and equality has never impressed the Chinese elites. Their political culture expressed through 2,000 years of political exhortation has always emphasized the enduring security that came out of prosperity and stability within and respect and admiration without. I suggest that, even to the current leadership, this is a goal that is more credible than the kind of ranking in league tables that modern quantitative methods favour today.

WINNING RESPECT

It is worth recalling that foreign views about China varied considerably over the past 3,000 years. Overland, the tribal confederations close by that conquered China regularly coveted its riches and showed scant respect whenever the Chinese state was divided and weak. Beyond the seas, notably in South and Southeast Asia, trading with China was profitable but, apart from some ceremonial genuflections, little attention was paid to what Chinese ideas and values stood for. And, except for Japan and Korea in Northeast Asia, nothing much was written about China's civilization and cultural achievements. Most neighbouring states did not even bother to flatter the Chinese by learning from its culture or by copying its social and political institutions. And the Chinese state was content with having occasional contacts and demonstrations of ritual respect through an evolving feudal system of foreign embassies coming to pay tribute to Chinese rulers. It was only after Western maritime power reached Chinese shores and industrial capitalism led to a new kind of global economy that the power landscape was radically changed. Even then, China could assume that there was respect for its dynastic empire, for the antiquity and continuity of its civilization if not its principles of governance.

Thus, at no point in China's long history did its ruling elites doubt that respect for their success in enabling such a large territory to be united, and staying united and stable, was a measure of its worthiness. The record shows that respect for China was the norm, it rarely lost that respect and, when it did, it was never for long. To expect that the time has come for China to be respected again can be said to be something much to be desired by all Chinese. The issue today is how much the criteria for winning respect have changed. To what extent must China conform to what is described as international norms before it can regain respect?

In this context, the relations between the US and China hinge more on the question of an expected respect between the two than any notion of equality that is merely legal and abstract. For China, at least, sustained displays of respect, however symbolic, are much more meaningful than regular measurements to determine equality. The story of the relationship here is mixed. During the past 150 years, the Chinese state can recall the many times when the US came to China's aid against imperial powers like Britain, France, Japan and Russia and offered to treat China fairly. Whenever that happened, China has taken it to reflect a respect that it greatly appreciated. Of course, it is on record that large numbers of Chinese merchants and labourers were ill-treated in the US. That was regrettable, but there was a lack of national consciousness under Manchu Qing rule and this partly explained why there was no official outrage at the time against such offensive treatment. Most Chinese now celebrate the new US immigration policies since the 1960s that have enabled hundreds of thousands of Chinese to settle and ultimately integrate into American society. These policies may have raised expectations too high but the main trends have marked a welcome change and done much to ease Sino-American relations at other levels.

But there remain uncertainties that stem from different ideals and ideologies. At the heart of it is what the US stands for as the sole super-power, one that, knowingly or otherwise, has inherited the ambitions of the British empire to protect its global interests by setting international stand-ards and siding with the weak against the strong. There is no question of China challenging that or even wanting to do so, certainly not on a global scale. China has no stomach or ambition to be equal to the US in that regard; I think that China is not so foolish as to even try to emulate the US. But, in the eyes of some Chinese, the image of the US as a superpower that is tempted to take on the British burden and surpass their achievements is still before them. When that ambition is seen as bolstered by a strong missionary tradition, then the Chinese must surely fear that, ultimately, they could never conform to, or satisfy the standards of international behaviour that the US demands.

Let me take a few examples from recent events. When the United Nations Security Council voted unanimously to impose sanctions on the government of Colonel Gaddafi of Libya, the PRC agreed, for the first time, to refer a case of state violence to the International Criminal Court. China and the US voted together on this matter, both countries displaying a degree of equality and respect they have not often shown to each other on the Security Council.

About the same time, the US media picked up the analogy of Tahrir Square in Cairo (and other similar centres of demonstrations in the Arab world) with Tiananmen Square in Beijing, and dwelt long and hard on the fact that the Chinese media were unable to report fully on the Middle East disorders. Chinese dissenters, mainly in the US, were also actively blogging with calls for brave Chinese citizens to meet in several major cities to display their discontent with the PRC government. Even the US ambassador in Beijing was involved with the police action at Wangfujing against possible or potential protesters.

Clearly the media saw the US on the right side of history and memories of China's record at Tiananmen have encouraged some to think that this was an opportunity to shame the Chinese leaders to make the political reforms they had been promising. There was no question of equality here, certainly no American respect for Chinese sensitivities and no Chinese niceties about foreign journalists, least of all American ones. It was striking that there was widespread use in the Chinese blogs (and the media outside China) of the word *biantian* (meaning change of heaven/weather) to describe what was happening in the Middle East. The word *biantian* is an ambiguous reference to regime change in certain contexts, and the word has been used to remind Chinese readers that a change in the weather or regime change could come about peacefully, without violence and many deaths. One reference to Tiananmen that was picked up in several blogs was a particularly painful reminder to the Chinese authorities. It came from Colonel Gaddafi when he loudly equated his actions with those of the Chinese government in the use of military force to quell the protest in the Beijing square in 1989. He showed China respect by promising that he would be equally successful, respect that the Chinese leaders would not have welcomed.

I shall not go into the rights and wrongs of using such analogies. It is interesting enough for China to live up to its apparent equality and act together with the US in the Security Council and, at the same time and in the same week, have its use of violent suppression in 1989 quoted approvingly by Colonel Gaddafi as comparable to his own actions 22 years later. Similarly, it is instructive that, despite decades of attention and support and billions of aid and arms sales to several states in the Middle East, the US was surprised by the fall from grace of their friends in Tunisia and Egypt (and possibly others elsewhere in the Arab world) and is struggling to show respect to the Arab peoples that their less than equal political friends had kept down for so long. The burdens of a superpower are truly onerous and unpredictable and China would not be slow to take note of that.

One other comparison is worth making. The size of US oil investments in Libya had been growing; similarly the number of Chinese companies that were operating there. The difference lies in that the former is capital-intensive while the latter involved labour-intensive enterprises. The difference in financial terms I have not been able to ascertain, but many more Chinese citizens, some 35,000 of them, were caught in the fighting as compared with a few hundred Americans, and evacuating them was a much more difficult task for the Chinese. Also, the US has bases in Europe and its naval and air forces are close by in the Mediterranean and the Red Sea. The Chinese government, in contrast, had a tough time diverting its airlines, including commercial flights, to pick up their workers who were forced to leave the violence. That they did so quickly and successfully is remarkable, something they had not had to do since they evacuated ethnic Chinese out of Indonesia after the fall of Sukarno. On the other hand, what is comparable is the way both countries are equally committed to saving their nationals and, on this occasion, the Chinese demonstrated the capacity and determination to do so in ways that the Americans can but approve.

For the past thirty years, China has come a long way towards adjusting to international norms and, where it has not gained allies, has been exceedingly cautious not to offend friendly countries globally. It has been meticulous in examining every action in terms of how it can defend its national interests, however narrowly those interests might seem. At times, for example, on questions of legal equality associated with issues of sovereignty, it has been correct and stubborn to a fault, even at the risk of angering erstwhile friendly neighbours with contentious disputes. Those disputes that involve treaty allies of the US will be potentially destabilizing for other relationships in the region. Both China and the US are equally aware of these obstacles to their future relationship. They know that failing to handle them successfully would undermine efforts for the two nations to treat each other with respect.

Where respect is concerned, there are also different threats. To many political leaders in the US, respect has hinged on expecting China to proceed with systemic reforms that would provide its people with more political liberties. China has not been willing to accept criticisms that threaten vital interests as its leaders saw them, whether they came from inside or outside the country. Indeed, China's record in the treatment of dissenters and whistleblowers has been openly contrary to ideals of justice and fairness that most people expect of civilized nations. Some of that stems from poor governance but others are rooted in selfish interests that protect those in power from public scrutiny. The contradictions are obvious and it is likely that these will remain for as long as Chinese leaders feel threatened by reforms the outcome of which they cannot determine.

China's progress in economic equality has been reassuring to the country and the issue of equality in general with the US and the West is not the problem it used to be. Respect, however, is more elusive. Each generation of Chinese leaders has to face growing complexity in the social and political changes taking place as their people become richer and better educated. Each generation will have to be more sensitive to the fact that respect for China as a country will be closely linked to how the ruling party can continue to win greater respect from its own people.

CHAPTER 11

A CHINESE WAY*

When we talk about China, we tend to think only of the People's Republic of China (the PRC). This is certainly understandable in the language of international relations, where the PRC insists, and most members of the United Nations agree, that there is only one China, and officially, that refers to the PRC. At the same time, it is accepted that this 'one China' recognises the historical position of Taiwan as part of a divided China. In short, China has always been broader than simply the PRC. In the near future, China will incorporate Hong Kong and Macau, and it may well in one way or another, either juristically or physically, include Taiwan sometime in the 21st century. Thus, the difference between China and the People's Republic of China lies largely in current usage. In Chinese eyes, China, Zhongguo or Zhonghua, can refer to a civilisation, a society, or a political entity. For Chinese people, it is both accurate and natural to include all three, the People's Republic or Mainland China, the Republic of China on Taiwan, and Hong Kong-Macau (abbreviated as Hong Kong here) as China. This has been confirmed by the fact that Hong Kong and Macau will very soon be part of China, and that the government of Taiwan still considers itself to be part of China, having always claimed to be China, albeit a temporarily separate part. Nevertheless, when the name 'China' is used, the focus is on the PRC, especially in the context of its position in international relations.

It is also important to note that the Chinese have many words to describe themselves. These vary depending on who the different groups of people are, and on the different historical and geographical contexts in which they need to be identified. But in other languages, there would only be a single word: 'Chinese'

---

*The article was published in *China's Political Economy*, edited by Wang Gungwu and John Wong, Singapore: World Scientific Publishing Co. Pte. Ltd., 1998.

in English, and similar equivalents in all the others. Thus, this one word, 'Chinese', is used loosely and widely. It is used to translate the many words in the Chinese language for the people, as well as various adjectival words and phrases to describe everything that pertains to China. As the name of the people, the word describes one-fifth of the world's population as well as their written language. The same word also includes millions of people of Chinese origin who do not reside in any part of China but have settled abroad, are foreign nationals, and may not speak the Chinese language at all. Thus, the word itself almost invariably needs an adjective before it like, Mainland Chinese, Taiwan Chinese, Hong Kong Chinese, the Overseas Chinese or ethnic Chinese, or is itself used adjectivally, as in Chinese diaspora and Chinese-Americans, just to mention a few examples. There is little doubt that, most of the time, the word 'Chinese' has been made to do too much.

In short, 'Chinese' may merely refer to a national name, like Belgian or Norwegian. Or, it would be used more like a term comparable to 'European', or even similar to the word 'Westerner' as well as to the many varieties of Chinese mentioned above. Obviously, this usage could be relevant to China's position in international relations, especially when it is ambiguous, or not clearly defined. Thus, it is important to account for 'China', and 'the Chinese', each in its respective parts.

My other starting-point is that, despite the differences in geography and modern history that have divided China, there is a great depth and breadth in China's continuous cultural heritage. This China has also claimed that, in its undivided manifestation, it could be a country like other countries. It suggests that whenever it can speak and act as one such country, it would expect to behave and be treated like other countries. During the 20th century, all three parts of the country have been sharply separated, and there have been times when Taiwan and Hong Kong people have been encouraged to behave as if they came from independent countries. In recent years, some of them have, together with foreigners, deliberately and habitually used the name China to apply only to the People's Republic. Sometimes, of course, this use of China is a convenient shorthand, but it would be misleading if this usage is employed to suggest that Taiwan and Hong Kong are no longer part of China.

For the past decade, however, the relations among the three parts have become increasingly open and interdependent, and mainland China has joined both Taiwan and Hong Kong in seeking to be open to the rest of the world. Of course, the specific experiences of each part, whether in terms of its internal experiments or of its external environment, have had clearly unique features. These experiences determine to a large extent if each of the three is more or less open, and if any one of them is more willing to resist global interdependence than any other. However, there is no question that the PRC, Taiwan and Hong Kong have also much in common. For example, during the 20th century, the following have been striking: their speed in changing themselves and taking up opportunities, the spirit of defiance they each show when challenged by outsiders, and the propensity for their people to migrate, something which their respective governments alternately forbade and encouraged.

Thus, I shall use the term China here to include the PRC, Taiwan and Hong Kong. However, we now increasingly encounter the term 'Greater China' (*The China Quarterly*, Special Issue, no. 136, 1993). What does this mean? When we speak of Greater London or Greater Tokyo, no one is alarmed. The word 'great' in Great Britain does not conjure images of expansion beyond the British Isles, although some of my Irish friends might object to having any part of the island of Ireland included. But when 'Greater' is attached to large countries like India and China, we risk being asked about their imperialist ambitions. In Asia, we have had the experience in the 1930s of scholars referring to Greater India, or ancient Hindu colonies in Southeast Asia, when they described Hindu-Buddhist influences in the region. There were objections to this usage, even among Indian scholars themselves, and the term was eventually dropped. Why then has a similar term 'Greater China' emerged during the late 1980s? The main reason, of course, is that people have narrowed the name of China to mean the PRC. Also, developments since 1978 in all three parts of China have shown how readily they can approach a condition of economic integration. With that possibility, it is natural to look at the three areas as a virtual economic entity again. But then, why not simply China? Why add the adjective 'Greater'?

I have been skeptical of the term from the start, but have also been surprised by its staying power. It seems important, therefore, to try to understand why it has attracted so much attention. It is, of course, a useful way for me to lead into the subject of these lectures which approaches China's international position and the future Great Power role for that entity, through perceptions of China's historic empire, of a China-based civilisation, of China's ultimate nationhood, as well as of China's divergent market economies.

DIVERGENT ECONOMIES

The origins of 'Greater China' may be found in the success of Deng Xiaoping's economic reforms in mainland China, coupled with the powerful economic performances by the Chinese entrepreneurs of Taiwan, Hong Kong and Singapore. Tentative efforts were made to find terms which would highlight the remarkable developments in South China during the 1980s and connect them directly, first with Hong Kong, and then with Taiwan. This is because the capital, business expertise and skills came mainly from these two territories. The initial concept was largely Hong Kong-centred. Some notable earlier examples to describe the increasing economic integration were: The China Economic Circle, or China Economic Zone, The China Economic Community, even The China Economic Sphere. Yet others introduced terms like 'Entity' and 'Commonwealth', and many began to add 'Greater China (*Da Zhonghua*)' as an adjective before the various nouns. Unconsciously, these terms extended the concept to imply all of China, or even all Chinese. But there were some terms that were more modest, carefully restricting the idea to the three specific areas of Hong Kong, Taiwan and South China, and referred to 'a potential Free Trade Area', and to the three as forming the 'China Economic Triangle', or the South China Economic Zone, or even Greater Hong Kong. And Greater China somehow became shorthand for some or all of these.

As Greater China became more widely used, first by businessmen and journalists and then by scholars at several major international conferences, various definitions were offered. The most practical and the one that raised the least alarm was to have the term narrowed to refer to the original areas of Hong Kong, Taiwan and South China. But in the excitement in having such a striking image of China, other usages expanded the term to include all of the People's Republic of China, that is, unconsciously returning to the broader concept of China. Some went even further to include all ethnic Chinese settled in foreign countries in different parts of the world on the grounds that many of them have invested, and are investing, in all three areas of China, and are therefore contributing to the enrichment of the PRC.

The main justification for Greater China has been the virtual economic integration of Hong Kong, Taiwan and coastal PRC. This is, of course, more apparent than real. The networks of relationships in this region which have been built up are both subtle and complex, and involve processes carried out through informal interactions between industrialists, financiers and traders of all three areas. These interactions are a part of, and can hardly be separated from, the international interests of the entrepreneurs of both Hong Kong and Taiwan, and increasingly, those of the entrepreneurs of the mainland as well. They are all dependent on the world's open markets, and none of the links have to be specifically Chinese at all. Indeed, the success of both Hong Kong and Taiwan clearly depend on their access to the markets of North America and Western Europe.

But if the concept is extended to include the rest of mainland China, and especially if it were to include the ethnic Chinese residing in foreign countries, it does become alarming and needs to be closely scrutinised. In the economic context of how 'Greater China' evolved to include all of the People's Republic of China, it is different from the historic idea of China, and it becomes totally different from the original concept that was centred on Hong Kong. We would find that, far from looking only to Hong Kong and Taiwan, most of mainland China really look elsewhere for their external relationships. For example, East and North-Central China would look more readily towards South Korea and Japan; similarly, North-east China would look to the Russian Far East, Mongolia and North Korea; and North-west China towards the Muslim states of Central Asia as well as Russia and Afghanistan. As for Western China (including Tibet), it would more likely lean towards Nepal, India and Pakistan. And then there are the trading routes out of South-west China, through Yunnan and Guangxi, which have already linked themselves closely into the economies of Burma, Laos, Thailand, and Vietnam. Surely, 'Greater China' was never meant to cover all that.

Furthermore, if Greater China is extended beyond that to include all the ethnic Chinese living in foreign countries, this raises even more problems. Eighty per cent of all ethnic Chinese abroad, the Chinese diaspora, live in Southeast Asia. In order to include them, and the majority of them are nationals of their respective countries, Greater China would certainly acquire imperialistic overtones in the region. As for the remaining twenty percent, they are spread widely throughout the world, but at least two million may be found in the Americas, the majority being Chinese-Americans and Chinese-Canadians. To have all these ethnic Chinese linked to a Greater China makes little economic or political sense. It also would create considerable difficulties for the economic freedom and viability of these ethnic Chinese in their home countries, especially for those in Southeast Asia, and would also undermine their need to identify with their countries of adoption and to which they owe ultimate loyalty.

It is clear that some of the uses of Greater China are more emotive than others. In particular, if politicians and the media in Southeast Asia use the term to warn and frighten their own peoples about how Chinese economic power could lead to ultimate political dominance and control, there will be repercussions that could be destabilising to the region, and have considerable impact on China's international relations. All the efforts of the Chinese overseas to show their loyalty to their local countries would be suspect. Any suggestion of a vigorous and aggressive revival of Chinese power and wealth, and any use of Greater China to symbolise that rejuvenation, would be disturbing to China's relations with its neighbours. The term could also be used by these neighbours as a warning of future Chinese imperialism, of the possible restoration of early imperial borders, and even as reminders of the tributary system that China had used to control its external relations for over two thousand years.

All these reminders of the past deserve attention if we look at China's international position today. But let me begin with the present economic dimensions on which the term 'Greater China' was based, that is, with perceptions of what most Chinese seem prepared to recognise as the socialist market economy of the PRC. The relations that such an economy will have with more conventional economic developments elsewhere, and the possibility of it being any kind of model for others in the region deserve our special attention.

Much has been written about China's position in international relations following the Chinese revolutions earlier this century and the transformations of the past decades. My lectures cannot hope to cover all the issues, most of them controversial, which so many studies have raised. They will focus mainly on two questions. For reasons of size, influence and potential power, the People's Republic will deserve much more attention than the other two parts of China. And, because of the way I have framed my argument, my lectures will begin with the present, and then return to the past in order to help look at the future. This lecture deals with the impact of divergent economies. I ask if the different experiences of all three parts of China can lead to a new model for the region and beyond. The next lecture will deal with the emergence of new frameworks for political and cultural change. To understand how these frameworks have propelled changes as well as inhibited them, it is necessary to look more closely at the past. From that background, we can explore some of the potentials for a future Chinese way. By looking back as well as forward, we may derive some longer perspectives that would link China's past with its future as a global power.

Among both Chinese and foreigners, it has often been asked, why is China not a 'normal' country? By that, the questioners mean, why is China not a nation-state that behaves like most other countries? It seems clumsy in its dealings with other countries, inviting impatience with its seeming intransigence over various international issues, for example over its nuclear testing or over trade disputes. It is seen alternately as a civilisation, an empire, or a potential superpower. At times, the PRC is condemned as the last communist giant. At others, there are predictions of disaster and mainland China is seen as a precarious polity teetering on the verge of becoming a group of fragmented and warring states. Or, China is considered an unstable hybrid, a strange creature that has a socialist body, but with parts of that body dressed in capitalist clothes. There are numerous paradoxes and contradictions, all leaving the impression of instability and the capacity to destabilise the region if not the whole world.

These different images, and the questions they beg, are found not only among those outside China, but also among those within as well. We can usefully explore these images through descriptions of China that reflect the different ways the country is being perceived by the Chinese themselves. The reactions of the Chinese to pressures from outside would then be more readily understood. The views vary from those about the present to those about the past, and also include hopes for the future. There are several layers of such perceptions which are current. By layers, there is a suggestion of chronological sequence, with the present on top and the past arranged in order below but, like the way historical events surface in our minds, each layer of the past can be conjured up whenever appropriate to any discourse and is not necessarily chronological. That is how Chinese people habitually make use of their past and that is how I intend to treat those layers. This does not imply that any of these perceptions are shared by all Chinese. Not all layers may be found among every group of Chinese, neither do they co-exist in people's consciousness at any one time. Also, natural to a large and diverse people, each layer, while they are not equally important, could be dominant for some Chinese some of the time.

SOCIALIST MARKET ECONOMY

By divergent economies, I refer to two current terms, the socialist market economy and the developing economies. The first term, 'socialist market economy' has aroused puzzlement and even scorn among Western and other economists and all those interested in economics or politics. It would seem a contradiction in terms and many have interpreted the Chinese use of such a term as a means of hiding their embarrassment that capitalism is now rampant in the country. Or it is thought that the Chinese leaders do not understand modern economics and therefore use the term 'market economy' incorrectly. But from all accounts, the leaders are perfectly serious about the concept of a socialist market economy that they have evolved over the past

15 years, and have tried to adhere to their interpretation of the term in the face of the many doubts expressed. For whatever reason the term may have been used, and however odd we may think this term to be, we should not underestimate the determination of the present leaders to develop this economic concoction successfully.

I have explained earlier why I begin with the present, with the most immediate issues of wealth and power that concern all Chinese. Firstly, the Chinese face the challenge of socialism in the PRC, that is, the way its communist leaders want to maintain the ideals of socialism as an ideology for the state as well as to develop the economy; they thus have to deal with a market economy in transition. Secondly, they see the various parts of China competing with other developing economies, some more successfully than others, but none conforming to the expected norms. And thirdly, they wonder if a powerful and united China might formulate a universal model from the integration of socialist and capitalist ideals and means. By considering divergent economic solutions to basic problems of livelihood, could Chinese leaders develop a way to position China to play its rightful role in global affairs and thus establish a new basis for its future position in the world?

In less than a decade, the economic reforms of the PRC have transformed the country from a highly centralised planned economy to one that is learning from capitalistic practices. There was nothing automatic or inevitable about the decision to carry out economic reforms without political reforms. There were other routes to radical change and there were examples from Central and Eastern Europe which the Chinese economists did closely study. But, in the late 1970s, partly in reaction to the consequences of the Cultural Revolution and partly because those consequences included the loosening of many of the instruments of central controls, Deng Xiaoping decided to promote market reforms as the path to follow.

The Chinese Communist Party and the Beijing government had little choice but to seek reform. Without reform, the country would have had to face further disasters to the national economy, disasters that could have threatened everything that the Party leaders had fought for. They could even have ended with the collapse of the regime. But the evidence is clear that the driving forces behind Deng Xiaoping's efforts were more positive than that. His zeal to bring modernity to China had not been dimmed by his years in the wilderness. His dedication to a revolution to restore wealth and power to China remained strong. In his own words in 1984, "We regard reform as a revolution" (Talk with Chancellor Helmut Kohl on 10th October). The lessons he learnt from the mistakes of Mao Zedong had heightened his natural pragmatism. In addition, he was correct in believing that the people were deeply disappointed at the PRC's poverty after 30 years of communism.

The idea that socialism brought betterment not only through a more equitable distribution of wealth but also through its efficiency in creating more wealth had been a promise that the people still expected the Party to keep. I recall the stirring call by one party leader at an international conference in 1979 (An Gang, a former editor of *People's Daily*) that "socialism should make money", and how that was soon echoed as "Get rich first" throughout the country, with the additional exhortation that socialism should be more successful than capitalism! This was when it was obvious that capitalistic Hong Kong and Taiwan, the 'little China's', were each producing greater wealth than their big brother.

The leaders who had fought in the battlefields still believe that socialism is superior. But, after the bitter and uncertain thirty years of experimentation since 1949, they now agree that learning from the capitalists conforms to historical necessity. Capitalism is a stage that cannot be skipped on the way to socialism. It is hard, however, to know how many of the younger leaders still believe in that superiority. Insofar as the picture of capitalism remains that of 19th century satanic mills and exploited workers, there certainly remains the faith that socialism is superior. But younger party members and intellectuals can now read about what capitalist countries have achieved during the past five decades, not only the obvious examples of Japan and the U.S., but also the territories where millions of other Chinese live, Hong Kong and Taiwan. They can see how all of them have been able to raise the standards of living for the vast majority of their peoples. Many PRC leaders can also travel and see for themselves how competitive developments in industrial practices, innovations in financial institutions and managerial methods have made it possible for wealth creation to co-exist with the principles of equitable distribution. They can see for themselves that the evolution of elaborate welfare safety nets for the weak and disabled have ironically been most developed and successful in these capitalist societies. There is no contradiction in places like Hong Kong and Taiwan; on the contrary, there is actually a direct correlation between newly generated wealth and higher incomes for the working classes.

Nevertheless, despite many vigorous debates, the bulk of all writings emanating from the PRC today remain loyal to key Marxist principles. The Chinese Communist Party still dictates all analysis of social and political phenomena, even when the economics of the market have been accepted in key aspects of reform policies. Capitalism in its modern and mature form is now recognised as more pluralistic and flexible. It is also seen as more being and a necessary means to an end. All the same, the official judgment still regards it as a force that will, in the longer run, stand in the way of progress towards the socialist ideals which the revolutionaries had lived and died for. But the crude form of anti-capitalist rhetoric and righteous pronouncements are now rarely made. Instead, there is widespread acknowledgement of the strengths of capitalist organisations and the relevance of their skills and experiences for the revival and development of the Chinese economy. The examples of Japan, South Korea and Taiwan (and cities like Singapore and Hong Kong) have inspired a younger generation of economists as well as the newly emerging private and semi-private sectors on the mainland, and also provided lessons for all levels of officials to learn from. And in every way possible under a rapidly changing economic system, the most enterprising people are responding to the extraordinary stimulus that Deng Xiaoping had released among them.

Indeed, it is this very speed of change, the bypassing of party and government structures, and the excitement generated by ongoing battles against ingrained bureaucratic habits, especially among more enterprising officials in the provinces, that have alarmed the leaders in Beijing. It is not capitalism in the abstract that is threatening, it is the perception of a market economy, however modified, that will inevitably unleash social forces that have hitherto been under severe controls. Every day, there is evidence that some of the worst features of the pre-1949 world have returned: the unemployment, the corruption, the greed, the selfishness, the immorality, the inequalities, even the dangers of runaway inflation that all the textbooks say the revolution had put an end to once and for all.

Thus, the perception of a successful market economy that would become less and less socialist hangs like a cloud over the recent triumphs. Ultimately, if mainland Chinese behave like the Chinese of Taiwan and Hong Kong, that economy could be heading towards a capitalism that would appeal to the young and ambitious, the newly rich and successful, the natural malcontents and rebels, the exploiters, and the potential traitors. How could the Party then maintain its tight control? Parts of the outside world, especially the western world, anticipate that it is inevitable that there will be a radical change in that capacity to control everything centrally. Some are already portraying the political reforms of Taiwan as the necessary next step for the mainland to follow. In coming to the support of the laws and freedoms of Hong Kong, they are pointing to similar democratic reforms as essential to future continued progress on the mainland. The Chinese experiences in the two smaller parts are expected to have a profound impact on the mainland.

The achievements of Deng Xiaoping's reforms have created a new volatile environment in which the hopes for ever better economic performances are matched by fears of social turmoil. The next generation of leaders urgently need to reinspire their people to believe that the socialist way to a market economy is the best road to socialism. For the past fifteen years, they have enjoined their economists and policy advisers to define that road more clearly and convincingly. These loyal supporters have been asked to map out how to sustain such a socialist market economy without becoming capitalistic like the Chinese Taiwan and Hong Kong. They must demonstrate, in addition, why such an economy is different from what social democrats in the West have been content to accept, that is, the various forms of mixed economies in so-called welfare-states. The time has come for the leaders to stop, if I may use their own words, "taking one step forward and looking around before taking another", and advancing as if they were, using their own words again, "wading across a river by feeling for the rocks under the water" (Zhao Ziyang in January 1985). They still seem to be some way from convincing their people that they have a found the right formula to enhance, and renew faith in, Marxism. But the perception remains that retaining the ideal of the socialist political order is essential to their particular variety of a market economy.

Despite the examples of Taiwan and Hong Kong for most Chinese people, the key to this primary self-perception of the PRC today is the word 'superiority', that is, the superiority of socialism over other systems. The PRC leaders have to believe that the revolution as they see it has not failed. Mistakes have been made and these are now being rectified through radical reforms. Capitalistic methods, where usable, are but the means to an end. To paraphrase an old Chinese saying, "socialism (now with Chinese characteristics) is the base, and capitalism (but avoiding its liberal excesses) is only for application". Therefore, greater efforts are needed to show that capitalism may be enough for a city like Hong Kong, or a small 'province' like Taiwan, but it has no place in a vast country of a 1.2 billion people. If the PRC can sustain its successes for another decade or so, it could enshrine the concept of a socialist market economy as the Chinese way for all Chinese, and perhaps for the region as well.

In short, what counts is whether market socialism will take root and produce the wealth that the country needs without political reforms. So far, the results have been extraordinary, but how convincing have they been for other countries in similar positions? The dramatic successes seem to have had surprisingly little influence among the former communist bloc countries. The Soviet Union under Gorbachev had chosen a different solution by putting political reform ahead of economic reform, a solution that the PRC leaders see as having led to the collapse of the Soviet Union and the end of communism in Europe.

But none of the twenty or so countries that emerged from that debacle have followed this Chinese way. They are trying to adapt their economies to that of the capitalist West, but are seeking to do so at their own speed. Their various kinds of socialism have, on the whole, accepted new approaches to representative democracy, or at least paid lip service to its principles. Except for Russia and its North Asian outreaches, of course, they are all much smaller than, and have nothing in common with the PRC. Those in Europe have, in any case, economies that are much more like those in the neighbouring European nation-states. In addition, there is also a greater cultural affinity.

Only the five Muslim states of Central Asia, which have remained more loyal to their communist past, might have looked to China. But they all have good reasons to stay close to Russia in the face of a very volatile Muslim world nearby. For similar reasons, in view of their own Muslim minorities in the neighbouring border province of Xinjiang, the Chinese are themselves cautious of intimate relations. Of the remainder, Mongolia and Vietnam seem to have found parts of the China experience instructive, not least the Taiwan and the Hong Kong parts. They are certainly studying all three with care, and, despite their reservations about Chinese power so close by, have not hesitated to follow similar market economy methods when they have found them appropriate. But they might also look more to Japan and South Korea in the long run. Only North Korea has chosen not to change, still being enmeshed in its rhetoric of self-sufficiency. Elsewhere, communist countries like Cuba really have no reason to look to China. When Cuba decides to move, it is more than likely that it would learn from Mexico and make its peace with the United States.

In short, the Chinese version of the market economy has won no converts among former communist countries. What then has made the Deng Xiaoping experiment important to the rest of the world, especially to the capitalist world?

From one point of view, it is obvious. The size of the labour force and the market, and the bold decision to open the country to outside investment, have attracted foreign capital from all over the world, and from both large and small trading companies. No less important is its location in Eastern Asia, close to Japan and the Little Dragons of South Korea, Taiwan, Hong Kong and Singapore, and to the newly emerging economies of the Association of Southeast Asian Nations (ASEAN) countries. Among the developing countries of the 'South' or 'the Third World', this is the region that has responded most successfully to development aid and international trade over the past two decades. China's interactions with the region, and with the West, constitute one of the most important economic phenomena in recent world history.

Thus the importance of the China experiment may be due more to its size and location than to its intrinsic qualities.

I shall come back to the perception of what might be called the China model and its future. What does need to be said here is that the PRC's faith in the superiority of socialism, and the China-U.S. relationship, which is being treated by the American government as the end-game of the historic capitalist-communist struggle, together provide a dynamic backdrop for the economic and political transformation of the region.

From the outside, two facts stand out. The first is that communist China has chosen its own way, even though it is yet without followers and allies from the former communist camp. The second is that China has been drawn into a larger Asian region of rapid economic growth. It is one that is likely to expand and, what is more important, it is one that offers an interdependence that all three parts of China will increasingly need. These two facts have encouraged the capitalist world to have great hopes for China to be further transformed by the eventual integration of its three economies, indeed by the very evolutionary changes that the Chinese leaders believe will prove the superiority of achieving 'socialism by capitalist means'.

In the PRC's own perception of itself, however, the emphasis is likely to be on the impact their success will have on other developing economies of the world. It could give others hope when it is remembered that China had stood with them during the Cold War period and, despite its limited resources and its many tragic mistakes, had challenged both the United States and the Soviet Union.

DEVELOPING ECONOMIES

This brings me to the second layer of self-perception, that China has many of the features of the developing Third World and is not greatly different from most of those countries still considered part of the so-called South. By developing economies, I refer to most of the former colonies of the West which did not come under communist influence, and those countries which had been under Western dominance or under some kind of tutelage, in Asia, the Middle East, Africa and Latin America. The exceptions are the oil-rich countries, which do not fit the description so well.

The obviously successful examples of countries modernising their economies are found in East and Southeast Asia, that is, in China's neighbourhood,
notably South Korea, the ASEAN states, and Chinese territories like Taiwan
and Hong Kong. They have done this by learning from, depending on, and
trading with, the capitalist West. The ones that have attracted the most attention in the PRC were, of course, Taiwan and Hong Kong, where Chinese
business and professional leaders have demonstrated their capacity to modernise rapidly by adopting an export expansion strategy. Taiwan had, earlier
in the 1950s, implemented a successful land reform programme and a
systematic upgrading of education, which led to considerable upward mobility. Similar successes in South Korea, Hong Kong and Singapore, had led the
four to be grouped together as Newly Industrialising Countries, or NICs, the
Four Dragons, or Tigers, and seen as models of effective development
strategies.

However, the PRC leaders have not compared their country directly with
any of the developing economies or any of the NICs. They would claim that
the PRC has both Chinese and socialist characteristics, and would point to
the unique features of their revolutionary experiences which have made the
country stronger and more independent. And they would insist that their
recent reform programmes were both original and exceptional. But they
would not deny that, where there are similarities, these are striking. While the
PRC is no longer desperately poor, it is still poor. It needs outside help with
both capital and technology, it needs to strengthen its education and training
institutions, and it needs all the trading and financial concessions that have
been granted to other developing countries. For these reasons, it is in fact to
the PRC's advantage to be treated as a developing economy.

The barrier to equating the Chinese variant of development with that of
most developing countries is that it had long been grouped with the alternate
model of the Second World, that is, the Soviet Union and all its communist
allies. That was a world that was thought to have the solidarity and, therefore,
the strength to challenge the First World, the capitalist West. Now that the
communist bloc has been wound up, this picture of the PRC's former place in
a Second World is clearly no longer applicable. Habits of historical classification

are, however, not easy to discard. By insisting that it is still dedicated to communist goals and is successfully reforming its way to a more sustainable form of socialism, the PRC would seem to be in a state of limbo between the West and the Third World. There are indeed many ambiguities which do not fit the country into the mould of a developing economy. China is a nuclear power; it is an economic giant; its size and location in the 'North', with Japan and Russia as neighbours, and its proven capacity to replicate the latest science and technology to match the West and Japan, would tend to put it into a different category of development.

The concept of 'Third World' was, of course, not exactly the same as that of 'developing economies'. There was always a strong political element in the way Third World countries were the targets of competition and rivalry between the capitalist West and the Communist bloc. Thus, strictly speaking, the PRC was never part of the Third World. However, the intense Sino-Soviet rivalry that started in the 1960s gave the PRC an opening to redefine its role. It distanced itself from the Cold War rivalry between the U.S. and the Soviet Union and offered leadership to the Third World. It reached out to the Afro-Asian and Latin American countries as a 'fellow-sufferer' of superpower ambitions, and wanted to join them to resist being pawns in that 'Great Game'. There was much writing at the time to justify placing this China among the post-colonial developing countries, but one that was separated sharply from Hong Kong, the British colony. It was also quite distinct from Taiwan, the instrument of U.S. intervention in Chinese affairs and therefore a U.S. satellite.

The PRC leaders did so for a variety of reasons. Despite the aid missions in the 1970s to help industrialise Africa (and many Chinese were sent to the continent to manage these missions), the country never had the resources to offer more than friendly gestures to the developing countries. Then the Cultural Revolution of 1966–76 destroyed most of what credibility and capability its aid and diplomacy might have had. Therefore, there was no question of setting up as a third superpower offering choices to Third World countries. Also, as an agrarian society still struggling to lift itself up, it was easy to portray itself as undergoing the same developing experience as all the others.

By the 1970s, with closer relations growing between China and the West (including the U.S.), there was the unexpected opportunity for the West to see China as a powerful counterweight to the Soviet Union. Deng Xiaoping's open door policies further broke down barriers to trade and investment. The PRC then joined those parts of the Third World which eschewed import substitution policies, including those which have always looked to the West. They adopted instead export oriented solutions to development, learning directly from Taiwan and the other 'Little Tigers'. It became an advantage thereafter for the PRC to continue to be seen as a developing country by institutions like the United Nations and the World Bank and many others. That image was also helped by policies which encouraged joint ventures with, and investments by, foreign multinationals. Ironically, Chinese entrepreneurs from Hong Kong, Taiwan and abroad, were specially invited to invest there. With the latter group, their investments were regularly treated as patriotic contributions by fellow Chinese.

All at once, measured by economic indicators alone, the country could see itself as a supremely successful developing country. Its performance in social and economic transformation over the past 15 years has been breathtaking. It is now possible to present itself as a 'Newly Industrialising Country'. Only its size makes it ridiculous to call itself another 'Little Dragon' or 'Little Tiger'. In fact, there is considerable ambiguity here. Both in terms of land and population, it could be compared with other developing countries like India and Brazil. Yet the comparison lacks the one dimension which has aroused controversy both within China and also with the leaders of the U.S., Japan, and China's immediate neighbours. India and Brazil are non-communist and practise versions of democracy which are acceptable to the West. Neither toyed with radical social experiments as the PRC had for decades. Theirs had never been the 'brave new world' of socialist man that Mao Zedong tried to lead his people towards. Their little successes and failures have been mainly incremental. They developed on the margins of capitalism, and in the case of Brazil, by being dependent on foreign governments as well. Neither had tried the bold leaps into economic revolution the way the PRC did. Neither experienced the dramatic ups and downs that brought, alternately, exhilaration and tragedy to hundreds of millions of people and, in the course of that, destroyed a whole ruling class, as had happened for China. These bold experiments with social and economic engineering have really no equal among the other developing economies.

For these reasons, the PRC does not readily fit the image of a developing country, but had identified itself as one partly for strategic reasons and partly for short-term economic and diplomatic advantages. Nevertheless, it is today more like a developing economy than it has ever been before. By opening its doors to foreign investment on such a large scale, it may seem to be even more of a developing economy than India. Indeed, if the Chinese leaders should lose their nerve now and pull back from a greater liberation of the economy, and from going ahead with more thorough reforms of its laws and its administration, its economy could end up being like that of India. Like India, China could share the fate of a developing economy with great potential which, for reasons of inertia, conservatism and lack of courage and imagination, has become stuck in a deep groove. If Chinese leaders see China as a developing economy, they would do well to examine the Indian experience carefully. There are lessons there, as in the former Soviet Union, which the Chinese believe they have already learnt, lessons from mistakes which they are unlikely to repeat, or at least hope not to repeat.

One lesson seems to be outstanding. India had its variety of socialism, but rejected the revolutionary communist road in favour of a representative democracy. The Soviet Union under Gorbachev also chose political reform, starting with more democracy in order to support economic change. The PRC claims to have avoided both these ways in order to concentrate on using strong central control to modify and reform the economy. The fact that the four NICs in the region, between the 1950s and the 1980s, did not need democracy to be economically successful has given the Chinese much encouragement. Their success supports the Chinese position that radical economic reform must precede political change.

Any study of the modernisation process would show that it is a very recent idea to have democracy coupled with economic growth as part of that process. The imperial powers in Asia and Africa had never thought democracy was necessary when they were administering their colonies. Britain and France experimented with democracy only at the last stages of an involuntary decolonisation. During the late 19th and the early 20th centuries, neither Germany nor Japan needed democratic institutions to achieve their own rapid rates of growth. Nor did the new post-colonial nations in the Third World produce any evidence that democracy was necessary for economic development. In many former colonies, democratic institutions did not survive and were never given the chance to prove whether they would have helped or hindered economic development.

In short, one may well conclude that the Western model of liberal democracy could only come about in three ways. It could evolve organically after several hundreds of years under certain favourable conditions, as it did in Western Europe. This would include going through an industrial revolution, though not always necessarily so. It could also be part of the colonial heritage, something which the British, the French and the Americans, each in their distinctive way, tried to leave behind on the eve of their departures, for example, in India, Malaysia and Singapore; in parts of Africa; and in the Philippines. Even Japan could be said to have had democracy imposed on it by an occupying power, the United States, after a disastrous war. Or, thirdly, it could emerge after decades of economic growth and the rise of a sizable middle class, as in Taiwan and South Korea, and perhaps Thailand. Some may point to a fourth example, one following de-Sovietisation in the late 1980s, as in Russia and some of the Eastern and Central European countries. I would rule this out where China is concerned. The Chinese firmly believe that all attempts at democratisation prior to economic reform in communist states were disasters. Thus, of the three roads to democracy, the first is too slow and depended on unique historical and cultural conditions which cannot be repeated. The second would not apply to China because China was never a British or French or American colony. Then, if the third were valid, democracy would have to await further economic growth. This would fit in with the PRC's contention that it would take much more time before some kind of democracy could appear in China.

The new kinds of developing economy like those of South Korea and Taiwan could be said to have produced 'models' that challenge the idea that democracy is essential for development and should therefore precede it. Instead, their examples show that the people's energies could be channelised towards growth and the production of wealth from the top down, by firm leadership, clear goals and administrative controls. It is possible for development to succeed by using capitalistic methods without the precondition of liberal democracy. And, if either South Korea or Taiwan is any guide, democracy would follow after successful development. Why could not Taiwan's form of capitalism and the PRC's form of socialism be brought together? Could the two not combine the free and outward-looking structures of Taiwan and Hong Kong with the national power of the PRC to promote China's international position and bring it closer towards finding the Chinese way?

CHINA AS UNIVERSAL MODEL

I suggest that China's recent economic successes cannot be separated from how the Chinese see the integration of socialist ideals with capitalist means as a model for the region. This is the third layer of self-perception. Let me start with some earlier Chinese ideas of being an advanced universal model.

Indeed, China is used to the idea of being a model for its neighbours. Many institutions introduced into Korea, Japan and Vietnam, and adopted in the kingdoms established by the tribal federations of the Turks, the Khitans, the Jurchens and the Tanguts, and the Mongols and the Manchus even before they ruled over all of China, were directly modelled on those of China under the Tang (7th–10th centuries), Song (10th–13th centuries) and Ming (14th–17th centuries) dynasties. So accustomed were the Chinese to being the model for others to copy that their ruling elites have been, for centuries, particularly resistant to learning from others. Similarly, they have never lost the urge for China to be a model for others. Hence the zeal to be a revolutionary model for the developing world after the communist victory in 1949 was almost inevitable. Although this model was inspired by the Bolshevik Revolution, it was seen as having been advanced by the vision and character of Mao Zedong. It was thus natural for the Chinese to expect their country to be a model for other countries again. For a couple of decades, the fact that it could be such a model was also a source of national pride for most Chinese.

This included the many Chinese who joined the missions to bring the Chinese model to Africa in the 1970s.

Deng Xiaoping's economic reforms were launched with the purpose of saving what had survived the anarchic decade of the Cultural Revolution. Reform was essential in order to protect what he and his colleagues still believed to have been a great historic revolution. It is in that context that we note that it is too early to say that the model for export to the world is free from the shadow of Marxist-Leninism. I mentioned above that the PRC appears to be in a limbo between the West and the Third World. From that point of view, more comparisons might be made with the new Russia. But the Chinese perception here seems to be different. The Russians have failed the revolution, the Chinese have not. China is being rescued from the mistakes of some of its leaders, and its success in doing so proves that the revolution is alive and well. Therefore, the earlier Soviet model is seen as irrelevant today only because it was imperfectly implemented, or inadequately adapted to Chinese and Asian conditions. But in its socialist essence, and after due reform, it could still be viable as a model and may still have universal features for others who seek the revolutionary way. If this perception is valid, what kind of model can China present to the world? How universal can that model be?

The literature that describes and extols the original model in China is vast and erudite. The whole country was saturated with the Thought of Mao Zedong. Every word he ever wrote or ever uttered was near-sacred, so the most careful editing of his works was done at the highest levels to ensure that there would not be any inconsistency between current policies and what the Great Helmsman had said. Then followed the massive effort to popularise his thought and enable every man, woman and child to understand the profundity of his vision for China. The Little Red Book served as a catechism, and every party member and cadre was expected to act as a priest in this secular faith. Although this is well-known, it is important to remind ourselves of how long and deeply the people on the mainland were subjected to this ideological bombardment and how many Chinese rejected it and voted with their feet to Hong Kong and Taiwan and elsewhere.

We should also remember that the classics of revolution originated from the west and were the works of Marx and Engels. Great efforts were also made to translate everything they wrote and annotate their most important texts for the whole population. Not far behind were the writings of Lenin and Stalin, and similar complete editions of their works have been made available. Scholarly analyses by generations of young Chinese ideologues of all the antecedents and contemporaries of these four men in Europe have also been made. In addition, all other revolutionary thinkers in the same mode have been given close attention, if not for their originality, at least to demonstrate the universality of the Marxist-Leninist canon. I do not need to add that thousands of scholars and commentators outside China, in the West, in Japan and elsewhere in Asia, in Africa and Latin America, have also contributed to this vast corpus of writings, whether critically or in admiration. It is also necessary to remind ourselves of the vitriolic debates between certain Russian and Chinese leaders over the interpretations of the classic texts of revolution. They formed a shared experience which few would care to remember today, but it did exercise many minds to what, in Chinese, is traditionally called 'the end-point of a bull's horn', that is, the epitome of futility.

I have recalled all this to make a point about the great paradox of this layer of self-perception in China. The paradox is that Marxism-Leninism brought an international dimension into the lives of mainland Chinese which they had never experienced before, but this dimension was given a narrow focus by Mao Zedong's appeal to the traditions of a peasant rebellion. The narrowness was the very opposite of the universal features of the socialist ideal, but Mao the Chinese was really a provincial patriot, and this feature was further aggravated because of the intense rivalry between Chinese and Russian leaders and their respective national interests. In particular, Mao Zedong's ambition to be the leader of the socialist world after the death of Stalin, and his conviction that Stalin's successors had perverted the cause of internationalism, led him to excesses of liturgical exposition and in the end to the Cultural Revolution that finally, and ironically, weakened the Chinese people's commitment to socialism and to revolution.

If that is the case, is a commitment to an old faith still valid? Up till now, it still seems to be among the leaders of the Communist Party. It provides much of the rhetoric in all pronouncements about the ultimate goal of Deng Xiaoping's reform programmes. Here I am not referring to the statements simply affirming the authority and existence of the Party. I am referring to the justifications for gigantic state projects like the Three Gorges Dam, or massive industrial enterprises to make steel, refine oil, or build nuclear weapons, aeroplanes and automobiles, and more recently, to create a massive central bank. Despite the reforms and the frequent calls to respect market mechanisms, we observe the survival of Marxist and Maoist ideas in large-scale management, in the practice of law and the administration of public order. Of particular importance is the survival of all the control mechanisms to ensure that central policies are being implemented. This is because the reforms are limited to economic affairs only and political structures, in particular, are not included.

The reforms clearly do not constitute in any way a rejection of the revolution. It presupposes that the revolution of 1949 and its achievements and failures remain the starting-point. Therefore, the injunctions are to learn from the failures and build on the successes. Clearly the centrally planned policies had failed. The isolationist closed economy out of touch with the developments in the capitalist world outside had also failed. Their structures need to be dismantled whenever necessary, but not to the point of endangering the achievements, and thus the regime and its leadership.

What are the achievements of the revolution that could strengthen the model for others to follow? It is difficult to be certain how many such achievements most Chinese people can now agree on. The main works of history on the Communist period have been written under party supervision. But more and more writings are based on data not previously available to the scholars in the universities and research institutes. There has also been revisionism in the writings about some aspects of revolutionary mistakes. Foreign scholarship about the revolution is now accessible; many foreign books and articles have even been translated into Chinese and widely read. Despite the constraints, independent thinking has surfaced. At this stage, there is neither wholesale rejection of the post-1949 years, nor uncritical praise for the successes during that tumultuous period. Nor is there much regret for what might have been had the revolution been better led, or led by other leaders who might have been more nationalist or more practical. Instead, we see sober preparation for reappraisals which I believe will soon produce more authoritative writings. As for more recent events, like the corruption, inflation, and lack of channels for redress and political dialogue that led to the tragedy at Tiananmen in 1989, these are new failures that have yet to be fully addressed. Unless that is done, they will tarnish any model that the PRC has to offer.

In the meantime, there have been some widely accepted claims about the successes. For example, the destruction of the old landed classes that had supported an inefficient and corrupt system of government is seen as a permanent achievement. Also, some of the advances in agriculture, science and engineering have been widely regarded as outstanding. By and large, enough was produced in the countryside, and the famines that had occurred regularly during the last century were brought to an end. And there is even some nostalgia for the relatively egalitarian policies which used to prevail but have now been superseded by the universal drive to make money at all costs. But, of all the achievements that are mentioned from time to time, it is probably the unification of China after decades of division under a variety of warlords that is seen by most Chinese as the revolution's greatest achievement. This is what saved China from further imperialist advances by Japan and the West. It protected China from bullying by the Soviet Union at its height. It raised the status of China in international affairs and made it a major player in the Cold War, and in particular, earned the respect of the one country for which most Chinese shared a deep but ambivalent respect, the United States.

All this despite the fact that the unification had not been complete. By a deliberate decision, Hong Kong was left alone after 1949 as a window to the western capitalist world. By default, arising from the lack of air and naval power, and because of U.S. support for Taiwan as well as other distractions on the long land frontiers to the north and the west, the Beijing government could not cross the Taiwan straits. This unfinished business has probably been as important to the Chinese leaders as their visions of communism throughout the past half century. It has always been on their political and military agenda.

What is unfolding today is an intriguing picture of how recent economic developments may alter Chinese perspectives on the issue of integration and eventual unification. The prospect of a coming together of socialist and capitalist ways of achieving progress could determine the shape and nature of a new universal model. In addition, the possibility of new wealth-making partnerships and ventures coming out of all three parts of China even before its unification is a riveting subject for China's neighbours. And it is breathtaking to imagine the potential for some degree of globalisation of trading and financial organisations that would be centred in the East and Southeast Asian region. If there are chances for that to become reality, it would transform the international relations of the world for the next century.

POLITICS AND CULTURE: FROM HISTORIC EMPIRE TO GLOBAL POWER?

Most Chinese believe that the PRC (mainland Chinese) leaders today got it right by starting with economic reforms and leaving political reforms till later. The Russian experience of the past decade has confirmed the wisdom of their practical approach. With wealth, there will be strength; with wealth and strength, China's power and influence will grow. My second lecture shall concentrate on the political and cultural aspects of China's relations with the world. It shall look in turn at China as a modern nation, as an historic empire, as a civilizational challenge, and as a potential global power.

THE MODERN NATION

Let me begin with China's perception of itself as a modern nation, or nation-state. China's desire to be a nation predates the launching of the socialist revolution, but not by much. It was really only during the early years of the 20th century that the idea of nationhood and nationality began to take shape in the minds of Chinese leaders. The emphasis was never on the question of citizenship, nor on political participation by all those who shared a common identity, nor on acquiring an international persona and seeking the protection of international law. What the Chinese leaders saw as nations were clearly the powerful ones like Britain, France, Germany, Russia and the United States; in short, the Great Powers with which China compared unfavourably. The importance of national unity, therefore, was from the start seen as a source of wealth and power, something China badly needed before it could take its rightful place in the world of nations. This picture remained the dominant one during the first half of the century while China struggled for survival against foreign intervention, especially the Japanese invasions.

But how strong is this self-perception today? It is remarkable how much attention has been given to Sun Yat-sen on the mainland since the early 1980s. What Sun Yat-sen, the father of Chinese nationalism, stood for had never been given as much attention in the PRC before. He had begun as a Han Chinese rebel leader against foreign Manchu rule, but when the Manchus were overthrown in 1911 and the Republic inherited the imperial borders, he was forced to change his concerns to those of a multicultural, if not multinational, state in defence of its national borders against other foreign enemies. In terms of China's needs today, Sun Yat-sen's original concerns are hardly relevant. Clearly, some of the attention paid to him is due to the use of United Front tactics by the Beijing government to win over those who still support the Guomindang, and the ideals of Sun Yat-sen's 'Three Principles of the People', in Taiwan and overseas. Thus, in the name of unification and the ideal of One China, Sun Yat-sen the nationalist would certainly have more appeal than Mao Zedong and Deng Xiaoping.

But this specific aspect of nationalism is misleading. China as a nation is much more than the question of reunification with Taiwan. The idea of national identity was a powerful discovery at the turn of the century for the intelligentsia who saw the imperial system collapse. For a people who had lived under an empire for two thousand years, it was remarkable how quickly they accepted the idea of a republic and have not seemed to want to return to any sort of imperial or monarchical system since 1911. Indeed, these nationalists started with radical political change. Dynastic overthrow was followed by the complete replacement of the system of government, including elected national constitutent assemblies. When that failed and the country was dominated for a decade by warlords, both the nationalists and the communists who were allied to fight the warlords were agreed that political res-tucturing was essential.

The first priority was national reunification, seen as political reform or revolution from above. The leaders looked for an alternative to the main-stream Western model which was seen as an exploitative system that was impoverishing China. Ironically, they looked to the West for an ideology that was more powerful than orthodox capitalism and liberal democracy, some-thing that would help China stand up against the West itself. Some found it in Mussolini's Fascism, others in national socialism, and yet others in anar-chism, socialism, and communism. In all of these, economic development was subordinated to the political goal of unification and centralised power. And this remained so under both nationalist and communist leaders on the main-land until Deng Xiaoping's reforms after 1978. Only then, for the first time in modern history, was economic reform given the highest priority, an under-standable reaction against the Maoist slogan, "Put politics in command". This emphasis on putting prosperity before further political reform has brought a totally new dimension to China's nation-building process.

The idea of nationalism itself was an inspiration for all Chinese who felt humiliated by the successive military defeats that led to unequal status for Chinese everywhere, to extra territorial privileges for foreign residents within China, and to the increasing dominance of foreign enterprises on Chinese soil. Nationalism was tied to anti-imperialism and anti-colonialism as the key to almost all the political struggles of the 20th century. Both Chiang Kai-shek and Mao Zedong were propelled into politics by their nationalistic urges. And, despite the romantic internationalist slogans since the communist victory in 1949, national pride and interests remained in the forefront of the goals of the People's Republic. With the collapse of communist ideology, there is now little to stand in the way of the current leaders returning to nationalism to seek a stronger mandate for their rule. In familiar language, this would mean a return to the quest for wealth and power on behalf of the nation-state.

This part is obvious. But nationalism could be either a very blunt weapon, or it could be supported by a sophisticated body of ideals for a loyal citizenry, ideals that would inspire political consciousness and democratic participation, and a fervent dedication to common goals. As a blunt instrument, however, it could still be very powerful. It could inspire zealous support or arouse open hostility and fear among those within the country who feel they do not quite belong. If nation-building is not done with the greatest of care, problems of identity could become the cause of much more serious divisions among the ethnic minorities who live within artificial boundaries, or who are forced to accept historical boundaries defined by other than national criteria. Examples abound of what happens when nationalism becomes narrowly defined and fierce passions are aroused both among, and against, those who do not feel that they really belong.

Among former empires, China is more fortunate than most in having a Han majority that numbers more than 90% of the total population. The Republic of China in 1912 inherited the boundaries which the Manchu Qing armies had extended into North and Central Asia. Some territories acquired in the 17th and 18th centuries, like Outer Mongolia, had their boundaries redrawn this century to acknowledge political changes following Russian intervention and support. Most notable, although its government is now not entirely secure, was the independence of the modern Mongolian state. Other territories like Manchuria, Xinjiang and Greater Tibet had also undergone changes when China renegotiated new international borders, but they also had their internal provincial boundaries modified, not always with the consent of the minorities living within them. And there are many more autonomous provinces, counties and districts created to accommodate recognised minority peoples who remain culturally and linguistically quite different from the majority Han peoples. In drawing up criteria for these autonomous areas, the Chinese had followed Soviet practice based on Stalin's ideas of nationality. Now that the consequences of those practices have ended in the split up of the Soviet Union, the Chinese are concerned about how they might affect ethnic loyalties in China itself.

Indeed, at various layers of self-perception, China cannot but be conscious of the Soviet model which had led China to the position it is now in. The failure of communist ideology is matched by the principles of national differentiation that came from the same source. On the other hand, turning to the West for nation-building principles does not make the problem any easier for China. According to those principles, even the smallest ethnic group may, under certain conditions of history, location, language and culture, seek independent nationhood. The numerous small nations of Western and Central Europe attest to the complexities which these national principles could bring. Most notably, the Chinese leaders must view the developments in Europe in recent years with concern, if not alarm. For example, there is the separation of Slovakia; the independence of Slovenia, Croatia and other parts of Yugoslavia; the three Baltic, three Caucasian and five Muslim republics, not to say, both Ukraine and Belorus, that pulled out of the Soviet Union. As for other periods of history, following the end of empires in the past, the number of new members of the United Nations has grown at a very fast pace and continues to grow. And there is pressure everywhere for smaller entities to seek their national identities and, should they still feel insecure, find other means, like bilateral alliances, to commonwealth associations, regional groupings, communities or 'unions', and what I have called 'Anti-empires', to strengthen their capacity to defend themselves against the larger powers that remain.

In this context, the idea of China being a new nation or nation-state is still a very crude one. The government in Beijing seems to be sensitive enough about the dangers of wielding such a double-edged weapon not to make too much of the act of nation-building right now. Official documents today do not attempt any clear exposition of what a Chinese nation could mean in the future, and there is no sense of urgency that the country needs such an exposition. Given the unusual fact that the major ethnic minorities have their homes on the extensive land borders of China, it would appear to be wise for China to leave the concept broadly and inclusively defined. Thus, despite the obvious power of nationalism as a unifying force, it is not really open for the Chinese to beat the nationalist drum. China remains in the ambivalent position of encouraging national pride in becoming a Great Power while dampening the national dimensions of minority peoples on the borders of the country. Instead, the focus would have to be, in the long run, on the development of a larger national culture for an 'imagined community' that could attract the loyalty of all peoples who live in China.

Here the example of the Union of India in a divided Indian sub-continent provides an interesting comparison. It is almost as large and as populous and in may respects equally poor and backward. It too espoused socialism, but implemented it through representative democracy and in what is effectively a confederated form of state governments. India's form of socialism has been no more successful than China's communism. But, most of all, India's greatest fear is of secession and division into various linguistic or religious states and thus bring about the end of its national identity. As an example of a multinational state, of course, India is very different from China. But as a continent-size country guarding carefully its national unification goals, China would have similar concerns. The energies and resources that both central governments have put into the duty of keeping the states and provinces together are immense. But the respective leaders have shown equal determination to succeed in strengthening national unity and preserving their new nation-states. There is little doubt that this matter will be of central importance to the Chinese leaders in the country's international relations until it is finally resolved to their satisfaction. If other powers actively seek to prevent China's national unification, or worse, encourage parts of China to secede, that would become a permanent source of instability in the region. Hence the Chinese concern to maintain a strong central government, something their history inclines them to in any case.

HISTORIC EMPIRE

This leads me to another layer of self-perception in China, which is of China as an historic empire. This is quite distinct from the idea of a modern nation discussed above and the pride in China's ancient and continuous civilisation which I shall come to later. This view of itself is a deep-rooted one which has always been linked to the question of power.

The importance of a glorious imperial past is well-attested in all the thousands of books written by both nationalist and communist historians about China during this century. But let me not suggest that the Chinese are more obsessed with their history than other peoples. All countries which also have full records of a long and distinguished past are equally fascinated with their own history. When there is such a vivid, continuous and concrete record about the activities of various people living in an extensive territory, which the people themselves recognise as having always had a unified core, it is inevitable that stories of specific successes and failures would be regularly invoked. What is unusual is the Chinese attitude towards the uses of history, one that has particular relevance to the idea of an historic empire. The attitude has always been a didactic one, one that believes that history is valuable for the moral and political lessons they might teach to future leaders of that empire.

It is this oneness of the historical experience and the didactic quality of historical judgments which make this self-perception of an historic empire specially interesting. Let me take the question of oneness first. Unlike Europe, Africa, and other parts of Asia, where kingdoms and empires rose and fell to form different nations, this sustained picture of historical oneness is unique to a continental territory like China. Most of the core lands of North, Central and South China, where the Han Chinese have always been the majority people, have had an unbroken history of about 2000 to 3000 years. Others further north and west have been alternately inside or outside the borders of Chinese empires, but have been regarded as an integral part of the ebb and flow of Chinese history. The fact that many of the more powerful tribal federations, such as the Turks, the Mongols, the Tibetans and the Jurchen-Manchus, have actually ruled over all or parts of the core lands, for example, has established the tradition that they all shared a common heritage with the Han Chinese. That many of these people have also been assimilated into the dominant Han culture over time has further confirmed this common heritage. Thus, although China has been divided in the past because of the fall of dynasties or foreign conquest, the driving force of all governments has always been to reunify the empire. The inclusive rhetoric used in historical writings to represent such a theme of unity in diversity is seen to have sanctified the idea that it is the land that is China, and all those who rule it whatever their origins, or all those who live there, become Chinese.

The problem with this self-perception is that much of the long land borders to the north and west has never been clearly defined. Understandably for the time, there was no concept of boundary demarcation. Nor was there one of sovereignty and jurisdiction. The most important factor was the reach of the central government. However, there are two exceptions in all of Chinese history that were products of special circumstances. This was when the tributary system was manipulated by non-Han peoples to secure a large measure of independence. The northern example was that of Korea, which kept itself out of China by a combination of geographical location, self-restraint and diplomatic skills. The southern example was that of Vietnam. The Vietnamese had to fight itself out of China, then struggled for centuries to define its own nationhood, and finally used both military and diplomatic skills to preserve its lands from Chinese invasions. Both were further helped by the crucial fact that neither was ever a threat to China. For all other kingdoms, principalities and tribal groups that accepted the Chinese tributary system, however, there were either no clear boundaries, or they were not contiguous with China and their tributary missions arrived by sea.

From the above, it is clear that China's concept of its historic empire was unlike those of the Persians, Greeks and Romans, or those of Asoka, Tamerlane or Babur, or in more modern times, like those of the Ottomans, the British, the French or the Tsarist Russian. These had been empires by conquest; in recent times, they have been by conquest over long distances and even across oceans. They lasted only as long as their military forces were victorious. For most of the two thousand years of 'imperial' history, this was not the case with China. With the exception of the short Mongol period of 90 years, when China was itself part of the world-empire of the Mongols, no armies marched out of traditional Middle Kingdom (*Zhongguo*) lands. The Mongol expeditionary bursts far into Eurasia, and across the seas to Japan and Java, were strictly un-Chinese. On the contrary, the successor dynasty of the Ming, which was led by Han Chinese, strongly resisted the Mongol world-view. After three decades of the exceptional voyages of Admiral Zheng He early in the 15th century into the South China Sea and across the Indian Ocean to the shores of East Africa, the Ming emperors insisted on returning to the control of traditional lands and forbade foreign adventures. They saw these voyages as aberrations and turned inward toward their land frontiers.

The Ming reaffirmed what had distinguished the Chinese historic empire for more than a thousand years, that was, its self-centredness, and its belief in its invulnerability and self-sufficiency. This was reflected in the history of growing complacency and arrogance, and in the empire's adherence to the tributary system that the Chinese rulers had developed internally and then applied in varying degrees beyond China.

I shall return to the tributary system and its relationship with the Chinese concept of empire. Let me now turn to the didactic quality in the Chinese historiographical tradition. In that tradition, history was to be studied in order that lessons can be learnt from the past. This didactic quality has persisted to this day. In all the histories down to the 20th century, the lessons to be learnt from the imperial past were that China was a land power, that adventures outside China should be avoided, and that Chinese rulers who had been ambitious on the borders usually exhausted the empire's resources and failed to profit from their efforts. And there are records of a long list of negative and positive role models for future rulers, from examples of those who had impoverished the empire in pursuit of foreign adventures to those who defended the sacred lands successfully with minimum effort and cost, and to those who used the tributary system skilfully to keep the imperial peace and foreigners in their place. Thus the lessons of political and institutional history were as important as the celebrations of past imperial glories.

But, since the turn of the century, modern historians in China have been greatly influenced by their studies of modern Western history. There has been a sharp departure in historical interpretation since the new historiography of Liang Qichao (1873–1929). Liang had read European history in Japanese translation. He was influenced by the same books that had inspired the Japanese to break from their traditions and embark on modern empire-building along western lines. Liang had also travelled among the overseas Chinese in British territories and admired the empire that the British had established around the world. With that background, and with the weakness of Qing China in mind, he was the first to record his regret that the Ming navies under Admiral Zheng He did not expand Chinese power into the Indian Ocean and thereby preempt the Portuguese by building a chain of Chinese trading ports all the way to East Africa. He, also for the first time, acknowledged the courageous Chinese pioneers in Southeast Asia and showed admiration for those who gained fame and wealth outside China without any help from the Chinese governments. These Chinese were considered to have been criminals for having left China without official permission.

Ever since then, a new breed of historians has tried to reinterpret 'empire' to compare with European empires in Asia. For these historians, the Chinese empire was no longer seen in traditional or 'historic' terms, but equated with Western empires. In their eagerness to equate Chinese history with European history, they tried to match what had happened in China with historical developments in the rest of the world. One of the consequences of this reinterpretation was to cast the tributary system in an unhistorical frame, one that tended to match tributary states with European colonies even though the Chinese had not conquered or governed any of the states outside imperial borders. Without perhaps intending to, they began to depict past Chinese empires as comparable, if not superior, to modern western ones.

Late Qing imperial policies had begun to show this tendency, largely in order to defend the dynasty against European imperialism, especially along its borders, for example, in Burma, Vietnam and Korea. As it turned out, the efforts were ineffective, and in the end counter-productive. In fact, it occasionally even strengthened the moral position of the European powers in allowing them to argue that their incursions had helped to liberate Burma, Laos and Vietnam from imperialist China, an argument which continues to be used against China today. The new interpretations were certainly used to justify Japan's claim to have freed Korea from Chinese imperialism.

Consciously or not, it was the modern nationalist historians who tended to distort the function of the tributary system and the relationships it spawned. Their work continued to influence some of the histories written after 1949. Since then, of course, other changes have occurred which have changed the way China's historic empire has been presented, and therefore perceived by its people. The most important factors include the internationalist perspective laid down by Marxism-Leninism and sinicised by Mao Zedong.

In particular, the dominance of Soviet historiography during the 1940s and 1950s led historians to try to fit all of Chinese history into a grand Marxist framework, with the communist revolution portrayed as the inevitable end-product of earlier stages of development, from primitive communism to slave society to feudal society, and then to capitalist-imperialist invasions from which the Communist Party had saved China. In addition, there was the not insignificant fact that, for the first time since the Mongol empire, China had the longest land boundary with one single powerful country, that was with the Soviet Union itself. The combination of all three factors had profound effects on Chinese history-writing from about 1930 for at least half a century. It has not been easy for the present generation of Chinese historians to free themselves altogether from that tradition of thinking.

One consequence, however, is clear. For many decades, there developed a tendency to write all Chinese history to take into account the existing land borders with the Soviet Union. Meticulous care was taken to avoid contro-versy about overland boundary disputes, and this practice was extended to include all land borders with countries regarded as friendly to China. This might have been done for the sake of good diplomacy. But it did lead to important results. One of them was to strengthen the sense that the central lands of China were sacred, and that its borders have been legitimately (and historically) extended to where they are today. The other was to play down the function of the tributary system altogether. The former has encouraged the habit of respecting the borders of friendly neighbours. The latter has also produced something positive and correct. It has reversed the nationalist claims to historic tributary states as former Chinese 'colonies'.

Finally, let me relate the historic question of tribute and trade to the issue of Greater China. John King Fairbank had called the tributary system a key part of 'the Chinese world order' in his book, *The Chinese World Order*. Many readers have queried the use of 'world' because China's political con-cerns were only with its neighbours, and the use of 'order' because the tribu-tary relationships were largely unsystematic and unenforceable, and the institution was most useful only where it helped to monitor official trading relations. Although the rhetoric in China was that various rulers and chieftains from near and far came to pay tribute to the emperor, in reality, the system evolved into one that dealt with foreigners who wished to have trading or diplomatic relations with China. The detailed study of these tributary relationships would show that there was really no Chinese empire outside Chinese lands, and the self-perception of historic empire is misleading, if not actually false. What is important about this kind of empire, however, is the way Chinese rulers had used an essentially feudal relationship, that was meant to serve defensive and diplomatic purposes, in order to regulate foreign trade.

There is today no place for this kind of historic empire and such a tributary system. The Chinese scholars who know this have made it clear in the many histories written in recent years. However, this memory of the historic empire may linger in the minds of the political leaders of the region. It would be interesting to see how the current understanding of the system can overcome the deep suspicions that have been aroused in the region that China has an underlying expansionist nature. In the context of the speculations about Greater China, some of the old fears have surfaced. These fears have run parallel to the earlier fears expressed about the Japanese empire which, having failed to achieve its Greater Asian Co-Prosperity Sphere as a framework for its imperial ambitions, then used its economic power to bring it about. Is this what China might do? Is the idea of an economic Greater China another way of achieving a new economic empire in the region?

If so, it would be a new phenomenon that has little to do with the historic dynastic empires of the past. The region has changed beyond recognition. So has the world. There is no return to the past. The new nations of the region may each appear relatively weak, but they have learnt the most important lesson of the colonial era. When they were divided, they were easily picked off, one after another, to become bits of other people's empires. They are unlikely to make that mistake again, and China can hardly fail to see the determination within the region to avoid doing so. Small and larger regional groupings, with or without China, will intensify their efforts to bring about peaceful solutions for all potential disputes. If they are successful in ensuring that peace, the concept of empire itself should be discarded.

CHINESE CIVILISATION

Until after 1945, the Chinese have not needed to think in terms of nation-building and forming some kind of 'imagined community'. The return of Taiwan to Chinese rule was followed soon by the division into the PRC and the ROC which continues to this day. The appearance of China in both names reflects the heritage of the Qing borders, but the oneness of China has another source, that of a common civilisation. But Chinese civilisation cannot be equated with either the idea of nation-state or the idea of empire. Parts of the empire in the north and in the west had never shared in that civilisation, and parts of the civilisation had spread southwards and eastwards beyond the confines of the empire, into non-Chinese kingdoms in Korea, Japan and Vietnam.

This leads me to another layer of self-perception, that of China as the home of a great civilisation and the Chinese as a people who share a common cultural heritage. Given the revolutionary changes that have occurred this century and the various perceptions outlined above, is this still significant? Do people really care? Even if the Chinese continue to refer to the glorious past, surely that past belongs to the museums, to displays for the tourist industry, or to the class of private hobbies that antiquarians and connoisseurs cultivate at their leisure. It is true that there are scholars who argue that China has always been a civilisation-state rather than a nation-state. Therefore, the fact that there is a China that people can identify with rests on the existence of that civilisation. But, if China is a modern nation, would that not contradict this residual perception of a civilisation that originated with the Chinese and still belongs to them? How would the Chinese see a civilisation that is not only shared with people of other nations, but may actually be better appreciated outside than inside the borders of the PRC?

As I have suggested above, the concept of a modern Chinese nation is imperfect, and is contingent on China having a larger national culture for the Han majority and all its ethnic minorities to share and embrace. To that extent, a cultural heritage that is both modern and based on the continuous civilisation that everyone recognises as belonging to China could be the foundation of new national loyalty. Until this century, the Confucianism that supported the imperial system, together with the popular culture based on a mixture of Confucian, Buddhist and Daoist practices, provided that heritage. But for nearly a century, nationalist and communist revolutionaries have done their utmost to lighten China of that cultural baggage. What then is left for those who still see China as the home of Chinese civilisation? Insofar as the Beijing government acknowledges the validity of Confucian role-models and ethics in the schools, and permits the revival of some Buddhist and Daoist groups around the country, the heritage is still real. To understand how important this is likely to be, we need to survey the extent of the damage done to Chinese civilisation during this century and the kinds of repair being attempted to make this heritage viable again. Is it possible for this heritage to be modernised? If so, how relevant would this heritage be for China's position in international relations?

It would be true to say that neither the nationalists nor the communists set out to destroy their proud civilisation. When confronted by the military power of the West in the nineteenth century, the Chinese struggled to adapt their civilisation to the challenges and dangers from the West. On the whole, they subscribed to the view so succinctly encapsulated by Zhang Zhidong (1837–1909) in *Quanxue pien* (Exhortation to Study), which he published in 1898:

> *Zhongxue wei ti, Xixue wei yong* (Chinese learning as base, Western learning as application).

Thus this 'learning', or civilisation, belonged to a deeper layer of consciousness which both nationalist and communist governments have tried, from time to time, to bring to the surface. But, as will be seen, the results were unpredictable and often contradictory. The Chinese were unable, like the Japanese, to retain the core of their values and institutions while learning what they needed of science and engineering from the West. The Chinese felt they had to redefine their civilisation in order to modernise their country and their ideas. It was thought that their civilisation could be revitalised anew as modern and progressive, if carefully selected bits of western learning could be grafted on to it.

But it was not to be that simple. To begin with, for most Chinese, the great Chinese civilisation had been associated with the ruling class of mandarins who dictated artistic taste and endorsed all forms of orthodoxy, especially those pertaining to government and to religious and ethical systems. That small and privileged class was generally seen as having served the foreign Manchu rulers in the context of Confucian ideals, and therefore, highly suspect in the eyes of the nationalists who overthrew the Qing dynasty. Thus when the Guomindang leaders tried to revive traditional values during the 1930s, they turned to a new generation of activists. But this consisted largely of radical intellectuals who found the whole exercise artificial, irrelevant and self-seeking. The best brains among them had turned to the professions, or to the study of science and technology, or to modern economics, business and management. They were more familiar with Maynard Keynes, Mussolini, Henry Ford, Madame Curie and Einstein and the latest artistic ideas in Europe and the U.S. than with the unglamorous efforts to keep traditional values alive. Already, the Great Tradition was seen by the best and brightest as more dead than alive.

Of the intellectuals who remained interested in cultural values, many of them had converted to anti-Confucian nationalism, to liberal ideals and capitalist practices. They were the first modern generation. But they then found themselves unacceptable in turn to the progressive revolutionaries who regarded them as scions of the landlord and new capitalist classes, who were condemned as the exploiters of the people. They were thus losers twice over. They had lost most of their own cultural bearings as well as their credibility as cultural leaders in the eyes of their contemporaries. After the communist takeover in 1949, some of them escaped to Taiwan and served a more sympathetic government there; others found new roles as scholars, and 'loyalists' in the Confucian tradition. Yet others went abroad, particularly to the United States, as bearers of the civilisation, rather like the 'loyalists' who went to Japan and Vietnam after the fall of the Song and Ming dynasties.

Who then remained on the mainland to claim the mantle of cultural heroes? Whoever they were, they would first have to make their peace with Marxism-Leninism and the Thought of Mao Zedong. Ironically, Mao, the romantic revolutionary, saw himself as a bearer, and an arbiter, of all that was great and worth preserving in Chinese civilisation. Thus, at the highest level, men like Guo Moruo (1892–1978), who was flexible enough to enjoy the personal trust of Mao Zedong, was able to offer some measure of protection for traditional scholarly values. Others less fortunate, like Liang Souming (1893–1988) and Fung Youlan (1895–1990), were criticised; yet others were marginalised. If they managed to survive through the 1950s and early 1960s, they were then either totally ignored, or brought out to serve crude propaganda purposes during the Cultural Revolution. The image of formerly famous scholars of Chinese culture being made to support the politics of those Cultural Revolution years remains sharply etched in many minds. It was a degrading and tragic experience. Although many understandably had to submit in order to survive, what they were put through certainly did not inspire confidence in their authority, or faith in the values they were supposed to support.

Since the 1980s, the more independent minded have taken advantage of the relative freedom now enjoyed to resurface and write on controversial subjects, like intellectual freedom, liberal democracy, legitimacy, the rule of law and human rights. Understandably, most of them were more excited by the fresh ideas from the West than by any return to Chinese traditional values. However, with a loss of faith in communism, and given the tight limits on publishing and the media, there seems to be a spiritual and ideological vacuum, especially among the young. Chinese leaders are worried at the materialism and corruption in the country today and are seeking ways to bring back some of the revolutionary purity of the early days. All the same, amongst them are the cultural loyalists who find the atmosphere now more congenial, and openly advocate that 'Chinese learning' be given back its rightful place in the curriculum before it is too late. How late it is, and how the extensive damage to China's cultural roots can be repaired, will not be known for some time. But it is impressive to see authors, editors and publishers all around the country, and in collaboration with their counterparts in Hong Kong and Taiwan, busily producing new textbooks, literary and artistic collections, and annotated editions of the classics, for all levels of students and scholars. The print and electronic media in all three parts of China have also joined in to a lesser extent, less didactically but, through entertainment and recreational activities, probably more effectively. The will to revive interest is not in question, and the number of people keen to do the work seems to be growing. It is possible to say that, at least among the Han Chinese, the glorious civilisation and the new nation idea can co-exist.

In what way then is the cultural heritage generally meaningful to the Chinese people today? I have attended several conferences on subjects like Chinese culture, Confucianism and the interface between modern and traditional society, and have followed several controversies on historiography, archaeology and the preservation of cultural artifacts, as well as more general issues like the future of the Great Tradition for the younger generation. There is undoubtedly official interest. There is also the popular conviction that the government must have a clear and strong position about the importance of the heritage. There is awareness that there are more people, including non-Chinese scholars, outside mainland China who are appreciative of traditional culture than there are within, and that the quality of that knowledge may even be superior. But the inescapable impression is that much of the attention on the mainland is still formal and dutiful, and that, most of the time, paying lip service to tradition is all that is officially required.

At the popular level, however, there is a different picture. This is particularly true in the countryside and in the small towns, both in Taiwan and on the mainland. Religion and local cults are gaining followers. Much of it is superstition and fills a need. Following the decay of Guomindang ideology and of the secular religion of Maoism that the PRC government had sponsored so vigorously for decades and that had caused so much confusion among the people for so long, it must be refreshing for the country people to find something different they can believe in. Unlike in the historic cities, temples, mosques and less obvious places of worship are being built or restored, not in support of tourism but for popular use.

Most notable has been the increasing concern to revive respect for family institutions everywhere. This is particularly relevant following the demise of the extended family and the one-child policy of the state. Not only can this be seen in the new school textbooks, but also in the increasing number of primers and catechisms dedicated to *jiaxun,* or 'family instructions'. These have been significantly revised and modernised, but still presented along traditional lines. They are popular not only because they embody the deepest levels of cultural consciousness among most Chinese, but also because they express a practical need when other institutions seem to be failing to sustain each local community. This is particularly true on the mainland. The new pressures towards private profit, the inadequacies of the welfare system, the trends towards insecure employment and the growing threats of falling real incomes for the rural majority, leave most people with little choice but to turn again to their families. Fortunately, the cultural heritage within the country concerning the family seems to have remained strong. Furthermore, as a common area still appreciated by the Chinese in Taiwan and Hong Kong as well as those overseas, this can be easily reinforced through regular contacts wherever family relationships can be established.

It has been suggested that a new concept of Cultural China (Tu Wei-ming, The Living tree, *Daedalus,* 1991), that takes China in its broadest non-political manifestation, could inspire a Chinese revival. This concept accepts that the greatest damage had been done to traditional civilisation in the PRC. Therefore, the future of that civilisation would depend on whether modern intellectuals in the two other parts of China, and among the Chinese diaspora, could transmit their heritage to the younger generations who have grown up in freer environments. Unless these intellectuals outside the PRC can demonstrate that the Great Tradition is still essential to China and inspire fresh confidence among themselves and their successors, there would be little chance of much of the civilisation surviving. But, for many Chinese today, it would be enough if certain core values still remain strong. For example, the major ones are: the respect for education and a meritocracy, including the readiness to upgrade knowledge and acquire the best in science and technology; then, there is the willingness to work hard and postpone gratification; the importance of both these, taken together with qualities of thrift and trustworthiness, is well recognised when they are integrated in the service of modern business and industry; and, perhaps most of all, there is the loyalty to family networks that most Chinese people still believe is not only natural and profoundly central to the civilisation, but also to all areas of practical activity. If all these values could serve to bind the Chinese peoples together, they would play a key part in producing a future culturally united country.

In any case, the question of civilisation is primarily a matter of choice for the Chinese themselves. Whether it impinges on China's relations with the rest of the world depends on whether it has anything universal to offer to non-Chinese peoples. Sifting through the heritage and finding qualities in it which arouse more than simply pride and nostalgia is a task that the past three generations of Chinese have so far failed to do. Until that is done and the result is to produce not merely some defensive walls for the use of the Chinese alone, that is, to strengthen China as a modern nation-state and a Great Power, but also with a fresh vision of how the values of East and West can together work for all humankind, then Chinese civilisation would have little to contribute to the world in the future.

Today, further new tasks await the Chinese. These derive largely from the need to protect the rights of all human beings as a universal principle. The principle has been thoroughly aired for decades, and there is little dispute among civilised people about the principle. The debate is about how these rights should be respected and by what means. But two problems have dogged it in recent years. One is of timing. Some have argued that full rights must be implemented immediately, no matter at what cost. The other is of approach. The issue of human rights has not been presented as one of civilisation and morality, but as a diplomatic, commercial and political weapon, and it has been done confrontationally as one between East and West, between inferior Asian values versus superior Western values.

This is unfortunate. If human rights and democracy still appear remote and difficult to realise, it is because the Chinese people have failed to create the political and legal structure for the new values to grow among them. On the other hand, if these values are insisted on from the outside, and by foreign governments, it is bound to be interpreted as either ignoring the fact that there are still immense problems in the country, or reflecting the desire by these foreigners to overthrow the present regime no matter what the consequences. Such an approach has also been interpreted variously as interference with China's internal affairs, or as an attempt by politicians in the West to slow down its development. The attitude towards China's tough birth control measures best illustrate that failure, or unwillingness to understand. If China does not control its population, it would be accused of irresponsibility, but if it tries to carry out such policies, it is accused of being draconian and inhumane. The way the one-child policy is used as a reason for refugee status in the U.S. until recently marks the dilemma sharply.

Chinese civilisation, it would appear, has bequeathed the following deep-rooted concerns: China's size gives priority to collective and public goals over individual and private goals; the necessity for immense infrastructural projects, and the continual danger of the country being invaded or falling apart, give support to the historic tradition of strong central control. However, since the ideas of democracy were introduced, there have been changes in emphasis. For almost a hundred years, democracy has been accepted and desired by the Chinese people as a civilised goal. Human rights, too, as another marker of modern civilisation, has been acknowledged as important for at least half a century. We can only hope that it will not be long before they receive the priority they deserve. But it will be surprising if the form of the democracy which emerges eventually and the legal and administrative framework established for the support of human rights will be the same as those that have been evolved in a Judaeo-Christian and Greco-Roman cultural context. That may not, in any case, be as important as having the ideals incorporated in the Chinese way to meet the challenge of the modern civilised world.

GLOBAL POWER

I have now reached the point when we might look at the future of China as a global power. Here I am obviously looking at China as represented now by the PRC, soon with the addition of Hong Kong, and later possibly in some special relationship with Taiwan. Many Chinese may hope that this China will soon be such a power, but I do not think that this is an important part of its self-perception today. From what has been surveyed above, it is clear that, whichever perception such a China may focus on, the ingredients for being a regional power are already all there, whether in terms of a rejuvenated economic presence, or a modern nation built on its historic past, or as a potential model to challenge the Western models of the 19th and 20th centuries. But how those ingredients could contribute towards China's capacity to project itself globally would be harder to say.

For China's neighbours, the view is simpler. The fact of China's size and location is itself a powerful reminder of past superiority and possible future threat. China's very existence, however passive and inwardly-looking, has always aroused interest and concern. What would be new and alarming to the region is if a modernised China finds that it has to behave like the modern Great Powers of the West. For example, is it likely that China should behave like 18th and 19th century Britain and France in their quest for maritime empires, or like Russia in its overland drive towards the east? Or, would China model itself after the doubly aggressive latecomers Germany and Japan, or aspire to the American 'manifest destiny' to take over from the British as a global power? With all those 'glorious' and recent examples before them, could the Chinese resist the dynamic urges of modern competitive expansionism? Could China's neighbours be assured that future regional relations will be based on fraternal cooperation, or at worst, merely the benign neglect of a patronising 'big brother'?

This is not the place to predict what is, or is not, likely to happen to China's growing power during the coming decade or so. As all scholars of 20th century China know, there are many political variables at work inside inherently unstable systems, especially when so much at the centre depends on dominant personalities exercising control, and on factional struggles among such small numbers of protagonists. Although that has not prevented many brave ones among us from crystal-gazing, the casualties among those who predicted confidently are great. What I have suggested so far is that we look not only objectively for relevant facts pertaining to China's potential power, but also for more subjective dimensions that are illustrated in past and present self-images. While this will not guarantee accurate predictions, it will add depth to our efforts to see larger trends and thus anticipate future developments. It is in that same spirit that I shall now point to five significant examples which, because of their international dimensions, and despite an apparently local and regional focus, might make a difference to China's future global ambitions.

Firstly, the unequal relations between the PRC and the U.S. that symbolize the global ramifications of anything that China does. This would include China's participation in international organisations like the United Nations, and new bodies like the Asia-Pacific Economic Cooperation (APEC) Conference. China's attempts to join the World Trade Organisation and the opposition of the U.S. are symptomatic of some of its problems to be a player in international affairs.

The Beijing government believes that the U.S., by its very nature as a superpower, would interfere globally wherever it can. The PRC is forced to deal with the U.S. at most forums and has to have a global strategy to keep up with U.S. plans and ambitions. It does not have the wherewithal to restrain the U.S. everywhere, but it can try to limit interventions in its own region, that of East and Southeast Asia. Indeed, it has to if it is to have any credibility as a future power. It can do so by being active in bilateral relations, by involving the American multinationals and financial institutions in China investments, by opening itself up for more trade, by being extremely careful in Northeast Asia (especially over the two Koreas) where U.S. interests are sensitive and unstable, and by responding positively to U.S. overtures as much as possible elsewhere where China's own interests are minor. For the period since the tragedy at Tiananmen Square in 1989, the generally cooperative moves made by the PRC have been extraordinarily successful. Outside of Asia, only where U.S.-Russian relations are concerned have the Chinese leaders experienced some anxiety. But as long as Russia is busy within its own borders, and more preoccupied with its future in Europe than in northern Asia, Sino-American relations need not be affected.

All the same, it is not clear how well the Chinese and the American policymakers understand each other today. Neither side has any advantage here. It is probably true to say that more Chinese understand the West than vice versa, if only because the West is more open and the Chinese written language is so difficult to learn. But the quality of that understanding among the experts remains uncertain, and their access to power-holders seems to equally limited. There have been gross misunderstandings in the past, and the results were destructive to both countries. Can the new generation of experts rise above the historical obsessions with the evils of capitalism on the one hand, and communism on the other? Would they be allowed to look at present problems with fresh eyes?

There have certainly been major changes in perspectives. The U.S. is still adjusting to the fact that it is the only superpower. This is at a time when its people are increasingly discontented with its politicians and critical of the country's financial burdens overseas. The very successes of the past decade in stimulating economic growth in East and Southeast Asia, and in trying to do the same in Eastern Europe, have led to the perception that the U.S., as the leader of the West, is in relative decline. If the Chinese should misread this as an opportunity for them to lead future challenges against the U.S., the world will be in for troublous times.

Continued fears and suspicions of China as a communist state, however, may fail to give sufficient weight to the determination to make its form of market economy successful. The PRC has passed the stage when concentrating resources on making the country powerful while keeping the people's standards of living low was a policy that was both patriotic and ideologically correct. The government's commitment to economic reform is deep and far-reaching, and the people who have endured poverty for decades will not stand for a return to national self-aggrandisement at their expense. What is truly challenging for China's leaders and their advisers is to show the world that the existing structures within the country can cope with the agonies of modernisation. They have the task of convincing the world, and especially the U.S. leaders, that failure in China will harm everybody. It is no less difficult to persuade China's neighbours that its success will not endanger peaceful relations in the region and that there is no need to call for the U.S. cavalry.

There is hope that matters will improve. De-linking the Most Favoured Nation provisions from China's human rights performance was the right decision. Both sides need a greater concentration on mundane but concrete commercial issues at this stage of an economic revolution in China. However acrimonious the debate, the unflinching attack on copyright infringements in China produced results. There are genuine business problems to be solved, and solving them openly for all to see is the best way to dispel conspiracy fears. The experiences of the past decade in bilateral relations have much to teach the expert advisers on both sides. The problem is that both sets of experts remain handicapped by political and cultural environments which insist on fighting the old wars by new means.

Secondly, the treatment of Hong Kong. This would mark an early test of China's readiness to play a global role; this is one of the reasons why Britain and its allies are pressing hard to ensure that Hong Kong's international position will not be constrained after 1997. It is easy to underestimate the PRC's hostility to any suggestion that there should be any British influence left in the territory, or that China's sovereignty over Hong Kong after 1997 should be questioned. To the PRC, Hong Kong should have been a purely internal matter to be resolved between the PRC and the colonial power. But the city's extraordinary importance to Chinese economic reforms since 1978 has given it international clout. Had there not been the June 4th tragedy and the collapse of the communist bloc in Europe, China could have expected a low-key transition, with Britain, the U.S. and Japan assisting in a smooth transfer of sovereignty.

But the international dimension became a much more central issue after 1989. The Hong Kong people, who are used to a considerable amount of freedom, are understandably fearful of the loss of that freedom. Attention has shifted from economic matters to questions of political rights, press freedom and the legal system. Increasingly, comparisons are being made with the lack of such protections in the PRC itself. In their efforts to preserve those protections, Hong Kong people have begun to insist on establishing the principles of universal human rights before 1997, and sought to draw international attention to their territory. Chinese officials are increasingly irritated at the widening range of foreign concerns about Hong Kong. It will require considerable diplomatic skill for the PRC to dampen the urge to interfere by outside interests to protect the excellent financial and business environment in Hong Kong. But if the transfer of sovereignty is well handled, it will enhance China's global status.

The third example concerns the independence pressures within Taiwan. This is an even more difficult test, for China would have to defend fiercely the principle that this is an entirely internal matter. The mixture of caution and blustering rhetoric has been revealing of the great tensions underlying this relationship. For over 45 years, the PRC has looked on this as a U.S. thorn in its side. The U.S. has supported the left-over regime from a bitter civil war that has lingered on for almost 50 years. During the latter part of this period, Taiwan's economic success has led to political freedoms which now challenge the very fundamental principle that there could only be one China, one nation and one set of historical roots. This was the principle that gave the Guomindang its legitimacy to rule Taiwan after they left the Mainland.

Now, however, among some Taiwan people, there are serious questions about the validity of sharing that one civilisation. There are calls for independence, which the PRC finds intolerable, although it has been surprisingly restrained in the actions taken so far. It probably has little choice now. But it is not clear whether the mainland government will remain calm if some of the excitable Taiwanese take their independence calls much further. What is clear is that if the calls developed into action, the threat of war across the straits would be great indeed.

Within the region, Taiwan is diplomatically contained, but trading relations with other countries, including the mainland itself, are growing faster than anyone expected. The biggest challenge would come if Taiwan's position gains sympathy as China's power rises. For the rest of the world, the efforts to isolate Taiwan globally are still continuing. It is a manageable problem, but nevertheless one that calls for the greatest vigilance. Taiwan's persistence in not allowing itself to be ignored by the rest of the world has frequently put the Beijing leaders on the defensive, and this takes away some authority from China's global position.

The issue of Tibet is the fourth example. This would need patience on all sides; it is a long term problem that will not go away and will call for statesmanship of the highest quality. China has stood firm that this is an internal matter, and international law and U.N. practice protect that position. The challenge today is really neither political nor military. The special quality of Tibetan culture and history, its unique religion, and the loyalty and faith which they arouse, have produced a moral authority for Tibet which will continue to bring it considerable sympathy from the rest of the world. China's comparative wealth, its power and influence, and even its legitimacy will not help. Even if conscientious laws, good intentions and humane administration were to be consistently applied in Tibet, China would still not easily overcome the image of having been the invader. It is the one exception among the various autonomous regions and districts along the whole length of China's land borders where normal methods of control seem to have been adequate to stop secessionist demands. It is ironical that this internal issue pertaining to a region so strategically important to China should have become such a cancer in the system. But it highlights China's difficulty with concepts of both nation and civilisation which I referred to earlier. Neither fits the Tibetan story, and the appeal to the idea of historic empire has simply not been convincing enough. As a future possible global power, the real test here is of China's patience and humanity.

The fifth example is the most immediately challenging. This is the issue of who controls the Spratly islands in the South China Sea. It will be most difficult to prevent this political and economic issue from becoming a military one that could spill over beyond the region. The recent flare-up with the Philippines over a few reefs may well remain a purely regional affair, to be resolved between China and members of the ASEAN states. It would, of course, be best if that could be done and done with the minimum of ill-will. In terms of China as a future global power though, China's approach to the issue will be scrutinised with great care. Which of the perceptions by China's neighbours will come to the fore?

The territory of an 'historic empire' has been invoked; obviously it is not a matter of civilisational ambit or revolutionary socialist superiority. But this is not a traditional claim for, as I have mentioned earlier, there is no concept of clearly demarcated international boundaries in the past. There is nothing in the dynastic records, not even that of the tributary system, that validates China's claim to these islands. In fact, it is a modern claim first made in answer to western imperialist or colonial practices earlier this century. Thus, it is really a matter of national strategy. Or, perhaps, equally one of resources and economic interests. The Spratlys, therefore, remind us that modern Great Power and nationalist politics now govern Asia just as much as appeals to history and culture, or to past practices and principles. China's road to global power will have to balance its various perceptions of itself and take all these into account.

All the five examples outlined above concern relations that have direct repercussions on China's leadership image in the region. From what I have outlined in these two lectures, I hope to have provided a broad base of historical background, of traditional ideals, of modern goals and ambitions, of critical self-images, of strong commitments and residual sentiments, to help examine what China may do given the major problems it faces. How the Chinese leaders deal with these issues would determine China's position in international relations, and help us to understand some of the possibilities for China's future development as a global power. And how they do that will depend on how they balance their various layers of self-perceptions as nation, empire or civilisation, as development model or a unique socialist market economy.

For years, I have had to argue with my European friends that Communist China is not the same as Communist Russia, and China is not a 'normal' country, not even a 'normal' communist country. Some have agreed with me by pointing out that the Chinese communists had got both Marx and Lenin wrong, and did not really have much clue as to what communism really was about. What I have outlined above, I hope, does illustrate how China is different. The way it perceives itself shows where its rich heritage as civilisation and empire has complicated its claims to be a modern nation; why its unique linkages with Hong Kong, Taiwan and parts of the diaspora have eased the pains of economic reform; and how it derived socialist ideals from its chequered revolutionary history. Together, they have made China an entity of paradoxes. China is all the above, and yet more than the sum of its parts. It is still divided and incomplete, but it has political weight. It is multi-layered, it is large and extensive, it is modernising, but it is also inclusive and is able to use traditional values and networks to reach out for new knowledge, new technologies and new investments. Finally, the transformation of China has been a most painful one and has dragged on for a more than a century, but the Chinese people have never given up and still seek to be modern and global and quintessentially Chinese.

INDEX